Midwest Portraits

A Book of Memories and Friendships

By
Harry Hansen

New York
Harcourt, Brace and Company

PRINTED IN THE U. S. A. BY
THE QUINN & BODEN COMPANY
RAHWAY, N. J

TO MY MOTHER

AND

TO THE MEMORY

OF MY FATHER

CONTENTS

1. Of an Ancient Tavern on a Well-Traveled Highway.

A literary movement consists of five or six people who live in the same town and hate each other cordially.

A. E.

WHEN this book began to be written the hands of the big wall clock at Schlogl's had already advanced to half past two, and as I looked up at the great disc of the pendulum, somnolently swinging back and forth like an animated moon, I saw reflected within its highly polished surface a merry and leisurely company that gave no signs of going home. Grotesque and disproportionate the scene, distorted in this concave mirror—a strip of olive-colored ceiling above and a flare of light from cut-glass chandeliers, then a strip of brown which I identified as the paintings indigenous to a tavern, then tables and chairs, and men bent over the polished wood in all sorts of easy attitudes. They might linger there for hours, unaware that the deepening gray outdoors was brought on by something more unalterable than descending soot; unmindful, too, of the pounding of iron wheels high up on iron trestles, or the clanging of street cars, or the churning roar of motor trucks. They were placid and comfortable even as that old patron at the third table, *un vieux*, if ever there was one, who had sat in that self-same chair thirty years or so, save for the time lost in the distraction of home and business, partaking of his hasenpfeffer with paprika, *etwas ganz feines*, pulling lazily at his long filler havana, sampling now and then his goblet of Rüdesheimer. Thirty years—that went back almost to antiquity in Chicago, where the calendar began *anno incendi*, in fact this very house had remained unchanged since the day that it was reared upon smoldering embers and charred walls, and if one dug deep enough the spade would strike bricks and debris that are all that remain to tell of the great fire—as in ancient Troy. Thirty years—and he might sit there another thirty years, toying with his hasenbraten and spaetzle, pulling at his long havana, if life could be endured that long again without the Rüdesheimer.

This, then, was a hallowed spot. One sought it, mistakenly, under another name, just off the Strand, in London, and thought it worth the journey; jaded souls, tired of insensate dining on Manhattan, imagined it near the Place du Tertre high up on the Butte; *feinschmecker* extolled its cuisine and dreamed for it a site near the Kürfurstendam in Berlin; the Rathusplaads had it too, they said, in Copenhagen. I had explored them all and traveled up and down their *carte du jour;* I had indulged in delights gustatory and olfactory, and bewailing the fact that America had no cuisine worth the name, I had come back reluctantly only to find Schlogl's within three hundred yards of the desk where I performed my daily task. And everything was as it always was. "Good day, and how are you?" asked Richard, as I hung my hat upon the hall tree, which scrambled over the wall like an illuminated initial from an ancient Celtic script, and then: "Your order is coming right up."

"But I haven't seen your little black book," I pleaded.

"No matter. The baby turkey is very fine to-day, so I have ordered it."

Naturally. Baby turkey. And *sauce meunière*. Potatoes browned just to the point of crispness. And here on the table unsalted butter in generous pound blocks, thick slices of fragrant rye and pumpernickel, and scattered about the plain, unpretentious silver service of an unpretentious age. The little black book that held the *carte du jour* was an adventure in itself; one found such dishes as eel in aspic, partridges and mallards in season, roast venison, and a morsel that never failed to disturb the newcomer: "Owls to order."

The reminiscence faded; the clock ticked slowly on. I surveyed the small service bar and its white-coated attendant, carefully measuring a schoppen from a long-necked bottle of Rhenish wine. I glanced at the lithographs of Berncastel; they, too, belonged; and the big oils in massive frames, long since mellowed to a rich brown by the tobacco smoke of a generation come and gone, depicting rotund tavern keepers tapping a tun of generous girth and hooded friars content at a well-filled refectory table, and men and maids of an alien country-side in the frivolous pursuits of a less jaded century. The worn linoleum, the polished cuspidors, the screened windows, the great black walnut tables of an age that knew no art but that of dining well.

Voices—they are always haunting one, particularly on a drowsy afternoon, when sleep would be a welcome variation. Voices—they ring in one's ears with strange snatches of conversation, odd banter on the trivialities of existence, rambling phrases that mask a momentous personal decision, perhaps, or merely repeat a platitude. Voices—but some one is speaking, in a drawling, gentle monotone, some one who loves the words that slip so easily from his lips:

"Our architecture, our streets, our buildings, typify after all nothing but energy. We have just emerged from barbarism. We are taking the first steps in civilization. Geometrical patterns all about us—that is all. Barbarian peoples and peoples emerging from barbarism are obsessed with admiration for geometrical patterns. Their thinking falls into conventionalized patterns. When they draw a picture it becomes conventionalized. Early peoples never draw portraits, always conventionalized patterns. Take the Aztecs . . ."

"But listen . . ."

"They look at the stars, study the sky, reproduce it in a zodiacal system, in a pattern, making a much better calendar than we use to-day. There is no real building in America. Only masses. Only heaps of energy. Utilitarian masses. No ideas, only energy. . . ."

"But what do you think of . . ."

"Streets, houses, walls, elevated tracks, doors, windows. Geometrical patterns. Barbarism."

Ben Hecht is speaking, speaking as he writes, always with a ready flow of words, with energy and forcefulness. Patterns. Buildings. Walls. Ben stops speaking because one must eat. The conversation lags. Walls. Patterns. The refrain repeats itself endlessly. Somehow even the elevated trains keep time to it as their wheels leap over the iron frogs outside. Bells clang in unison. Whistles blow in conventionalized rhythm.

"But, Ben," reiterates the low insistent voice, "have you got any new scheme to-day for making a million dollars?" Then follows a low, delighted chuckle. The speaker has launched his query for his own amusement. The spell is broken.

That is Sherwood Anderson. He leans forward and smiles across the table. His eyes are big and gentle and there is always a sort of friendly look about them. His hands are clumsy and soft but active; you get the feeling that he must hold a pen clumsily, that he must pound a typewriter mercilessly. He is the only man of whom one can say that he speaks caressingly. He rarely argues. He never expounds. He merely chuckles a bit to himself, tells a story when he has been prodded long enough, preferably an anecdote about somebody he knows. He and Ben Hecht are old friends. Back in the old salad days, oh, ever so long ago, when Ben was a cub reporter reading the "Arabian Nights" between assignments and Sherwood was the world's greatest unpublished author, reading his manuscripts aloud by candlelight in studios, in the back rooms of saloons, in forlorn lodging houses, the two men met and learned to respect each other's gifts. For years Ben predicted a big writing career for Sherwood Anderson. For years Sherwood Anderson looked with kindly eyes on Ben's ripening powers. "He thinks I am the greatest writer living," said Ben once, "that is, next to himself."

Out of the limbo come faces—faces. The table's full. In fact there are more here than the table will hold—and yet they all belong here. Memory is playing me a trick, the past is coalescing with the present. No matter. Keith Preston is here, nimble-witted, proficient in the argot of Chicago and of Rome; the mantle of Eugene Field has fallen about his shoulders and he wears it a bit askew, letting it trail a bit, for Field was a tall man compared to Preston. Gene Markey too—who draws with his pencil the literary lights of the modern age—suave and urbane and immaculately attired; it might have been Markey who inspired John V. A. Weaver to write those revealing lines in his "Élégie Americaine": "He was a darb; the swellest dresser, with them nifty shirts—" And Maxwell Bodenheim, uniting nouns and adjectives in morganatic union, giving birth to epigrams with a deep frown on his forehead, a cynical smile on his lips, and an admonitory forefinger tapping the table. A voice: "What I want to know is where Bodenheim gets the idea that he is a maligned character, a pessimist, scornful of men." Henry Justin Smith speaking. He handles a cigar carefully and smiles wryly at the frowning man whose blond hair falls like wet hemp across his forehead.

"I am. I have a healthy contempt for the whole human race. I despise these fawning sycophants. I am the only one of four major poets of America who has never received a prize. . . ."

"All bosh. Just a pose." Smith is pleased with his manœuver. Ferreting out a pessimist and showing a lamb beneath the lion's hide. Smith himself has fought the fight with pessimism and come forth victorious. He will tell you that all the world is like the past Carl Sandburg writes about—just a bucket of ashes. But he will not want you to believe him. He is an editor and he has found out that the editorial code demands on his part a certain amount of asperity and cynicism. All to no avail. Beneath his coat beats the heart of a romanticist, a man who idealizes his friendships. He has poured it all into "Deadlines," his novel of "the game." A romance of editors, and reporters, and copy boys. Into its writing went nothing but the pure love of the newspaper. He sent it east and the best houses rejected it. It was too short, or too provincial, or too western—besides there was the failure of Jesse Lynch Williams' book, "The Stolen Story," to warn them that a newspaper story cannot succeed. Smith took his manuscript under his arm and went sadly home. His mien was perturbed, his heart lonely. He had proof to himself of his failure—he, whose encouragement had meant life and hope to so many others. Until Pasquale Covici and Billy McGee came and decided to print the book. Smith's love of life has come back. He can afford to poke fun slyly at Bodenheim's pose.

Again the voice:

"I have seen people stand on Clark street bridge and look at the warehouses and the lights without knowing what they were looking at. They saw no significance in the masses. They didn't know what sort of civilization conceived those buildings. They could not think. Their minds were filled up with images drilled into them for hundreds of years; ten thousand images, and not one real picture. No ideas. A painter can draw a face without looking at a face. But he draws nothing real, nothing with an idea."

"Does he always talk like that?" This from a visitor, a poet from Indiana, or maybe a schoolmaster from Iowa. Yes, always. Always with an onrush of words. Always with a preoccupation with his own ideas. One might as well try to stop a mill-race. But no one wants to.

Forms move about the table; faces appear in the memory. There is Carl Sandburg, perhaps, peering out from under his black-visored cap like a traffic policeman, wearing his coat about his shoulders like a cape and stalking forward like another Ibsen in the streets of Christiania—Carl, come in for a bite to eat and a cup of coffee and to listen rather than talk, for Carl greatly prefers a hole in the wall where he can dine *à deux* and pursue his topic to the end. There is a reminiscence among us still of the memorable debate waged between Carl Sandburg and J. C. Squire when the latter with A. P. Herbert sat at our table, the debate that Gene Markey has sketched in caricature in his "Literary Lights." On Carl's part, an indictment of the London "Times" for the conservative attitude of A. Clutton-Brock toward modern art; on Squire's part a gentle evasion of responsibility for the views of an Englishman whose department he had not read and whose ideals he knew little about. "But you will admit," thundered Carl, raising his voice to bring home his bolt, "that the 'Times' was entirely wrong in the Whistler-Ruskin controversy," and Squire parried with his parting shot: "Yes, and in the matter of George the Third too, but they reversed themselves on that. . . ." There is Vincent Starrett, the last Tennysonian, biographer of the Eighteen Nineties, grave and ponderous and happy over a Rabelaisian anecdote, quick at hand with stories of Stephen Crane and Arthur Machen, whose fugitive tales he has collected in much-prized volumes, a khaliff lost in an industrial Bagdad and dreaming dreams of scimitars and lutes and Scheherezade. . . . There is Lew Sarett, a woodsman in a suburb, wearing his heavy cowhide boots on the flat cement walks of the city, an Indian at heart, rich in the council talk of the Ojibways and the Chippewas, interpreter of Indian dreams and philosophies in a noisy, incongruous world. . . . There is Lynn Montross, modest in outward shew, a rebel at heart, who with Lois Seyster Montross wrote defiantly of college life in "Town and Gown" and who shrinks when captious critics cry: "What ho! A new Fitzgerald! . . ." There is Dr. Morris Fishbein, precise and pathological, and Leroy T. Goble, a gourmet in art as in life, the perfect amateur, and John Gunther, critical spokesman for the youngest generation, wearing an air of authority that bespeaks a high and mighty age. . . . There is Sam Putnam, learned and wise, biographer of the metaphysical poets, and Mark Turbyfill and Virgil Geddes, his two most proficient exhibits;

Llewellyn Jones, with an air of authority that sits well upon his generous proportions, and Samuel P. Rudens, with the psychology of the Russians at his finger tips. . . . One is minded to recall those incidents that somehow retain their place in the memory; of Hendrick van Loon narrating with gusto the Inside Story of the Bible, of Ludwig Lewisohn, telling how, after he had written what he thought a simple autobiography in "Up Stream," he awoke one morning to find himself become a prophet in Israel; of "Bobby" Edwards, mostly of Greenwich village, twanging his dodo-bird ukelele and singing "The sultan's wives have got the hives—Allah be merciful!" (He was.) Of Hugh Walpole, Louis Untermeyer, Clement Shorter, Gilbert Cannan and Sinclair Lewis. Of W. L. George . . .

The story will live after him. It was the occasion of his first visit among us, and none of us knew him save by the grace of "A Bed of Roses" and "Blind Alley," which he has never surpassed. Sandburg was there, and Hecht, and Llewellyn Jones, and a dozen more perhaps, and the subject had drifted around to the American woman. Mr. George sat in the center of the group, stuffed his pipe briskly and observed: "I am very much interested in the American woman. It depends entirely on her whether or not the American nation is decadent. Now we are all men here together, all interested in the same subject. So let me ask your opinion, that is to say, the sum of your own personal experience. Is it true that the American girl permits—ah, er—certain liberties of her person, without the impairment of, shall we say, her technical sex capital?"

"You mean—" began Ben Hecht—but the argot of Chicago, which Ben wields in picturesque fashion is a thing apart, and the common speech has moved on too rapidly for the printed page; we desist, the secret remains our own.

When I returned to my desk the personality of these men lingered with me and I observed to Keith Preston that thirty or forty years hence, when we were frail and toothless, we would stir the embers of a dying fire and try to rekindle the flame that once burned brightly in our hearts. These our contemporaries would no longer be subject to abuse or laudation; their stars would be fixed, and a younger generation of artists would be waging war upon a materialistic world under banners not yet unfurled. A couplet from one of Arthur Davison Ficke's poems kept recurring to me and seemed to fit the theme: "You whose old sins have in the later time become a legend perilous and sweet"—into what legendary stuff, thought I, will the dawning years transform Sherwood Anderson's boyishness, Ben Hecht's vivacious cynicism, Carl Sandburg's slow-spoken philosophy, Edgar Lee Masters' unwilling aloofness? Why wait until these living men have passed to transmit the story of how they lived, of how they built, of how they thought and spoke?

And then tradition rose up to caution me: there was Jules Lemaître's oft-quoted remark that writing about living men is not criticism, but conversation, and there was the apology Andrew Lang addressed to Thackeray, in the first of his Letters to Dead Authors, where he said that he "would not willingly be regarded as one of the many parasites who now advertise each movement and action of contemporary genius." Fair enough, and worth thinking about, but just then adventure called, and **romance** beckoned, and reason, as always, stood aside.

The adventure, the recklessness of it! To tell about living writers when their careers were still in the making; when their importance was, in the east at least, still a matter for debate; when one knew not whether their labors were the beginning of a new school or the echo of an old one, or a cry into the night; when the future lay ahead, like a golden river, leading either to the marshes or to the sea. One thing was true: if their place in literature was not certain, their place in our affections was assured. And so I said to Keith: "I think I'll write down the story of these men we know," and Keith responded simply: "Go to it. But," he added, leaning forward over his desk and raising an admonitory forefinger, "there is one great drawback. You will have to read their books!"

2. Carl Sandburg

Poet of the Streets and of the Prairie

> *The strong men keep coming on.*
> Carl Sandburg.

I

THERE remains in my mind an unforgettable picture: Carl Sandburg standing before the heavy hangings of red velvet in Mandel hall at the University of Chicago, twanging his guitar and singing into its Gothic recesses the gutter songs of America. Imagine the surroundings; the hall, almost monastic; the audience, cloistered almost, at least far removed from the spirit and atmosphere of the songs. And the poet—come with the very beginnings of folk lore to a spot dedicated to the refinements of literature, an intruder from a raucous, bellowing, swearing world, elbowing aside the stately verse of the ancients. Here have resounded more often the hymns of the English church; there is no place within these walls for "Blow the Man Down," "Jesse James," and "Frankie and Johnnie"; crude and formless they are, coarse as the roustabouts, panhandlers, and cattle rustlers from whose lips they come. . . . And yet, what was the first draft of the Iliad like, I wonder?

It is a conglomerate audience. Young men, fresh from their plunge in the swimming pool, lounge expectantly in their chairs; young women sit erect with black notebooks open and pencils poised; here and there in the sea of faces one finds lines that tell of late hours, anxiety, and approaching middle age, for many of the women have taught school in hidden, isolated districts in Kentucky and Tennessee, in lonely prairie schoolhouses in Texas and the southwest. They have come here for the summer to refresh their learning, come from places where these folk songs are native, and where no doubt they passed them by as ribald and coarse. What is going on in their minds now that they hear them sung in the sheltered university halls?

When Carl Sandburg talks to you he seems to have a bit of a stoop, to lean forward as he speaks; but before an audience he stands erect and seems much taller than he is. His long grayish hair, which he parts on the right side, falls forward over his forehead; his black bow tie gives him an appearance of being carefully attired; as a matter of fact he is not a fastidious dresser and you will find him wearing his heavy shoes, with their clumsy bull-dog toe, in any society. After he speaks you forget about his looks—his voice is a rich, deep monotone and he draws out his words slowly, which heightens the effect of his reading.

"The great iron cat" was what Witter Bynner once called him, when, in a spontaneous outburst of enthusiasm at Santa Fé, he wrote a group of verses beginning:

> Gray and sinewy and soft,
> Purring in a cosy loft,
> Prowling on accustomed feet,
> Courting a semi-friendly street,
> Aloof, but at home wherever men be,
> In town or on the prairie,
> Tender toeing round a child,
> Tigered with moonlight in the wild,
> Mysterious and more than that,
> Sandburg comes, the iron cat—
> Attic, cellar, alley, plain,
> A hunter, hunting poems again.

Like as not he begins on the defensive. He takes for granted that his audience is either unfamiliar with free verse or does not understand its place in our literature,

and most of the time he is right. Even though this movement is over ten years old and is an ancient tale among
writing folk there are audiences in Brownsville, Texas,
or Portland, Oregon, that have never heard of it; even
Dartmouth college, or a Browning society here and there,
or this audience at the University of Chicago, may profit
by the explanation. Carl's argument for free verse is
also an argument for the cultivation of our native resources, for an understanding of our humble folk lore,
for the plain speech of the people. Carl poises a lance
for the plain English idiom; his poems are filled with
the expressive words that he has picked up in his tramps
over the countryside: galoots, mutts, slant heads, jazz-
men, knucks, fourflushers, cheap skates, longhorns, work
plug, fade away, hanky-pank, bootleg booze. He takes
over whole phrases from the speech of the people and
flings them at you, as in "The Windy City," where,
standing on the bastion of a bridge, he hears the "black
cataracts of people jazz the classics":

> Since when did you kiss yourself in
> And who do you think you are?
> Come across, kick in, loosen up.
> Where do you get that chatter? . . .

"We do not always understand what you write," say
the scholars, reading "Gold Mud." "We don't get you
at all," say the unlettered workers, thrilled by "Smoke
and Steel" but confused by "Honky Tonk in Cleveland, O."

In reply Carl loves to tell a story:

"I've got a poem, 'Elephants Mean Different Things
to Different People.' It is reasonable to suppose that a
poem may mean many things to many people, and some-

thing entirely different to the poet himself. There was a merchant prince in Chicago who, when about to die, called in the highest-priced lawyers in the town and told them to draw up a will which should be fool-proof, so that after his death his heirs wouldn't have to fight in the courts over his estate. The lawyers drew up the will, and it was a good will, and after the man died it cost the heirs over a million dollars and took over seven years of litigation to find out what the will meant. After that I think people might permit a vagabond poet once in a while to write a poem or two which is not entirely clear to them.

"If a poem is a great big poem it will mean half a dozen things to half a dozen people; each one will get something personal out of it. Little children, with their minds free from rational images are quicker to grasp the fantastic pictures of poetry than grown-ups. I wrote a little poem: 'This—for the Moon—yes?' It begins:

> This is a good book? Yes?
> Throw it at the moon.
> Stand on the ball of your right foot
> And come to the lunge of a center fielder
> Straddling in a throw for the home plate,
> Let her go—spang—this book for the moon
>   —yes?

"Now a little child is delighted with the idea, but sometimes the elders ask me what it means. So too 'Primer Lesson';—'Look out how you use proud words'—you will find it in 'Slabs of the Sunburnt West.'

"Poems are the results of moods. I don't approach a subject in the same mood every day. Maybe some days I am in the mood for the prairie, the skies, the trees.

On other days I can feel the noise, the jumble, and the confusion of the city. There are days when I could not have written or even tolerated the idea of 'Smoke and Steel.' "

And then, perhaps, if his listeners prove receptive, Carl will launch into the thirty-eight definitions of poetry that he conceived one afternoon on the inspiration of a letter—but that is another story. The audience listens in rapt attention; the definitions are sometimes concretely put, sometimes intangible. At times the audience discerns an epigram and a ripple of laughter floats through the hall. And then again, puzzlement, and bewildered faces, as when Carl explains that poetry is achieved by a synthesis of hyacinths and biscuits. A vague suspicion floats through the audience; perhaps he is kidding us.

The origin of the definitions was this: About a year ago an eastern editor wrote Carl for an article explaining the new poetry. "I confess," he said in effect, "that I have grown up with the so-called older poetry and that I prefer it, and don't know what to make of the new poetry. The other day I picked up what seems to be a representative magazine of the new movement, "Broom," and read a poem by Miss Amy Lowell on lilacs in New England. This poem I understand, for every New Englander is familiar with lilacs. But beyond that— Now what I ask of you is, can you write me an article explaining the new poetry for our readers? . . ."

Over this letter Carl puzzled long. Explain the new poetry? But the new poetry was already ten to fifteen years old; even to his mind hoary with age, so well established that it appeared in school texts and conservative instructors in English presented it to their classes. Free verse, too, was an old story. Carl began thinking about poetry in general and his mind went off on a ramble. A definition jumped into his mind. He turned to his type-writer and transcribed it:

"Poetry is a projection across silence of cadences arranged to break that silence with definite intentions of echoes, syllables, wave lengths. . . ."

Then he went on:

"Poetry is an act practised with the terribly plastic material of human language."

"Poetry is a sliver of the moon lost in the belly of a golden frog."

"Poetry is a phantom script telling how rainbows are made and why they go away."

Carl's room is spacious and for the most part quiet. He remained uninterrupted, and in the course of the after-noon definitions raced to get on paper. He had written thirty-eight when the well ran dry. Then the inspiration passed— not another line could he write. The definitions may be found in the "Atlantic Monthly" for March, 1923.

One of the definitions shows how well Carl has built on the older sages. It reads: "Poetry is the achievement of the synthesis of hyacinths and biscuits." The phrase, when read, always brings about an outburst of hilarity, but its derivation is probably known to those who are familiar with the ancient Persian proverb: "If I had two loaves of bread I would sell one to buy white hyacinths to feed my soul."

"Nor let us forget the reverse of that," Carl added one day. "I have two baskets of white hyacinths and I wish to God I could sell one and buy me some bread to feed myself."

The auditors listen in rapt attention. They are lulled

by the speaker's voice; they drift with the rich melody, the singing note, and the cadence with which he reads makes them forget that his verses will not scan by any rules of classic form. There are many who say that they found no music, no beauty, upon reading Sandburg's lines but that they were captivated by his own rich intonation and discovered unexpected beauty after he had read to them; this is true, for perhaps more than any other poet, even more than Vachel Lindsay, Carl Sandburg is the master interpreter of his own verse. He is apt to begin anywhere—with his grotesques, his love lyrics, his balladry, his hymns to the prairie, to smoke and steel, his satires on civilization, his apostrophe to industry and the city—and carry his audience with him. With his voice he becomes humorous and ironical, sarcastic and contemptuous, whimsical and deeply serious. "Carl Sandburg's voice," said William B. Owen, head of Chicago Teacher's college, "should be perpetuated on records, for like the voice of Tennyson it is an unforgettable and essential part of his poems." And although Carl uses no gestures and rarely alters his attitude, his face is a sensitized mirror of his moods. When he aims a thrust at some inhuman practice that has aroused his indignation his lower jaw sticks out, his lip seems to curl and he drawls out his words as if taking careful aim; when he reads the Rootabaga stories he is as a big boy among children; his eyes are wreathed with happy wrinkles and he chuckles with inward mirth at his own lines.

II

Carl Sandburg's voice is rich and mellow and deep; his range is a few notes only and when he sings you get the impression that he is holding a low, sweet tone indefinitely and strumming a few changes of chords on his guitar. His singing is pure art; the art that disguises all artifice. He is at his best in a group of friends and toward the sobering part of an evening, when he will strum chords at a piano and sing ballads and chanteys. There remains in my mind a wonderful picture of Carl singing; he and Sinclair Lewis had visited the Lindlahr sanitarium at Elmhurst, Ill., to see Eugene V. Debs that afternoon and had joined us later in the evening at the home of Dr. Morris Fishbein, editor and lover of books, to whom H. L. Mencken once sent his photograph with the inscription: "To the philological pathologist from the pathological philologian." Lewis and Sandburg have a deep admiration for each other; Lewis' openness and generosity naturally appeal to Carl, who once said of him: "This great big husky fellow—he's got something stirring inside him; George Horace Lorimer wanted him to be one of his trained seals, like Irvin Cobb, but he kicked over the traces; I wouldn't be surprised if, in ten years or so, he gathered up all that is in him, Main street and all, and came out with something big." Well, Lewis was there, and Keith Preston, Fishbein, Dr. Arthur J. Cramp and Paul de Kruif, and I forget who else, and Carl chanted "Casey Jones," "Frankie and Johnnie," "Whiskey is the Life of Man," "Blow the Man Down," "Noah's Dove," the Boll Weevil song—heaven knows what else. There is this about Carl's singing: his themes are elemental, the words are often crude, uncouth, but his rendering is never coarse. I have heard some of our folk chants shouted by college boys with any number of foul innuendoes—I have never heard Carl sing them without realizing that his art raised the whole ballad to the height of poetry. One reason is that Carl has a feeling for strong, homely words, but not for obscenity. I suppose that "Frankie and Johnnie," which comes somewhere out of the southwest, and tells the story of how an underworld character becomes unfaithful to a prostitute, who thereupon shoots him, is about as profane a song, when all its implications are understood, as any in our folk lore; it has, singularly enough, penetrated our best circles and is beloved of college gatherings—but I have yet to hear Carl Sandburg sing it with all its coarseness. This has been, now and then, a subject for banter among us, and I have heard friends express disappointment that Carl, popularly considered the apostle of men with big, broad shoulders and hard-hitting words, should shun anything in our native speech. Carl's version before most audiences is entitled "Frankie and Albert," and is rather innocuous. One evening when he was addressing a college audience he announced that he would include not only "Frankie and Albert" but also "Frankie and Johnnie" in his program, and the ripple of hilarity that ran through the groups of college boys and girls showed that the ballad was no stranger to them. Carl even heightened the interest by facetiously remarking: "If a student of folk lore from Europe were to ask me which of the two songs was the most significant, I should say that the first is simpler and belongs to the earliest stage of our folk songs, the second to the more sophisticated period. To those who have heard Debussy a little of 'Frankie and Johnnie' is more important than much of Debussy."

But if any one expected Carl to sing all the obscenity gathered together in the song he was doomed to disappointment. Both versions carried the famous refrain: "For he was the man who was doing me wrong," but in

other essentials they bore a closer resemblance to
"Wyncken, Blynken, and Nod" than to the famous underworld ballad.

Carl Sandburg's love for folk songs goes back a long
way in his history—no doubt as a boy he first sang them
with no regard for their relation to our folk ways or to
their literary potentialities. Later it seemed but natural
that the poet, dealing in plain, homely themes in his
poetry, should become interested in folk songs as a
creative art.

Carl does not know when he first began to write them
down, but it was a long time ago; more recently, since he
began singing them in public, volunteers have come forward and contributed to his store from all over the
United States. The songs he likes the best, and the most
effective ones, are not found in books; many of them he
took down from the lips of all sorts of strange characters.
Like John A. Lomax, professor in the University of Texas,
compiler of "Cowboy Songs," who gave Carl a number of
his songs, the poet found a rich store of unrecorded but
widely known ballads in America. They seemed to have
originated among men who never read, but who chant
songs in lumber camps, in southern timber lands, on
plantations, on cattle ranches, in railroad yards, among
cow punchers and hoboes all over the United States.
They are like the great unrecorded stories that are passed
on by word of mouth, like the legends of Paul Bunyan
which Sinclair Lewis ran across in the lumber camps of
the northwest, and of which we have no authentic records
anywhere. The Anglo-Saxon strain seemed to have been
particularly prolific in balladry and there is current in the
Kentucky hills and West Virginia a great variety of
English and Scottish folk songs, some of which have their

roots deep in medievalism. Carl Sandburg has heard a great many unrecorded songs in his trips around the country; hence he has become an alert transcriber, writing down the ballads and humming over the tunes to himself whenever opportunity offers. The negroes, he found, seemed most addicted to balladry. Any outstanding catastrophe would lead some improviser to throw together a dozen or more clumsy quatrains telling the story of the event. One of these was a song on the sinking of the Titanic, first sung by negroes in the South, and sent to Carl by an inmate of the penitentiary at Atlanta, Ga. Naturally it makes much of the gallant captain and crew and the famous line: "Women and children first!" Sailors bring home all sorts of chants heard in the ports of the world. One of these, with the refrain "Blow the man down," Carl first heard in Boston; Robert Frost had heard another version of the same song on the wharves in San Francisco. It is interesting to find the originals of some of these maritime songs in "Sea Songs and Shanties," [*sic*] a compilation by W. H. Whall, master mariner, of some of the best known historic chants of the British marine. The Boll Weevil song naturally originated in the south where this insect has done much damage to crops. "Casey Jones" is a railroad song much used in vaudeville, and is said to have been written around the career of John Luther Jones, engineer of the "Chicago and New Orleans Limited," who died in a wreck on March 18, 1900. So much interest has become attached to this character that when the Dearborn station in Chicago was destroyed by fire in January, 1923, the information that this was Casey Jones' old terminal was carried in newspaper headlines. The song is most popular in the southwest and by the substitution of local railroad names it has been acclimated everywhere. The song about Jesse James is indigenous to Missouri and Kansas and demonstrates the close link between our folk songs and those of old England. Jesse James' career was a modern version of that of an ancient highwayman, and in the song he is raised to the position of a martyr. Carl is wont to remark with a smile: "Jesse James may yet become to the United States what Robin Hood is to England. He never robbed the poor but always banks and railroads." It carries the odd but catchy refrain:

> Jesse leaves a widow to mourn all her life,
> The children he left will pray
> For the thief and the coward
> Who shot Mr. Howard
> And laid Jesse James in his grave.

Most of the American ballads have this in common with the ancient English balladry; they deal with somber themes, death, infidelity, and destruction, and few have in them a note of ecstasy or exultation. To his well-groomed audiences Carl is apt to say: "There may be murder, crime and adultery in these folk songs, but after all not more than you find in the average grand opera."

It would be inutile to list all the songs that Carl Sandburg sings; he has acquired a large repertoire and his list is regularly increasing; those he knows best include besides those already cited the Sam Hall song, "Stacker Lee," "Noah's Dove," "Whiskey, Johnnie Whiskey," "Jay Gould's Daughter," "Zion City," "The Buffalo Skinners," and many more. At the University of South Carolina Carl found a group of men deeply interested in American folk lore, in fact Professor Taylor, and Dan Reed and his wife, Isadora Bennett Reed, who was at

one time on our staff at the Chicago "Daily News," have
sent him ballads and blues. But sometimes he finds folk
songs that have their roots deep in American history
repeated in the most unexpected places. One day when
he was visiting his brother-in-law, Edward Steichen, the
photographer, in New York City, he became acquainted
with a couple staying in the same house. It transpired
that they originated from Oklahoma, and a short conversation was sufficient to unlock a store of native material. They had retained a number of folk songs that
must have been sung in Oklahoma by the earliest settlers
who crossed the Indian lands in prairie schooners. One
day when Carl had stopped in Carney, Neb., to give a
reading he stumbled on an old civil war song about "the
Linkun gunboats." In Missoula, Mont., he found a
woman who in her youth had lived in the Kentucky
mountains. She recalled that the old mountaineers used
to sit in front of their cabins and sing:

> I don't like no railroad fool;
> Railroad fool's got a head like a mule.

This ballad, of innumerable verses, went back to the days
when the railroad prospector was cutting a path through
the mountains, when the locomotive whistle was disturbing
the quiet of the prairies, and the ballad reflected a hos-
tility that would be hard to comprehend now. There is
available a book, "Folk Songs of the Kentucky Mountains," by Josephine McGill, but for the most part the
historians of our folk ways, with their eyes glued to the
European keyhole, have neglected this rich lode of native
Americana, and forgotten that a great part of the history
of our nation had been sung by plain people in humble

balladry that awaits a native Liszt, Dvorák and Tschai-kovsky. It was after hearing Carl Sandburg sing ballads before the Chicago Woman's Club one day that Grace Williamson Willett wrote: "When Mr. Sandburg's musical voice and the soft strumming of the guitar ceased more than one in the audience thought: 'Here is the American poet who will some day create an operatic libretto about Chicago that will be to Chicago what Charpentier's "Louise" is to Paris.'" When I brought this to Carl's attention he replied half humorously, half seriously: "Yes, I have often felt the inspiration to do that, an opera in the native idiom, and there is a theme waiting in the Black Hills version of 'The Dying Cowboy' with its refrain, 'Bury me out on the lone prairie,' which is, I think, the best native strain I have ever come across and one full of drama and pathos."

On a parallel with folk songs are folk proverbs; these have also engaged Carl's interest, and he has found that in common with all nations America has a great fund of rich sayings which no one has taken the trouble to record. This led Carl to read the proverbs of other nations and compare them. American proverbs he finds brief and imagistic and often with a tang of slang in them that gives them particular piquancy; they are, he says, "fugitive and furtive like ground squirrels; they have to be smoked out."

III

In all my memories of conversations with Carl there is somewhere in the distance the roar of the city; the grinding of wheels upon the pavement, the pounding of elevated trains on iron trestles, the whistling of traffic cops, the shouting of drivers. Noises that are a part of us in our cloistered city life; were they not there we might sob out, with his teamster, en route to the penitentiary, "O God, there's noises I'm going to be hungry for." The city is always omnipresent; its tall houses shut out the sunlight, its smoke cuts off dimly-lit vistas like a curtain. The low, rumbling sounds are to me like the deep bass of a mighty organ, upon which rises the gentler, mellowing music of the poet's voice. And as I think of the city in terms of sight and sound Carl is thinking of men and women, of rugged, bent, broken men, and pale, emaciated, toiling women, of the twisted gargoyles of our life.

We were speaking of beginnings. Once the youth of this man is unveiled we realize how deeply his earliest experiences have colored his whole life. It explains his themes, his point of view, his intensity, his compassion, and pity. Carl Sandburg comes from Galesburg, Ill., where he was born January 6, 1878. Ostensibly he was of the city, but the great wide prairie was close at hand; he was to grow up with the music of the wind through its corn fields in his ears; like the young Lincoln he was to tread the furrows of rich, black loam and feel the soft grass of the meadow lands under his bare feet. "I was born on the prairie," he sings, "and the milk of its wheat, the red of its clover, the eyes of its women gave me a song and a slogan." His father put in long hours in a grimy railroad blacksmith shop. His mother became bent and worn in a life of unrelenting toil. His first little collection of poems, printed privately in Galesburg years ago, he dedicated to her with an expression of deep, sincere affection. His boyhood was filled with harsh episodes, with meager schooling, with little room for self-improvement. He worked hard, tried all sorts of jobs; the hours were long; the work unremitting. The fight for sustenance left deep scars on his sensitive nature.

One of the earliest jobs that left a lasting impression on his mind was driving a milk wagon in Galesburg at the age of thirteen. Later he obtained work in a barber shop as porter. "This is where I first got acquainted with the American congressman," said Carl. "A congressman from Galesburg died and about twenty to thirty congressmen and senators from Washington came on to bury him. I guess I had the usual kid's exalted view of these men until I blacked their boots. . . ." He worked in a brickyard and then decided to "go west." But going west was an arduous process—by freight and blind baggage mostly. The trip was a hard one, but the young Sandburg had the stars for companions; he could commune with the clouds, the wheat field, the great, wide spaces; the open appealed to him; life was harsh, perhaps, but his spirit was unperturbed. In Kansas he struck out for the harvest fields and got big skin blisters on his hands and hard callouses on his feet; in Kansas City, Omaha, and Denver he found jobs as a dishwasher in hotels. For a short time he was a carpenter's helper in Kansas; again he procured a pot of black asphaltum and a brush and went from house to house offering to paint stoves in exchange for a meal. Days like these were treasured in his memory; eventually they flowered in poems in "Cornhuskers" and in "Smoke and Steel." "Prairie," the long poem, is of them, and there are innumerable smaller ones in both books that are reminiscent of these days of hazard and uncertainty.

When Carl eventually turned his face homeward he found his old job on the milk wagon awaiting him in Galesburg. He took it for the time, but soon he obtained his first chance to become apprenticed to a trade—that of house painter. And then came 1898, and the Spanish war. "The fever to see Porto Rico and the West Indies got me," he explained. He enlisted as a volunteer in the Sixth Illinois Infantry and was sent to Porto Rico, where he served eight months. It was to prove the turning point in his career, for in the ranks he met a youth from Lombard college, Galesburg, who talked college at every opportunity. The opportunity to get some schooling looked big to Sandburg, and upon his return home his matriculation as a special student there was made possible.

Carl recalls vividly the hopelessness of his outlook when at work on a menial task; the depression that often came over him when he contemplated the lot of the worker who has aspirations and can see no way out. "There were times," said Carl, "when I might easily have stepped over the line that marks the honest man from the lawbreaker. I mean conditions often drive a man to hate the law. I used to like to play ball. I played a great deal after work, especially in the evenings. Once a gang of us played ball hard one Sunday in an open field near a deserted brickyard. There was an old pit near by where clay had been dug for bricks and this was full of water. The water was inviting and we pulled off our clothes and waded in. Some righteous character spied us from a hill and telephoned the police. The cops came in a wagon-load and rounded us up, tumbled us into the wagon and took us to jail. There was no judge sitting that day and so we were kept there, in a hot stuffy place, the rest of that afternoon and night and hauled up before the justice for a reprimand next morning. We had been boys at play, swimming for the pure joy of it, but the law had been broken and we had to suffer for it. That sort of thing makes a boy wonder about himself and what laws are good for."

Carl's early reading was desultory—the sort of thing a boy picks up without guidance, but the books that left a lasting impression betray his interest in two lines of activity that survive to-day. He liked to read biography and recalls that he perused the life of Napoleon by John S. C. Abbott with intense application. Biography is to-day one of his favorite themes. He also enjoyed reading two encyclopedias—one of persons and places, the other of common things; to-day his feeling for interesting, unrelated facts, for strange, out-of-the-way data is almost a passion. He read the Rollo Books by Jacob Abbott—which proves only that he was a typical lad of the eighties. Folk lore held him from the start—he read repeatedly Grimm's fairy tales, Hans Christian Andersen and the Zigzag journeys—and mayhap the zigzag railroad in "Rootabaga Stories" harks back to that earlier mental picture.

"My father was a dark Swede," said Carl. "He had dark hair and brown eyes and came from Asposoken, in the north of Sweden. I flatter myself sometimes in thinking that maybe somewhere back in my history there may be a Mongol or one of those old Asiatics. I have a sense for fantasy that runs through the Nordic folk lore, but I do not have the oriental's sense for plot.

"When I got to Porto Rico," said Carl, "I was already doing a lot of desultory reading and several sentimental poems had impressed me very much. Most of these ran to serious themes. I had a fondness for Herbert's

Sweet day, so cool, so calm, so bright,
The bridal of the earth and sky,
The dew shall weep thy fall to-night,
For thou must die.

"Then there was 'To a Waterfowl' and Gray's 'Elegy,' and I found a satisfaction in reading and committing some of the orations of Robert G. Ingersoll. His rhetorical speech at his brother's grave, for instance, I have never forgotten."

Carl looked out over the rooftops, over the elevated structure, and repeated slowly: " 'Life is a narrow vale between the cold and barren peaks of two eternities; we cry aloud but the only answer is an echo. . . . If every one for whom he did a kind deed were to bring a flower to his grave to-day, he would sleep to-night beneath a wilderness of blossoms.' Well, that's Ingersoll," said Carl, coming quickly back to the present.

No doubt other fine lads have hustled milk cans and swept out barber shops, but if at the same time they brooded over the lot of the worker they left no record of it. Carl came out of struggle with deep compassion and pity for the struggling, burdened toiler who can't help himself, can't see the way out, and with deep protest within him against things as they are.

Carl Sandburg's determination to write must have welled up within him even in the days when he was handling milk cans. At least when he reached Lombard college he had already laid the foundations on which his career has been built. A sentence in a personal letter of that time is characteristic of his attitude: "I am like Keats at least in this, that the roaring of the wind is my wife, and the stars through the window panes are my children. As for posterity, I say with the Hibernian: 'What has it ever done for us?' " He might equally well have asked this question of tradition, for his preoccupation has been with "the supreme possession of this hour."

IV

Carl Sandburg entered Lombard college in Galesburg, Ill., upon his return from Porto Rico in 1898, where he had served eight months with the Sixth Illinois Infantry during the Spanish-American war. This was due in part to the persuasion of a Lombard student whom he met in the ranks. Carl's army name was "Cully"—some time later he seems to have been known as Charles A. Sandburg. Lombard was to prove an important factor in his development. For here he found Philip Green Wright, a teacher of English, mathematics and astronomy, a gentle, refined character who was of tremendous inspirational value to younger men about him, and who wrote poetry and sought companionships in our traditional literature. Philip Green Wright sits to-day as secretary of the tariff commission at Washington, D. C., and few men who meet him casually suspect that he is at heart a poet and a pilgrim, a wayfarer among beautiful things. He was the first man to see the promise of Carl Sandburg. He called together Sandburg and two other students of literary tastes whose names survive—Brown and Lauer—and together they formed the Poor Writers' club, which met on Sunday afternoons in Wright's home and read prose and verse, criticized compositions of their own and developed their young enthusiasms. Later on, in 1904, when Wright became Sandburg's first publisher, he demonstrated his keen appreciation of the young poet's unformed talents. In an introduction to Carl's first book of verse—of which I will speak soon—Wright presented this happy portrait:

I do not remember that at that time there was anything particularly distinguished in his appearance—anything, that

is, to suggest incipient genius. He looked like one of the proletariate rather than one of the intellectuals—just a rough-featured, healthy boy possessed of indomitable energy and buoy-
ancy of spirit. But it is just these rough-featured boys whose
faces take on with the years the impress of that indefinable
quality we call character. I suppose the "god within" can
achieve more lasting results with granite and bronze than with
clay and putty. . . . He had seen a good deal of the world;
some of it, I believe, from the under side of box cars, traveling
via the Gorky line to literary fame. The boys called him "the
terrible Swede"—not such a bad characterization after all.
. . . The Poor Writers' club is now dissipated. Brown is like
myself, a pedagogue; Lauer is No. 834 on the payroll of a big
factory but Sandburg, true to his Norse instincts, disdains
harness. In these days of frock coat degeneracy he could
hardly build a dragon ship and scour the seas like his viking
forebears, but he is making the nearest approach to this which
modern manners permit; he is traveling, selling stereoscopic
views for Underwood and Underwood. And he is doing it
in quite the old viking spirit. "When one has the right swing
and enthusiasm," he says, "it is not unlike hunting, a veritable
sport. To scare up the game by preliminary talk and to know
how long to follow it, to lose your game through poorly directed argument, to hang on to game that finally eludes, to con-
front boldly, to circle around quietly, to keep on the trail,
tireless and keen, till you've bagged some orders, there is some
satisfaction in returning at night, tired of the train, but proud
of the day's work." And when he has bagged some orders
enough to keep him alive for a few days he is free. Free to
read, to observe men and things, and to think. He reads
everything: Boccaccio, Walt Whitman, Emerson, Tolstoi, and
enters with appreciation and sympathetic enthusiasm into all
that he reads. But literature, even the best, is but a pallid
reflection of life; he prefers impressions at first hand. . . .
And so he moves from place to place reading, reflecting and

growing inwardly from the deep impression of beauty and
grandeur which his soul drinks in from surrounding nature.
"We have been working in the country lately," he writes, "the
trees have massive and far-reaching roots. The marshes by
the sea are impressive in their loneliness. I have seen fish
hawks seize their prey—and more things." To me there is
something of the quality of a Norse saga; inchoate force and
virility, unconscious kinship of the soul with all that is beautiful and terrible in nature and above all the delightful bloom
and freshness and spontaneous enthusiasm of expression of
one who is witnessing the sunrise for the first time.

This panegyric comes from the little book of verse
which Philip Green Wright sponsored and which contains
the first published poems of Carl Sandburg. Carl is
rather glad now that its distribution was limited and that
few copies are to be found to-day—adolescent enthusiasms
stick out all over it, he feels—but what matter? It also
radiates courage, honesty, strength of purpose, and a
clean outlook. Philip Green Wright may have been
superlative in his praise, but then no young writer out
of his classes had ever come forward with so clear a
vision. The book is a little pamphlet bound in paper; it
is called "In Reckless Ecstasy," and was printed at the
Asgard Press in Galesburg in 1904.

Harking back to the first fruits of poets in their adolescence is sometimes a hapless task, sometimes meaningless, and we would spend but little time on this book of
verse if it did not happen to be so thoroughly naïve and
self-revealing. As in epitome here are all of Carl's aims,
aspirations, enthusiasms; here is that fine attitude toward
his work that has distinguished all his craftsmanship. He
took the title from a line in one of Marie Corelli's books—
of all places! She had written: "Ideas which cannot be

stated in direct words may be brought home by reckless ecstasies of thought," and in elaborating his thesis Carl had said:

"When I seat myself in the sumptuous saddle of 'The Ring and the Book' and ride upon its restless ecstasies, I get more light and truth and wonderment than in listening to any preacher who splits hairs and pumps platitudes for a living. It is well to make distinctions: it is the shades, the graduations, the lights and shadows, not the colors, that mark the artist. Nevertheless there are thoughts beyond the reach of words and these the seers transmit only by lurid splashes of verbiage that cannot be gaged by common sense but must be sought out by the spirit of sublimity in us. I try to express myself sensibly, but if that fails I use the reckless ecstasy. As Kipling has one of his untamed children of the forest say: 'I will be the word of the people, mine will be the bleeding mouth from which the gag is snatched. I will say everything.'"

Has any critic ever formulated a better expression of Sandburg's work than that contained in the last two sentences?

What we seek in this little book is the man himself— so the weak adjectives, the clichés, the unconscious imitations of older ecstasies, even though they spring from the heart, mean nothing to us. It is to be supposed that every poet begins his apprenticeship with discovering rainbows. Sandburg, too, has written lines to stars, flowers, clouds, grass; he has addressed the ideal in such wellworn terms as "O star, radiant, glowing orb, matchless, beautiful, scintillant"—yes, even he who thundered the sonorous lines of the hog butcher of the world could speak of a star as an "exquisite, piercing luminary, soft, superb, undying iridescence." But this book reveals something greater and stronger—sympathy with human suffering, a man with confidence in humankind, a lover of all men, proud to be alive. He writes:

> To whom my hand goes out;
> The unapplauded ones who bear
> No badges on their breasts,
> Who pass us on the street with
> Unfearing, patient eyes,
> Like dumb cart horses in the street . . .

Free verse? Or merely broken prose? Remember that this was 1904—when there was no *vers libre* controversy, no *imagistes,* no manifesto for workers in unrimed verse. Carl was already conscious of a cadence that he was to develop later into a characteristic verse form. It came easy to him, and naturally. This was recognized even by so captious a commentator as Theodore Maynard, who writes in his new book, "Our Best Poets": "Masters is a free verse poet by accident; Sandburg by fate; Amy Lowell by choice; Sandburg by natural bent; Amy Lowell by cleverness; Masters by shrewdness helped out by luck."

Tramping over the countryside, Sandburg saw with sympathetic eyes the puny struggles of frail human beings for bread; his arms instinctively reached out to them, for they were engaged in an uneven battle, just as he had been. He had come upon the glass blowers in Millville, in southern New Jersey, and been moved by the sight of boys who worked nine to ten hours a day at $2 to $3.50 a week at "carryin' in." "They are grimy, wiry, scrawny, stunted specimens, and in cusswords and salacious thought they know all grown men know. Their thoughts are only

those of the blowers and gaffers, besides views of a big
barnlike space lit up by white hot sand. This has been
their universe at those times of the day when they were
most alive, most wide awake, most sensitive to impressions. The manufacturers have endowed a night school
but the teacher told me the boys cannot keep their heads
up and their eyes open during the sessions. Therefore
their brains don't make much headway." Immediately
his mind turns to the future and with the exuberance of
youth he visualizes a time when this shall not be; in a
form of verse easily borrowed from Kipling he declares:

For the hovels shall pass and the shackles drop,
The gods shall tumble and the systems fall,
And the things they will make with their loves at stake
Shall be for the gladness of each and all.

But over ten years later his faith in a speedy reorgani-
zation is not so firm; he writes a poem called "Milldoors"
and we may wonder in how far the memory of the little
lads carryin' in for the glass blowers survived to create
this strain of hopelessness:

You will never come back
I say good-by when I see you going in the doors.

.   .   .   .

I say good-by because I know they tap your wrists
In the dark, in the silence, day by day.

And here, in this little book, at the outset of his writing
career, he stated his creed with the enthusiasm of youth,
and although he has never referred to it again, it still
deserves to stand as a creed that has been lived up to:

Make me a good mixer among people; one who always passes along the good word.

Give me a keen eye for the main chance, but give me to remember that I can take nothing home.

May the potencies of song and laughter abide with me ever.

I glory in this world of men and women, torn with troubles and lost in sorrow, yet living on to love and laugh and play through it all. My eyes range with pleasure over flowers, prairies, woods, grass, and running water, and the sea, and the sky, and the clouds.

V

After college all sorts of jobs came to him; none held him for long. But life beckoned to him, he rubbed elbows with his fellow men, he grew in understanding and sympathy. Joined with the under dog's lot in life, he had from the first a thoughtful lad's attitude toward more fortunate, more well-established men; a bit resentful he was, and belligerent, and contemptuous of men who fed their bellies at the expense of half-famished women and children. His social sense was always acute, his deep sympathy gave him radical leanings, but his habit of mind, of weighing, of reflecting sober issues, kept him from ever throwing himself wholly into any one political camp. He traveled about the country selling films for Underwood and Underwood; he went to Milwaukee and got into newspaper work, and there, on June 15, 1908, he was married to Lillian Steichen. From 1910 to 1912 he was secretary to the mayor of Milwaukee and there gained an insight into practical politics and the disillusionizing practices of actual city government. He got very close to labor leaders, to spokesmen for plain folk; he knew men who were Napoleons of wards and precincts, and saw through the crude political chicanery of the time. He then drifted to Chicago and obtained a position with "System" and here his knowledge of labor stood him in good stead, for he was able to write about factories and modern industrialism with an understanding that gave weight to his articles. There was a series on "Training Workers to Be Careful" which included an investigation of safety appliances. Moreover Sandburg here came in contact with the big employers of labor; interviewed them in their well-equipped offices and contrasted their lot with that of the teamsters, the bricklayers, and the sand shovelers of his experience. They were to him the "millionaires" of his earliest poems, and in his first usage of that word there is noticeable a contempt and a resentment that comes from the heart of a man who hates a social system that permits the wholesale exploitation of the many by the few, without his being able to suggest a remedy. Newspaper work of various sorts intervened; he came in contact with N. D. Cochran and eventually drifted into his employ. Cochran had a brilliant, absorptive mind with a strong feeling for social justice. Before he came to Chicago he had been associated with "Golden Rule" Jones in Cleveland and with Brand Whitlock in Toledo and had participated in their fights for better government. In Chicago he established a tabloid newspaper known as the "Daybook," which was to carry no advertising and to gain a general circulation on the merits of its news alone. Cochran argued that the newspaper, lacking advertising, could suffer no dictation from wealthy advertisers, hence it would be free and could devote itself to printing news without favor and to break a lance for the under dog. Carl Sandburg naturally found his interest enlisted in the cause; he also had a great admiration for the mind of Cochran, of whom he said, in contrasting him with Jones and Whitlock: "He got all they had, and something more." But a newspaper of this character, dependent for support on the unorganized proletariate and the wage earner, who had as yet developed little sense of class solidarity, could not hope everlastingly to combat the highly superior news-gathering forces of the big dailies, and eventually Cochran stopped his presses and went back to Toledo. Before that time, in 1917, Carl Sandburg, through his acquaintance with newspapermen, had come in contact with Henry J. Smith, news editor of the Chicago "Daily News," and had for the first time obtained employment under its kindly roof. In 1918 an opportunity to travel to Norway and Sweden in behalf of the Newspaper Enterprise Association beckoned him and he seized it; for the best part of a year he wrote voluminously for the N. E. A., immersed himself in old world philosophies, and sought to penetrate the historic background of his own people and gain a better knowledge of national psychology. Soon after his return he again became associated with the Chicago "Daily News" and that relationship lasts until this day.

During all this time his knowledge of men was being sharpened, his perceptions were becoming more acute, he was gaining interest in mass movements as well as in individuals. He wrote prodigiously the ephemeral news of the day, and always with much feeling. One cannot picture Carl Sandburg as the superficial reporter who cavorts from one cause to the next, measuring a strike, a murder, a wedding, a funeral, by the same rule—an opportunity to write a column. Carl's emotions entered into much of what he heard and saw and even though the impersonal newspaper account did not betray his sympathies he was never able to discourse about the events of the day without wearing his feelings on his sleeve. His knowledge of labor conditions made his assignment to labor matters a natural result, and for a long time he wrote much about them. Strikes, lockouts, boycotts, were his daily fare; he listened to the grievances of teamsters and garment workers; he heard labor leaders at their daily counsels and discussed "the men" with employers. From day to day he followed the fortunes of the Amalgamated Clothing Workers of America in their bitter but successful battle for recognition and justice in Chicago. For three years he attended conventions of the American Federation of Labor. With his strong leaning toward the poor and the unfortunate, it was but logical that the situation of the negro in Chicago should enlist his interest, and when the local race riots broke out in the summer of 1918 through the killing of a negro lad by a white man at a park swimming beach, he was delegated to investigate the whole affair. His series of articles on the subject, entitled "The Chicago Race Riots," were published first in the Chicago "Daily News"; later they were issued by Harcourt, Brace and Company in pamphlet form and have been sold widely to students of race conditions in America.

Carl Sandburg was never a hair-trigger reporter; he could never get into action quickly and weave a fanciful story as Ben Hecht, seated only at the adjoining desk, was wont to do; his work required meditation and leisure, and often he toiled far into the night, and Henry Smith would find his neatly typewritten manuscript on his desk when he arrived early the next morning. Special assignments soon fell to Sandburg, and when W. H. Hollander, for a number of years motion picture critic of the "Daily

News," resigned to become publicity director for the Balaban & Katz string of theaters, the place was offered to Sandburg. The fact that this poet of the prairies and of the city's streets should find contentment in writing about motion pictures for a daily newspaper often causes surprise when mentioned, but his editors discovered that it was one thing that Carl really liked to do. It was again close to the people; Carl saw them go into the theaters with their pennies, he began to speculate about the social consequences of the motion picture and its influence, proof of which was daily before his eyes. His stories about motion pictures have no place here, but it may interest many that they are dissimilar from anything else that is being written under the guise of criticism. With an absolutely free hand Carl Sandburg was enabled to pass such judgment as he wished; his criticism varied from sermons to vignettes, and often a strong dose of homely philosophy was thrown in after the manner of a poem in *vers libre*. Theater managers who looked for puffs and publicity could make nothing out of this strange, aloof creature who reported "movies" in a fashion contrary to all standards of exploitation; publicity men shook their heads sadly and cautioned the advertising department of the newspaper that with proper "coöperation" by an amenable editor they could gain much more advertising lineage—to no avail. The standards that Victor F. Lawson had set for the "Daily News," which included a divorce between the advertising and the editorial departments of his newspaper, were perhaps unique in this most exploited and ungodly of all nations, but to his glory and to the eternal advantage of the motion picture critic and those of us who labor as reviewers of books they held fast.

Those who have deplored Carl Sandburg's association with newspaper work, fearing that it would heap vulgarity on his muse, spoke first of all without knowledge of the fact that the newspaper was primarily Carl's research laboratory, and that he belonged there; moreover they did not know that his berth at the "Daily News" possessed advantages such as few poets have been able to gain in their formative period. The genius of Henry Justin Smith, whose fame will go down as an author as well as an editor, had another facet—this lay in his direction of men. To give young men a chance to bring out the best in them and to place no obstacles in their way was an unspoken but nevertheless hard and fast rule with "H. J." —by his kindly advice half a dozen men whose names are now nationally known were encouraged to persevere and work out their own salvation. No editorial shackles ever lay heavily on Carl Sandburg; he has been able, despite his close association with the "Daily News," to travel far and wide, from coast to coast, to meet his audiences whenever they beckoned, to obtain leisure and rest when something inside told him that it was needed. This elasticity has taken the curse of the treadmill off the "Daily News"; there are men throughout the United States to-day, and likewise in the positions of foreign correspondents in Europe and Asia, who will speak with gratitude of the fact that Victor F. Lawson has never insisted on his pound of flesh, and that in this organization at least there was no hindrance in the way of the man who had grit to make a name for himself.

See how the early influences have molded, have shaped the creative work of Carl Sandburg. Out of his association with the city came his first book of poems, "Chicago Poems" (Henry Holt & Co., 1915)—for his adolescent

writings do not rank with his mature work. But
although the city pulsated in his veins he was yet the
child of the prairie; great acres of the land lay in his
background and in his ancestry, and he celebrated his joy
in the majesty of the prairie and the open spaces in "Cornhuskers," the second book (Holt, 1918). "Cornhuskers"
has in it much that reminds one of his early tramps
through the middle west, and there are also little lyrical
poems that tell of his happy home fireside. Then came
"Smoke and Steel" (Harcourt, 1920)—again the city, the
industrial center, but not entirely so, for upon examination we find that many poems therein again celebrate the
lands, the countryside, and there are echoes of his trip
to Sweden in 1918. His tone is mellowing too, his bitterness is less evident, he has less acerbity and more melody.
Finally, in "Slabs of the Sunburnt West" (Harcourt,
1922)—the fourth book of poems—both the city and the
country vie for position, and perhaps in the end the country has a shade the better of it. Throughout each one of
these books of poems we can trace the result of his activities. This is because the poems were often a summary of
his thinking over the events that shaped themselves round
about him. There was a wire basket on his desk, and
often, after the day's work, he would sit at his desk, look
dreamily out on a little whitewashed brick court where
pigeons dozed, and write a poem, a few lines of reflection
and comment, and toss them into the basket. Day after
day the basket received its dole, these sheets to be looked
over carefully, and sorted and filed away—rarely to be
destroyed. For Carl has the acquisitive instinct in matters of paper which bear the printed or the written word,
and he is aware that the fugitive thought as well as not
may bear the germ of a living idea.

VI

One day Carl had a reporter's assignment in the district back of the stockyards. Drab, colorless streets; dwarfed, misshapen trees, if any; gray frame houses huddled together, and in them men and women with "hunger-deep eyes, haunted with shadows of hunger hands." Carl found facts that were not part of his assignment, and they wrung his heart. "I was told that seven times as many children die in the stockyards district as in Hyde Park, a little more than a mile away," said Carl, slowly. "I seemed to feel that I had the sort of authentic incident that Poe might have made use of. Out of that idea I wrote: 'The Right to Grief.' "

You know how it goes. Carl begins with those lines about the millionaire's child, which brought on a certain amount of criticism:

Take your fill of intimate remorse, perfumed sorrow,
Over the dead child of a millionaire,
And the pity of death refusing any check on the bank
Which the millionaire might order his secretary to scratch off
And get cashed.

Very well,
You for your grief and I for mine,
Let me have a sorrow my own if I want to.
I shall cry over the dead child of a stockyards' hunky . . .

And after he has pictured the hunky and his wife and kids crying over the little pinched face—the hunky, whose job it is to sweep blood off the floor for $1.70 a day—you can feel the defiant ring in the poet's voice when he hurls his lines:

I have a right to feel my throat choke about this.
You take your grief and I mine—see?

When Miss Amy Lowell read this poem she became
convinced that Carl was a propagandist for the lowly and
oppressed with a prejudice against wealth that blinded
him to any merits that men better favored in life might
possess. "To young men of this type," she wrote sar-
castically, when "Chicago Poems" appeared, "all cruelty
is man-made, they have but to sweep away the man who
made it and behold, it is gone, all study of the lives of
wild animals and fishes notwithstanding. If only life
were as simple as that! A man in a well-cut coat—he is
an evil thing, shun him; a man in rags begging on a street
corner—take him to your heart, he is of the elect. It is
but just to say that Mr. Sandburg tries to be fair to his
millionaires (all his well-to-do men are millionaires), in
fact, a great desire for justice is visible throughout Mr.
Sandburg's book; but prejudice is a firmly-rooted thing,
and try as he will, Mr. Sandburg cannot help feeling that
virtue resides with the people who earn their daily bread
with their hands rather than those who do so with their
brains . . . Through pity and sympathy, the poet is led
to a revaluation of human types in which those least far
on the evolutionary road, those least important if we
measure by scientific laws, come in for them at attention.
No one will deny that the brutal, unimaginative dinner-
eating millionaire is probably one of the lowest forms of
animals on our earth. But there is another type, the
high-minded, ideal-following, sober-living man, who needs
to be considered. He rather spoils the argument, so he is
usually left out of it. Not that Mr. Sandburg or other
democratic poets deny his existence, but they throw the

weight of their sympathy and their art into the scale against him."

Did Miss Lowell at that time know anything about the hard, unequal struggle in the poet's youth? Far from taking sides as a "democratic poet," he was expressing something deep down within him that he could not have eradicated if he wished to. It was his right to speak for these stricken people as much as it was Miss Lowell's right to speak for a beneficial, cultural aristocracy. It seemed as if Carl's jaw stuck out a bit farther than usual when he said almost in the lines of the poem: "Talk about my being a propagandist for the poor, I have a right to feel that revolt, that protest against stifled, needlessly defeated lives . . . William Stanley Braithwaite talks about my propaganda. Even if it were propaganda could he not recognize the defeated artist soul crying out against these wrecks, these misshapen hulks of houses; huge, ugly buildings that he has to pass day by day, the output of a purely utilitarian age that has no beauty, no joy in it— buildings so hopeless that you have to see them only at dusk or by moonlight to get any poetry out of them . . ."

> I have a right to feel my throat choke about this,
> You take your grief and I mine—see?

VII

Of all the poems by Carl Sandburg written within recent years few have had the influence and effectiveness of "And So Today," the poem inspired by the burial of the unknown soldier at Arlington, Va., printed in "Slabs of the Sunburnt West." Readers have tried to pick out of it various philosophies; audiences have been known to sit tense, moved alternately by pity, anger, uncertainty, desperation. The emotional appeal of this plain-spoken discussion of the objects for which the unknown soldier died, and which, in the eyes of the poet, remain unaccomplished, unrealized, is tremendous. The poem has a recurring theme of five lines that have a cadence that comes back again and again:

> And so to-day—they lay him away—
> The boy nobody knows the name of—
> The buck private—the unknown soldier—
> The doughboy who dug under and died
> When they told him to—that's him.

The poet pictures the scene as the procession rides down Pennsylvania avenue—"men and boys riding horses, roses in their teeth"—and also "skeleton men and boys riding skeleton horses." He sees on the one hand the great of the republic paying tribute, laying wreaths of remembrance on the grave; he directs attention to the roses, the wreaths, the proclamations of the honorable orators—but never letting you forget the skeleton horses, the incoherent, uncomprehending crowds, the conclusions that different men draw from the ceremony. "Feed it to 'em, they lap it up," says the cynical movie news reel camera man. "It's all safe now, safe for the yes-men," says the tall scar-face ball player. The honorable orators —"Do their tongues ever shrivel with a pain of fire across those simple syllables 'sacrifice'? The last refrain brings out the poet's irony:

> And so to-day—they lay him away—
> The boy nobody knows the name of—
> They lay him away in granite and steel—
> With music and roses—under a flag—
> Under a sky of promises.

And I recall one reading before a great audience in which the poet increased the effectiveness of his conclusion a hundredfold by looking up quietly and repeating the last line as if to drive home his theme: "Under a sky of promises." Carl said to me: "The poem on the unknown soldier was written out of the mood of that week."

The poem called out the most diverse sort of comment. One critic called the words of the tall scar-face ball player almost a parody. "Safe for the yes-men, hell," he wrote. "This is the lowest form of salesmanship and if I read him aright Mr. Sandburg approves." The comment of Prof. Stuart P. Sherman was typical of his stand during the war. Mr. Sandburg, he said, created for himself a purely artistic problem of great difficulty. "When Mr. Sandburg presents the official pageant of mourning for the Unknown Soldier as a farcical mummery; the president, the commanding officers, the 'honorable orators, buttoning their prince alberts' as empty puppets; and the people from sea to sea as stopping for a moment in their business—'with a silence of eggs laid in a row on a pantry shelf'—when Mr. Sandburg presents a great symbolic act of the nation as vacuous and meaningless, he creates for himself the pretty problem of showing where the meaning of the nation lies; till he has shown that, and with at least equal earnestness and power, he is in danger . . . of leaving his readers with a sense either that his conception of the nation is illusory or that both he and they inhabit a world of illusions—a world of dreams, violences, toils, cruelties and despairs, in which nothing really matters, after all." ("Americans," page 243.) Professor Sherman was not content to let the poet voice his protest at a prodigious show; he needed a moral, a constructive program, attached to the verse. It was for this reason that he found virtue in Whitman; the lack of it in Sandburg was to Professor Sherman unpardonable.

As a matter of fact the message of the poem is a very simple one; like that of all great poetry. The poet, bewildered by the horror of the war, benumbed by the outrageous catastrophe, beholds the pirouettings of the spick-and-span "honorable orators" with disgust and scorn. The lad in the box—he died for something; what, we don't know clearly, but it was not for the clap-trap of civilization, the smug pretense to respectability by the men who survive and are now fulsome in their eulogies. "It is as if some great majestic storm has gone whirling by," said Carl, "and played hell with a community, and then the solemn, sour-faced men, untouched by the war, who had their three squares a day, gather for a ceremonial, the object of which they do not understand. I want to know, what's it all about?"

The poem has been widely translated and the Swedish version, translated by Einar Soderwall and published in Bokstugan for September, 1922, is perhaps the best. The last stanza:

> Och så i dag—de lägga honom hän—
> ynglingen vars namn ingen vet—
> de lägga honom ned under granit och stal
> med musik och rosor—under en flagga
> under en sky full av löften.

VIII

I speak of new cities and new people.

I tell you the past is a bucket of ashes.

I tell you yesterday is a wind gone down, a sun dropped in the west.

I tell you there is nothing in the world only an ocean of to-
morrows, a sky of to-morrows.

Carl Sandburg wrote that for his song of the mother-
land, "Prairie"—the first poem in "Cornhuskers." In it
there is a spirit of exaltation, as the man flings his arms
wide as if to embrace the winds and waters and the limit-
less skies. In it there is a note of warning, a note of
defiance. "I tell you the past is a bucket of ashes"—that
defines the poet's whole outlook toward traditions. "I tell
you there is nothing in the world only an ocean of to-
morrows, a sky of to-morrows." Therein he faces the
light.

"Prairie" is the poet's eulogy of the land that bore him.
He is, for all his "Hog butcher of the world," not city
nourished. The prairie feeds him, makes him content.
This poem is his grateful acknowledgment. It is conceived in ecstasy. It sings itself. In another age it might
have been as treasured as the Psalms of David or the
Song of Solomon. It has no underlying philosophical significance; it is pictorial only; the poet tells what he sees
and glories in these plain, common objects of life for
themselves alone. "I was born on the prairie and the
milk of its wheat, the red of its clover, the eyes of its
women, gave me a song and a slogan," sings the poet.
"The prairie sings to me in the forenoon and I know in
the night I rest easy in the prairie arms, on the prairie
heart." Wagons, plows, horses, loghouse, sodhouse, towns
on the Soo Line, towns on the big Muddy—"Omaha
and Kansas City, Minneapolis and St. Paul, sisters in a
house together, throwing slang, growing up"—all these
are of the prairie. The wigwams, the flatboats, the smoke-
stacks biting the skyline with stub teeth, the Pioneer

limited crossing Wisconsin, the Mississippi bluffs, the cornhuskers—these and innumerable other objects are part of the poet's vision. There are in the poem half a dozen notable lines:

I am the prairie, mother of men, waiting.

O prairie mother, I am one of your boys.
I have loved the prairie as a man with a heart shot full of pain over love.
Here I know I will hanker after nothing so much as one more sunrise or a sky moon of fire doubled to a river moon of water.

I speak of new cities and new people
I tell you the past is a bucket of ashes.
I tell you yesterday is a wind gone down, a sun dropped in the west.
I tell you there is nothing in the world only an ocean of to-morrows, a sky of to-morrows.

Curiously enough one of these lines, which I single out for the strength and vigor of its homely imagery, has lately been brushed aside by Dr. Henry van Dyke as not made of the stuff of poetry. Writing on "anti-poetic diction" in an article on "The Fringe of Words" in the "Yale Review" (October, 1922) Dr. Van Dyke says pedantically: "Carl Sandburg says 'The past is a bucket of ashes.' Now ashes of the past was once a poetic phrase, though it has now become rather a cliché. But when you lug in the bucket it makes one think of the janitor and the garbage can."

No better example than this is needed to point out how free, how vigorous, how open to new forms and new images, is the poetry of our western homeland; how wedded to ancient usages and traditions is desiccated classicism. "It took one hundred years to get the lark out of English poetry . . ."

I have often heard Carl speak on this subject—for he is not only a poet who uses free verse, but a propagandist for it. It has always come natural to him and is in a way a part of the man's character, for in his thinking on social subjects, as on everything else, he is liberal and hospitable to new ideas, and often contemptuous of old forms that have outgrown their usefulness. His education embraced the English classics; Keats was once the star of his horizon, and Browning held him in turn, but he never went deeply into the Greek and Latin classics and his work bears no evidence that he ever absorbed them. A great many masters he has read in translation; his favorite method is to tear a book apart and carry as many pages as he can digest in a day; for several weeks "Rabelais" was thus his disjointed, daily fare. He began to express himself naturally, seeking for the right word diligently, with a feeling for its sound and its place in text, but it turned out that the words he hit on were never classical but seemed to come right out of the mouths of men, and so gained a living value that an older, less native symbol could not have held. It dawned upon him very early that American life was not being expressed in its own terms, but that men were writing about the street, the country, the plain, the valley, and the people who inhabited them in a tongue that was accurate, scholarly, and full of learning, but actually not used by the people; which was in reality an alien language, like a suit of clothes imported from London. He had a feeling for rhythm and cadence that will some day find its highest expression in glorious prose, but he broke his story up into lines that sang themselves, and because they owed no allegiance to Greek forms and did not rime at the ends they were called free verse. No doubt many of his poems are prose—especially those that contain long paragraphs of summaries, categories in the Whitman manner. No doubt many of them are exquisite poetry. Others are assemblings of cadenced phrases, rhythmic lines—lines that will not scan, but that can be sung or chanted. It has even been proved that they can be set to music, for Rupert Hughes has incorporated three—"The Prayer of Steel," "Bricklayer Love" and "Lost" in his "Free Verse Songs." "Lost" is one of the most exquisite of Sandburg's lyrics, and in commenting on its musical setting Anna Urie Lord said: "Hughes' slow and lonely sounding music brings one face to face with the fog, the steamer whistle out on the lake and the divine unrest in life itself." The appeal of the poem, which will live long after the "Hog Butcher of the World" is forgotten, is indubitable:

> Desolate and alone,
> All night long on the lake,
> Where fog trails and mist creeps,
> The whistle of the boat
> Calls and cries unendingly,
> Like some lost child
> In tears and trouble,
> Seeking the harbor's breast
> And the harbor's eyes.

When "Chicago Poems" appeared Carl Sandburg was recognized as the focus for an attack on free verse by the classicists; perhaps no controversy since then has omitted to cite him as the most accomplished poet in free verse, and the poet most untouched by classical beginnings. Even Miss Amy Lowell is excused partially by her critics because her classical education is self-evident, and her plunge into free verse was a deliberate conversion. But with Carl Sandburg writing in free verse was not so much an acquired habit as a yielding to "a natural bent"; he is not derivative even though he is often spoken of as the most successful follower of Whitman; he read Whitman early in his career but there is little of him in his poetry. He is familiar with the imagist, vorticist, and other schools, but it is doubtful whether he ever made an intensive study of them; his poetry is an example of a man writing himself down, and not attempting to pour his thoughts into a standardized mold. The attacks on free verse put Carl on the defensive, and when he began to address audiences he came like a campaign orator about to invade the precinct of the enemy; the audiences, often in the universities of America, were against his verse forms, and he had to win them over. So he frequently prefaced his readings with a talk on poetry, explaining the movement toward a greater freedom of expression in America, and why men needed courage to interpret their home life in its own terms; citing the results of revolt in architecture, music, painting, and education, and explaining the old truism that what one age rejects is frequently idolized by the next. He found that he had to contend with two types of mind; the mind of the scholar, who was against him on classical grounds, and who insisted that poetry to be beautiful must comply with certain standards and prohibitions laid down in the course of the ages and rarely departed from in English—a mind that could not be convinced because it refused to discard preconceived beliefs and demanded that a new structure must rise upon the foundations of an old one. The other mind was the popular mind, and this Carl found almost as firmly set against him as that of the scholar, for the people, although giving no thought to iambics, spondees, dactyls, hexameter or pentameter, had formed their poetical standards on sentiment and habit. For generations they had been nourished on stories in verse form, stories like "Horatius at the Bridge," "The Sky Lark," "An Old Sweetheart of Mine," and "Enoch Arden," in which the story was joined with a pleasing melody in regular rhythms, and these they accepted just as they accepted certain definite ideas about books and the theater. To convert this mind to the idea that free verse might be poetry was a gigantic task, like wiping out the altars of an ancient faith. But actually it was much easier than in the case of the scholars, for the people rested their arguments on sentiment and emotion, and although Carl's prefatory remarks made no impression on them, they became attentive listeners when he began to read his own lines. Perhaps he took an unfair advantage, for few poets have read their own verse with the appeal, the emotional beauty, the tenderness, of Carl Sandburg. It became customary to meet the remark: "I don't like free verse," with the retort: "You will, when you hear Sandburg." The people, always ready to be swayed emotionally, could not be expected to scan Carl's lines to determine whether or not he held firmly to iambic pentameter; his victory was easy and his trail across the country is like that of a conqueror, for he leaves eager converts everywhere in his path.

To bring home his argument Carl will often use a homely figure, a proverb. "When I think of what we are trying to do in poetry," he says, "I sometimes reflect on the motto of the society of California: 'The cowards never started and the weak ones died on the way.' And on the motto of the state of Kansas, which is sometimes translated: 'To the stars through difficulties.' For myself I prefer: 'To the stars, by hard ways.' "

"Think what Shakespeare could have done with the emotion behind the sonnets if he had been free, not bound by any verse form," is one of Carl's favorite remarks.

"Egyptian mysteries, Greek temples, Chinese dragons and many things European and Asiatic form the stuffs and figures that make up the writings of so-called American poets. Glance through any anthology of poetry and there may be found frequent delicate tributes to the gold-fish, while the muskellunge is neglected, even though the wild muskie, as it cavorts in North American waters, has more color and form.

"Out on the prairies where the wind blows men say there is no let-up to the wind. The ordinary newspaper writer however would feel compelled to say in his copy that there is no cessation to the wind. Unless we keep on the lookout we write book language and employ the verbiage of dead men instead of using the speech of people alive to-day, people whose tools, games, crimes, and sacrifices are wearing out an old language and making a new one.

"Young reporters and certain romantic oldsters get the habit of thinking there are women in Paris or Vienna or Moscow more wicked and mysterious than any women to be found in Toledo or Des Moines or Pasadena. By muzzing around in standard woozy books and magazines articles hashed up according to a formula as standardized as Aunt Jemima pancakes it is easy to imagine that all

Italian lake sunsets are superior to North Dakota prairie sunsets and that the play of dawn colors on the Jungfrau or Mont Blanc must intrinsically have a higher rating in esthetics than the morning lights of the Ozarks or the Rockies. Well—maybe so.

"But let it pass. Walt Whitman had a comment of his own on 'Leaves of Grass' that's worth remembering— 'My book is a candidate for the future.' He had a sense of the world in flux, the hobo aversion to all things fixed and fastened down, a habit of thinking and dreaming more about to-morrow than yesterday. Ever notice how much there is in to-day's paper about to-morrow—the atmospheric weather, the political weather, the financial weather, the labor weather, the war weather—to-morrow?"

IX

In his more recent writings Sandburg has been attempting the longer epic, the descriptive poem of several hundred lines that portrays a wide canvas, or a whole philosophy. "I have been writing a long poem on the Mississippi system," he said the other day. His latest book of poems, "Slabs of the Sunburnt West," although a slim volume of only seventy-six pages, contained three long poems—"The Windy City," "And So Today," and the title poem. "The Windy City" is a long potpourri about a conglomerate, heterogenous community, in which Sandburg attempts to capture the spirit of Chicago—and succeeds admirably. It is one of the most revealing epics of a city ever written. It tells its story pictorially, historically, emotionally—a story by sights, sounds, and smells. There is in it something of the broad-shouldered swagger, the braggadocio that was once more generally characteristic of Chicago than it is now. There is in it the voice of the city, expressed in its buildings and in its people, in its achievements and in its vile oppressions. There is in it the note of change, of constant upheaval and turmoil. There is in it compassion, pity, pride, arrogance, defiance, and sense of futility and progression joined, a going on.

The man who writes this epic stands with his feet on the city's pavements; the dust swirls about him, the throngs elbow him aside, the noises of the city ring in his ears. He is one of the throng; what they hear he hears, what they see he sees; he looks up at the tall buildings from their vantage point; he gazes out on the waters from the footway of the bridges, he hears the people talk the plain, direct vernacular of a living tongue. His poem is pictorial and representative; it is a monument that shows the futility of portraying the city as a woman in a coat of mail with the words "I Will" across her breast; it heaps irony on statues of "civic virtue" and other outcroppings of municipal vanity.

The origins of the city; the red men gave it a name, the name of a wild onion, but the city rises out of the payday songs of steam shovels, out of the wages of structural iron rivets. The clean shovel, the clean pickax, last. Here come its people; taxpayers, haberdashers, undertakers' stiffs, greased mannikins, children reading history, men and women. The voices of the city; they "jazz the classics" with their quaint phrases: "Bring home the bacon. . . ." "You said a mouthful. . . ." "Beat up the short change artists, they never did nothin' for you. . . ." You can fix anything if you got the right fixer. . . ." "Shoot it all, shoot it all." Then the effec-

tive, the forceful fifth section, the litany provoked by
the city's sins:

> Forgive us if the monotonous houses go mile on mile
> Along monotonous streets out to the prairies . . .
>
> If a boy and a girl hunt the sun
> With a sieve for sifting smoke . . .
>
> Forgive us if the jazz timebeats
> Of these clumsy mass shadows
> Moan in saxophone undertones,
> And the footsteps of the hungle
> The fang cry, the rip claw hiss,
> The sneakup and the still watch,
> The slant of the slit eyes waiting—
> If these bother respectable people
> > with the right crimp in their napkins
> > reading breakfast menu cards
> > forgive us—let it pass—let it be.
>
> Forgive us
> If boys steal coal in a railroad yard
> And run with humped gunnysacks
> While a bull picks off one of the kids
> And the kid wriggles with an ear in cinders
> And a mother comes to carry home
> A bundle, a limp bundle
> To have his face washed, for the last time,
> Forgive us if it happens—and happens again
> And happens again . . .

The spirit of the city lives in these lines: "Put the city
up; tear the city down; put it up again . . . The city

is made, forgotten and made again . . . Every day the people sleep and the city dies; every day the people shake loose, awake and build the city again."

X

This brings us to the two moods that are ever recurrent in Sandburg; the social and the lyrical; the note of protest, of indignation, of grief at the oppressive conditions under which the humbler brethren of this earth live, and the note of exultation that has as its basis love of life, love of laughter, love of beautiful, fantastic and colorful pictures in nature. In his own cadence Sandburg portrays moods, feelings, surface impressions. Sometimes it is the wisp of smoke on the sky that engages his fancy; sometimes it is the great sweep of the virginal prairie; sometimes it is a face that awakens thoughts of laughter that has died down, of an ecstasy that has been crushed by human woes. In taking his work progressively we find first a strong emphasis upon the social note, a desire to place before the eyes of the smug, respectable, sluggish middle-class tradesman and the sleek, swaggering "millionaire" a conception of the drudgery, the pain and the suffering of the under dog in society. With a defiant air he thrusts the picture forward. This in "Chicago Poems." Then strong emphasis upon the pictorial, unrelated to social significance, as in "Prairie," the first poem in "Cornhuskers," his second book, in which the fine exultation of a man in what he sees of his own homeland carries him away into ecstatic renderings of its pictorial values. If there is any social significance at all in his thoughts it is in the inter-relation of historic events, in the feeling of a historical sequence, of a progression, that comes over him when he contemplates first the prairie of the frontier days and now the prairie of the Pioneer Limited. Then "Smoke and Steel"—again a heavy emphasis upon the pictorial and the lyrical, for the title poem, which men might look to as a social document, proves to have very little in it about oppressed humans who work at the great steel ingots; rather is it a hymn to human achievement, in which all, big and little, high and low, have a part; yes, truly he writes: "In the blood of men and the ink of chimneys, the smoke nights write their oaths," but it is only an observation that comes to the poet as he considers the "curves of fire, the rough scarf women dancing, dancing out of the flues and smoke-stacks—flying hair of fire, flying feet upside down." No bitterness marks the poems, only a note of resignation: "Finders in the dark, you Steve with a dinner bucket . . . wondering where we all end up; Finders in the dark, Steve— I hook my arm in cinder sleeves; we go down the street together; it is all the same to us; you Steve and the rest of us end on the same stars; we all wear a hat in hell together, in hell or heaven. . . ." True, there are social poems in "Smoke and Steel," but already we find Sandburg moving toward general themes, rather than particularizing one instance. And when we come to "Slabs of the Sunburnt West" we realize how far he has moved from his first moods in "Chicago Poems"—his tone is less bitter, though no less effective; he aims at a general picture, rather than at the pointed portrayal of one or two specific incidents; and although he is still eloquent in the portrayal of a single tragic episode, as in "Ambassadors of Grief," he is dealing for the most part with bigger themes, themes of na-

tional significance in "And So Today," philosophies and
experiences of a whole city in "The Windy City," and
of a whole continent in "Slabs of the Sunburnt West."
It is a mellowing Sandburg, contemplating the mass
rather than the individual, flinging out his arms and
finding room therein for all humankind.

His first mood was a vital one, it brought him his name
as a fighter, as a propagandist. How deeply he felt, how
thoroughly he lived, the hurts that came to humbler men
—how defiantly he hurled these gloomy, depressing facts
out of the heart of life at the heads of our "best people."
No wonder they declared his themes were not of the stuff
of poetry; no wonder they stressed his uncouth manner,
his uneven lines, his plain words, not yet accepted in the
first circles. He was a rebel, a nonconformist, a man
using the sacred cows of poetry and yoking them to the
lumbering wagon of the barnyard. That he was forceful
they were willing to admit; courageous, too, but alas,
they made lament, his were not the graceful pirouettings,
the cadenced steps of the minuet—how attune his blaring
songs to the melodies of the poetic muse? And yet he
wrote on.

"Chicago Poems" is close to earth; there is in it the
tang of the soil; you rub elbows with the fish crier, the
hunky, the shovel man, the dago, the factory girl, the
cash girl; the ice handler, the gang on Halsted Street,
"the worn way-faring men":

> That pigsticker in one corner—his mouth—
> that overall factory girl—her loose cheeks . . .

He sees "tired empty faces, tired of wishes, empty of
dreams"; he hears on Clark Street bridge "voices of dol-

lars and a drop of blood." He becomes ironical when he contemplates:

> Tomb of a millionaire,
> A multimillionaire, ladies and gentlemen,
> Place of the dead where they spend every year
> The usury of twenty-five thousand dollars
> For upkeep and flowers. . . .

And then by simple contrast he paints the woes of the oppressed: "A hundred cash girls want nickels to go to the movies. . . ." Similarly he is affected adversely by the contemplation of a fine stone house on the lake front, around which workmen are erecting an iron fence with cruel palings, but he concludes, not regretfully; "Passing through the bars and over the steel points will go nothing except Death and the Rain and To-morrow." He tells how "I drank musty ale at the Illinois Athletic club with the millionaire manufacturer of Green River butter one night. . . ." All of these he uses for contrast. He has a contempt for the misuse of wealth and the millionaire of his poems represents that misuse, that abuse of the poor. He is calm, defiant, contemptuous; but he is never vindictive, nor is there in his philosophy any hint of violence. He is in love with the poor, as when he wrote later on: "And then one day I got a look at the poor, millions of the poor, patient and toiling, more patient than crags, tides, stars; innumerable, patient as the darkness of night. And all broken humble ruins of nations."

Contrasted with this is Sandburg's love for plain things, his glorification of humble occupations. Most notable is the widely quoted example of the fish crier on

Maxwell street. "His face is that of a man terribly glad to be selling fish; terribly glad that God made fish." The picture of a group of Hungarians out with their wives and children and beer and an accordion he labels: "Happiness." He contemplates the "muckers wiping sweat off their faces with red bandanas" with something of approval and satisfaction. The dago shovel man is a "child of the Romans." He is proud of Jack London and O. Henry because "both were jailbirds; no speechmakers at all . . . who knew the hearts of these boozefighters?" "Work Gangs" have to him a matured philosophy; it runs like this: "A long way we come; a long way to go; long rests and long deep sniffs for our lungs on the way. Sleep is a belonging of all. . . ." And many more.

Best of all he develops a fine irony; he contemplates the foibles of mankind with an appraising eye; he observes incongruities, injustices, oppressions. Has any one surpassed the forcefulness of "Man, the Man-Hunter"? with its terrible dénouement:

> In the morning the sun saw
> Two butts of something, a smoking rump
> And a warning in charred wood:
>
> > Well, we got him
> > the sbxyzch.

In that mood he has done any number of poems that depend for their power on contrast. There is "The Mayor of Gary" who wore "cool, cream pants and white shoes" pitted against the workmen with leather shoes scruffed with fire and cinders. There is "The Sins of Kalamazoo," an indictment of the small town, a "Main

Street" of poetry. There is that powerful little poem entitled "Knucks" which relies for its interest on the fact that he finds brass knuckles for sale in a store in "the city of Abraham Lincoln." In his irony he is forceful and direct, but rarely subtle. In only one or two instances does he achieve that bit of sardonic laughter that we can imagine comes from a man contemplating a joke played on him by fate. One of the best instances of it is "Three Ghosts." It might be a miniature ballad; it tells that "Three tailors of Tooley street wrote: We the People. The names are forgotten. It is a joke in ghosts." He goes on to tell how they sat cross-legged, working for wages, meeting after work to drink their beer to "the people." They are forgotten. It is a joke in ghosts. They wrote: "We the People." Laughter—the low, ironic laughter of the man who views life as a burlesque, a horrible joke on the frail idealists, runs between the lines.

In his love lyrics, in his sentimental moods, Sandburg reaches the heights. For he is never maudlin, never unbridled, even at his most ecstatic moments. Take the poems about the children—and they run through most of his books—and you will observe a quiet satisfaction, a peace and happiness in the lines that are dedicated to the doings of little folk. When he comes to write the simple love lyrics of which he is capable he dreams in homely metaphor and simile, never in fantastic, outlandish embroidery. He is always of the soil. "Home Thoughts" is a lyric of exquisite beauty because of its simple imagery:

> Speak to me of the drag on your heart
> The iron drag of the long days.

I know hours empty as a beggar's tin cup on
    a rainy day, empty as a soldier's sleeve
    with an arm lost

Speak to me . . .

His poems of the streets, his emphatic pounding with
hard words, have become so characteristic of him that
many persons know no other side of him; when they
think of Sandburg they picture the Sandburg of the "hog
butcher of the world" forgetting that in him live fantasy
and whimsicality, lyricism and lyrical beauty. His delicate images may be found in every book.

XI

Carl Sandburg seemed to grow perceptibly in stature
on the day that he first appeared before us as a teller of
tales. Up to that moment he had been a strolling player,
a minstrel twanging his lyre to songs of his own invention; now he came to weave together beautiful prose tales
that meant romance and adventure to grown men and
little children. The moment when he first revealed himself in this new mood comes back most vividly now that
a copy of "Rootabaga Stories" lies upon my desk. It
was at Schlogl's—Henry Blackman Sell was there, and
Jerome Frank, Carlton Washburne, and Keith Preston,
and many more, when Carl Sandburg strolled in and
nonchalantly called for his coffee and ham on rye. None
of the more palatable dishes for Carl—no pickled eel, or
baby turkey, or champignons—Carl has never conceded
that dining is more than partaking of plain food; and
more often than not he prefers to hunt up some hole in

the wall where he can "grab off a bite to eat." Nor
does he take part in the animated discussion that goes
with dining *en masse*—in the criss-cross of words and
banter—he is at his best when he has one auditor and
can speak at length on his favorite topics. So our prattle
did not engage his interest, but there came a lull in the
talk, and then Carl fished a manuscript from his pocket.
"I've been writing some stories for the kids at home,"
he said, "reading to them at night and this is as far as
I've got. I'll read it to you." It proved to be a fairy
tale—the tale of a little lad whose mother had called him
Petie-Patta-Tatta, because that is the sound the rain-
drops made on the roof the day he was born—pat-ta-
tat-ta pat-ta tat-ta—a little boy who lived in a town
destined to become a familiar mark on the chart of all
childhood; the Village of Liver and Onions. A fairy tale
—and yet an entirely new sort of fairy tale, one that wove
romance around familiar objects and unromantic scenes.
Carl Sandburg, like Hans Christian Andersen before him,
had tapped the source of our inspirations—he too had
found, as Francis Hackett wrote of Andersen, that fairy
tales are our dream and intuition, the hem of our garment of immortality. A new and wonderful vision of
Carl as the spinner of tales, sitting among the little folk
with his fine, graying head bent down toward them and
a wistful earnestness in his eyes, grew up before us.
"I've got another one," said Carl, when he had finished
reading, "about the Village of Cream Puffs and how they
wind it up every night on a spool when the wind blows
it away." "Are you going to publish them?" some one
asked. "I hadn't thought of that," said Carl, "I've just
been writing them for the children."

To tell something of "Rootabaga Stories" we must

make a pilgrimage to the home of the Sandburgs, out of Chicago on the St. Charles road. A long pilgrimage it is, for Elmhurst is one of those wooded villages that has slipped out from under the pall of smoke and fumes that hovers over Chicago. The Sandburg house—"it's that little white place with a wooden fence around it," is the way it was described—was once a farmhouse that stood in the center of a sizable plot, but time nibbled down its acreage until it became a city lot and now a well-paved asphalt roadway under the guise of York street runs by where once the cows went lazily to their barns. "Part of this house is over seventy years old," said Carl, and to us of the west that is the equivalent of the New Englander's boast that his home was raised two hundred years ago. A quaint, rambling place it is, a homey place, with many little rooms, cozy and comfortable and without pretense; part of the house was once a little old-fashioned school-house and there is evidence that bits have been added now and then. Mrs. Sandburg is the kindly spirit that hovers over the roof-tree with genial informality, and if you remain long enough three lively youngsters will come romping in, tossing their hats in childish abandon, radiating health and good cheer—Margaret, Janet and the little curly-headed Helga—you will meet them all in the dedications of several of Carl's books, and again in the poems. They are, as Carl will tell you, with a twinkle, "the heirs to the Sandburg millions—millions of clippings."

And that brings us to "Rootabaga Stories." For if it had not been for these three romping, rollicking youngsters, and their appetite for stories, it is doubtful whether their father would have turned from his rugged lyrics to fashion strange, whimsical stories in limpid prose. What an audience they made—generous, whole-hearted, insatiable. One day Carl was telling how the stories sprang into life and thus he put it in his own way:

"The fox drank cream in the kitchen, measuring himself between drinks, till he had just enough to let himself through the window and out again. The story was told to Janet. Now Janet comes saying, 'Tell me a fox, tell me a fox.' And we are trying to think of more foxes to tell.

"The wolf drank too much cream. He couldn't scrape his full belly through the kitchen window and escape. 'They killed him with an ax.' So the story was told to Janet and Helga, five and three years old. Now each blossom of a child goes saying to father, mother, rag doll Tessie, china doll Betty, and to the invisible spirits of bedtime, 'I kill you with an ax.' With laughing chuckles they keep saying with twinkling eyes that shine straight and merry into your own face, 'I kill you with an ax.'

"There is a blue fox lives under the front porch. The father and mother have told Janet and Helga it is so. And Janet and Helga have repeated it to each other. It has been spoken of so many ways, in relation to so many concrete and particular events, that we all know a blue fox is there under the front porch, alive, with shining eyes, shining white teeth, shining blue hair. 'Tell us a story,' we say to Janet. She will, she won't, she will, she won't. 'Tell us a story,' we beg. 'Blue fox under front porch. Man come. Fox say, "Go away." Man go away.' And that is the story. No adjectives, brief action—a ghost of a blue fox puts its footsteps on a child sky."

So we begin with Margaret, Janet, and Helga. You can see them home from their play, sitting at the feet of this tall, gaunt man, who bends forward to pull dreams out of the clouds for them. Gone are his searchings for powerful speech, for hard-hitting prose, gone are his pre-occupations with men of heavy hearts and strange op-pressions; he has stepped down among the children and his voice is attuned to childhood's ear. Here we find his strength giving way to gentleness, his love for clarity being superseded by a trick of using words not to be found in any vernacular, and yet words that delight the child mind, his character as a poet of the social order standing aside while he dons the cap and bells. It is an intimate, real, and lovable Sandburg.

The children have been often in Carl's thoughts. In his first book, "Chicago Poems," he writes of Margaret:

> In your blue eyes, O reckless child,
> I saw to-day many little wild wishes
> Eager as the great morning.

In "Cornhuskers" also there are poems about the chil-dren. The dedication of "Cornhuskers" reads: "To Janet and Margaret"; for there was no Helga then, but "Slabs of the Sunburnt West" is dedicated to Helga. What better beginning can any book of fairy tales have than that it was conceived solely to enrich the hours of little folk? Carl was telling these tales at home long before he thought of printing them. He tried one or two on his audiences and found that human beings are always chil-dren at heart—for the grown-ups loved them, too. Gradually the stories grew and he found himself in pos-session of a whimsical imagery that he had not known before. To sit down in the quiet of an evening and write another adventure of the curiously human folk in Roota-baga land became a strong man's play. Only long after did the idea come to him that they might provide joy to other children than his own and to grown-ups were they placed in book form.

Out of a strong man's playtime came these stories of Rootabaga land. Out of a man's realization that, for some of us at least, the play spirit never dies out of life; that we reach out into the unknowable and bring back gifts that enchant us, even though we cannot always justify them by the laws of logic and coherence. There came a time when the opportunity to sit down and meditate on the doings of Rootabaga folk and eventually to write them down on his typewriter was to Carl a hallowed moment of rest and exultation. They expressed the play spirit within him and soon he began to measure his fellows by their response to these fanciful creations. "The stories," Carl would say, "are pure unmuddled joy. They are only for people who understand—who haven't dried up. I've worked harder on them than on anything I have ever done. If the people who read books don't like these stories there is no joy left in the world." It was a happy moment when he found the book tightly clasped in the arms of half the world.

The most outstanding characteristic of "Rootabaga Stories" is that although they are properly fairy tales, none of the lay figures of the fairy story live in them. The objects one encounters have a familiar sound—cornfields, skyscrapers, furnace shovel, coffee pot, potato bugs, blue rats, popcorn hats, policeman's whistles—but truly none belongs to the fairy tale of tradition. And that is because Carl knows that fairy tales, after all, are but an inverted expression of the folk lore of a people, and that when the stories out of foreign lands tell us of princes, knights, giants, ogres, chivalrous knights rescuing beautiful maidens, kings in coat of mail charging across a drawbridge, we are dealing with an historical tradition that is not ours, as a race, save only by indirection. To the people who tell them these castles were as familiar as our skyscrapers, and the giants and ogres were originally the feudal oppressors of the poor. But America has no knights clad in armor, no kings in coats of mail charging across a drawbridge, and left to itself an American child would build the life of its imagination not with these objects but with the actualities of its own environment. That is why the fairies were helping Carl weave these stories just as truly as they worked at the elbows of the brothers Grimm, for just as those men set down the folklore of the people, so Carl crystallized the whimsey, the fantasy, the quaint musings of the child heart of a nation that has skyscrapers for its castles, policemen for captains, railroads for knightly cavalcades, prairies of waving corn, silver blue lakes like blue porcelain breakfast plates—the magic that you can conjure up any day from your bedroom window.

These men are the sprites of a strong man's playtime. They vary in mood, in significance, in treatment, as vary the moods of a thousand readers. The quaint embroidery of familiar objects in childhood lives in such fancies as the potato-face blind man and the man with a popcorn hat, popcorn mittens, and popcorn shoes; the more familiar tale that depends for its movement on a piling up of incidents and the repetition of names and speeches lives in "How Bimbo the Snip's Thumb Stuck to His Nose When the Wind Changed" and the tale of "Three Boys with Kegs of Molasses and Secret Ambitions"; there is humor that calls for clear, ringing laughter in the story of "Gimme the Ax" and his two children, who named themselves

Please Gimme and Ax Me No Questions; there is whimsicality and poetry and magical music in the stories of the sand flat shadows and in "How to Tell Corn Fairies if You See Them." There are tales out of the warp and woof of our daily life, as in the story of the two skyscrapers that decided to have a child . . . "a free child, not a child standing still all its life on a street corner. . . ." When it came it was an overland passenger train, the "Golden Spike Limited," and the ensuing tragedy is as heart-breaking as any in all fairy lore.

So much for subject matter. If the themes vary, so too does the treatment; there are tales that reveal plain, matter-of-fact story telling, there are others that seek for nuances and overtones. Most interesting is his understanding of the child mind. "Isn't it odd," said Little Ruth to her mother, "that only the fire-born understand blue?" "I don't know what you are talking about," replied the mother. "But it's true," said the child, "for it says so in my story." The child mind grasps readily facts that a grown-up needs to have explained, for the child is building fancies as it reads and has one ready for every image that comes. The more sophisticated oldster, measuring everything by past experience, leaves no play to the imagination. So, too, the odd words that Carl has put into his stories immediately call forth a burst of laughter and approval from little folks, who are ready with an image to fit the case. "I will give you a new ticket," says the ticket agent to Gimme the Ax, when he breaks away with his family to go to the Rootabaga country. "It is a long slick yellow leather slab ticket with a blue spanch across it." Spanch? The children laugh with glee . . . it is a new word, expressive, ready to fill a niche in their imaginations. In a lecture before the students at Northwestern University Carl told this story, using the term "spanch." "Many of you will want to know what sort of word that is," he explained, "but I have not time to stop and tell you about it. If you want to know what it is you will have to look it up." Several of the students took him literally. They wrote him letters beginning: "Dear Mr. Sandburg: We have been unable to find the word spanch. What does it mean? . . ."

The writing of "Rootabaga Stories" was for Carl an invigorating exercise. He could not drop it; it was a tonic to his nerves; it had to go on. And now, after long intervals a story comes from his typewriter, to be brooded over, read to children, and revised again. In time there will be another of "Rootabaga Stories,"—perhaps two, or three. Already the second volume is close to his heart; "Rootabaga Pigeons" it will be called. "It will have more real poetry in it than the first Rootabaga book," said Carl, "but the kids will get it." Sometimes he likes his Rootabaga Stories even better than his poems. When he learns that they have pleased others besides himself he chuckles with glee like a small boy. People write him about them; he learns that they have been read in hospitals, in jails, in the rush hours on trains. And although his reputation rests on his poetry this one volume has been much more widely distributed than any of his poems.

Carl himself regards them as the equivalent of simple folklore told in droll stories without the surplusage of most fairy stories. "The child's mind reels with the impact of lonely princesses and castles," he says. "There is nothing marvelous in these tales, they are folklore material in a modern mood, and for that there is no such word as marvelous. Even the pigs with bibs on—it is logical that the checker pigs should have checker bibs on and the polka dot pigs have polka dot bibs on. That may be strange, but hardly marvelous."

"They kept me alive," said Carl; "they have my heart's blood."

XII

No man has a keener sense for the significant phrase in homely surroundings than Carl Sandburg. He is always pulling something out of the air almost—something you want to remember, to reflect on, and then telling you that it came from the clerk at your elbow, the elevator man, the woman with the dust-mop. He has a faculty for alighting upon stray, nomadic items in newspapers and magazines that hold his attention. His pockets are always full of press clippings; invariably, at the end of a conversation he will pull a bunch from his pocket, extract one well-thumbed and curling bit of newspaper print and leave it with you with the remark: "Read that and tell me what you think of it. That fellow says something. I've had my eye on him. Give it back to me when I see you again." Then with a smile he departs. . . . Sometimes in an unwonted place in my desk I find a clipping which reminds me of a remissness in returning irrelevant gifts.

But out of the welter of words men use, out of the well-worn imagery, the stereotyped expressions of commonplace thoughts, Carl gathers a rich haul. Many of his poems have been inspired by a look, a spoken word, an inadvertent remark. He sees poetry in the commonplace—poetry before it is so labeled.

"Our lives are rich with poetry," Carl remarked one day over the coffee cups. "Did you ever hear the court bailiffs administer the oath? Some of them have a sense for rhythm." Carl reproduced their manner in a slow, impressive monotone: " 'I solemnly swear to tell the truth, the whole truth, and nothing but the truth, so help me, God!' Others just rattle it off without any sense or feeling for rhythm."

He paused and reflected. "Then take this: there was a woman I ran across in Milwaukee, her husband was the janitor of a building and they lived in the basement. They had had eleven children and buried six, from tuberculosis, and they still lived in the basement. She said to me: 'We work and we work and all that we earn goes into the grave.' " Carl's eyes took on a look of triumph. "That line has a rhythm and a power to it that makes Thomas Hood's 'Song of a Shirt' fade out of the picture," he concluded emphatically.

"And then you run across this plain homely philosophy, this summing up. I was talking with a man on the smoker going out to Elmhurst and we were holding forth on the mixup in local politics—the state's attorney's office or something. He leaned back and said: 'There always was politics; there was politics one thousand years ago; there is politics to-day; there will be politics one thousand years from now; when there ain't no more politics there won't be any human race.' "

XIII

Who reads Carl Sandburg? Who understands him best? To whom does he make the greatest appeal? One is tempted to call up the picture of a little Presbyterian church in an Illinois village. Carl Sandburg has promised to speak, and a class in domestic science, which gets its members from all the religious denominations of the village and from the farms for miles around, stands sponsor for the program. They come in motor cars—in Dodges and Fords—boys and girls, mothers with babes, brothers and fathers. The lads take the first few pews on one side of the center aisle, the girls the other side. The poet reads from his poems, and sings folk songs to the strumming of his guitar. I asked Carl how he liked his audience. He replied: "They knew I was trying to find beauty that lurks in the commonplace, in the everyday nooks and corners. I told them to avoid rules and doctrines. Ramble around among masterpieces; if you see what you like, go ahead. I talked to them straight. I gave them some songs. They liked that."

And another picture. The Chicago Public Library is observing its fiftieth anniversary, and there is the usual program. Carl Sandburg rises to speak, somewhat haltingly at first. Brahmins are massed round about him, seers, visionaries, and representatives of the established social order. He talks quietly in his plain vernacular, and reads from "The Windy City." As he finishes an elderly Brahmin leans forward and remarks in an audible whisper: "If that's poetry then a sheep is a goat."

Who reads Carl Sandburg? His style is his own, his technique differs from that of every one else, and yet he is national—as Maxwell Anderson said: "He has carved his reliefs and gargoyles on sidewalks and stone fences all up and down the land." There are critics in America —and chief among them Stuart P. Sherman—who say that Carl Sandburg is not read or even known by the

masses whose songs he sings and whose sufferings affect
him so deeply. He writes about the down-trodden, they
say, for the sophisticated arm-chair readers of poetry.
This criticism has just enough truth in it to make us
pause, but it is not entirely just. We may say that Carl's
poetry is not read by his dago shovelman, who sits by
the railroad track, or his stockyards hunky, whose job
is sweeping blood off the floor at a dollar seventy cents
a day, or the nigger—"singer of songs, dancer, softer
than fluff of cotton." We may also grant that as a class
the Babbitts of our land do not know him—there is no
melody in him for those whose favorite sentimental poet
is James Whitcomb Riley and whose eyes grow tearful
when Edgar A. Guest sings his uninspired lyrics of home
and mother and the little children's finger marks on the
wall. Let us also leave out most of the members of the
English departments of our universities—not all, but
most—the upholders of tradition and historical forms,
who frown on anything new this side of the Victorian era
and who see a menace to the Anglo-Saxon ideal in literature when Sandburg recognizes poetical qualities in
hunkies, dagoes, bohunks, and shovel stiffs. For whom
then does Sandburg write? The answer is both amusing
and inspiring. He writes for men and women in each of
the classes we have named, and for many more outside
of them, for youngsters in colleges and for men in offices
to whom tradition is nothing more than a name, for men
behind prison walls, for professors of English who are
classicists at heart, for bookkeepers spending long hours
at high-legged desks, for stenographers who catch a few
moments of reading on their way to work, for advertising
men who don't know Byron and can't get Shelley, and to
whom Eddie Guest is "sob stuff." The proof? Let us

begin with Prof. Stuart P. Sherman himself, head of the English department at the University of Illinois, principal spokesman for the Anglo-Saxon tradition in our national letters, and yet himself sufficiently big-hearted to say that "Many of the things which Carl Sandburg relishes I relish: the jingle of the American languages in the making, the Great Lakes, prairies, mountains, and the diurnal and seasonal scene-shifting of the elements; all kinds of workmen with their tools in city and country, and the feel of an ax or shovel in my own hands; the thunder of overland trains and the crossfire of banter in a barber shop; eating ham and eggs with a Chinese chemist at a wayside lunch counter at four o'clock in the morning, suntime; the mixed human contacts to be had, for example, in a common upcountry smoker, where black men, Italians, Poles, Swedes, Japanese, Indians, and Germans commune happily in a thick blue mist. . . ."

And then let us turn to those numerous proofs that come to the poet day after day from all over the land, and that show how he has touched a sympathetic chord over and over again. "Here's a letter," he will say, rummaging through a drawerful of papers, "from a quarryman in North Carolina. He liked my last book. And this fellow is doing time in Atlanta. He sent me the words for the folksong about the Titanic. This man—well, you know him yourself—he's a bright negro chap from Harvard and as keen a mind as I have ever met. That's a Yiddish magazine, 'Nei Yiddish'—they wrote a story about me and printed some of my stuff in Yiddish. This fellow's an I. W. W.—he got sent up during the war. There's a letter from the president of a life insurance company in Iowa. This is from a chap in Grinnell college—on the faculty there, and let me tell you, they are

up and coming there; the old boys whose faces hang on
the wall—Longfellow and Tennyson and that crowd—
they're ghosts, that's all. This girl wants me to auto-
graph a book—she was one of a group of sorority girls
in a university in Texas—they had me come down there,
took charge of the evening, hired a hall and guaranteed
the trip, and the whole university turned out for them—
a girl with a lot of force, I'll say. Then there's a letter
from Franklin K. Lane—he liked 'Cornhuskers.' And
here's the secretary of a labor union. I get to some of
the labor organizations—they read me. And the So-
cialists—I suppose because of my protest against things
as they are. They had 'Smoke and Steel' at Fort Leaven
worth, and at the detention camp there were dozens of
copies. Some of the American Federation of Labor men,
too, read my poems—but I never got to Ed Nockels and
Fitzpatrick. I think the fault is in me, although it may
be that their feeling for poetry has been blunted, as
Darwin said that his sense for music had been blunted
by his close application to science. I admire them—
Nockels and Fitzpatrick are honest; they have never
become snobs; they didn't give in to dressy clothes and
the airs of the labor leader who gets patronized by the
employers. . . . But you can't expect your poems to
appeal to every one. Here in the same day a friend sends
me clippings from an Oakland, Cal., paper that prints
'Sea Slants' as an example of the poetic quality in my
work, and another friend sends a clipping from a Los
Angeles paper which says that 'Sea Slants' is a fine
example of rot."

And Carl chuckles as if he has found a good joke. He
has a sense of the ludicrous, in spite of his deep serious-
ness. A friend tells the story of meeting Carl in Missoula,

Mont., just as he was being interrogated by a reporter for a local newspaper.

"What is your message, Mr. Sandburg?" asked the reporter, pompously.

"Message?" repeated Carl, "I didn't come out here to burn up the prairies; I'm just looking around, singing a few songs, reciting a few poems; tell your readers I am lazy as hell."

In June, 1923, Lombard College at Galesburg, Ill., determined to honor its poet by conferring upon him the degree of doctor of literature. Carl entered the office of the secretary to the president on the morning of the commencement exercises and inquired of the shocked attendant:

"Where do I get this Ku Klux regalia?"

But toward his own work Carl's attitude is one of intense earnestness. Edward Price Bell, just back from London, came in one day for a chat. "How do you feel when you read adverse criticisms of your poems?" asked Bell.

Carl leaned back in his chair, looked abstractedly out of the window, and then remarked slowly:

"A man was building a house. A woodchuck came, and sat down, and watched the man building the house."

And so it goes. To-morrow is a new day. Carl turns back to his desk, looks at the pile of letters and clippings that he has dug out of the drawers and remarks philosophically:

"Guess I'll clean out the drawers of this desk. There are some letters there I want to answer. But the trouble is, some of these people may have moved. . . ."

XIV

Out in the Sandburg house life flows on with something of the calm and poise and homeliness that one associates with the New England tradition, but which, unhappily, is so often absent in the private life of many of our modern poets. The youngsters who romp through the rooms reflect a mother's happy, adaptable disposition and a father's whole-hearted love of the life round about him. Carl Sandburg is not a prey to emotional disturbances. He and his wife are pals—she calls him "My Buddy"—she has held with him whether the sledding was hard or easy; it was through her persistence that his first poems were accepted; she is still his most sympathetic auditor, his most competent critic. There are evenings when dinner goes on without him; she then knows that he has hid himself away somewhere, to brood over a poem, perhaps, or that he is sitting in some humble workman's tenement, gaining a new insight into life's phantasmagoria, or that he is leaning his elbows on a table with a bunch of teamsters, carpenters, plumbers, and bricklayers—listening eagerly to the thoughts that fall out of the unimaginative experience of these men. She smiles quietly to herself; he will come back in a day or two, famished for the home board, eager for the bright eyes of the family circle, and then ready to enter his workroom and there write, reflect, brood, and compose until the early dawn. It is as if in "Accomplished Facts" he might have been singing of his own contentment:

Ride, ride, ride on, in the great new blimps—
Cross unheard of oceans, circle the planet.
When you come back we may sit by five hollyhocks.

We might listen to boys fighting for marbles.
The grasshopper will look to us.
So it goes. . . .

Up the steep little stairway we go, to Carl's workroom; it is on the second floor back, and through the little square window panes we can look out over a roof, and a barn, and a lot of cheerful foliage. It is the sort of workroom where the most precious things are ideas and words, and everything else is but a means toward an end —expression. The straw matting on the floor shows signs of use; the little flat-topped desk and the tables may have had several owners; the pine shelves, raised by Carl himself, are there to bear their burden of books, and not to support a scheme of decoration; throughout you get the impression that this is the room of a man without pose, without external furbishing; a man of wide interests and sympathies, as one may deduce from the varied character of Chinese prints, newspaper halftones, press clippings, pinned about. And the books one sees are of the kind he might be expected to have around him; innumerable volumes on songs of which "Sea Songs and Shanties" by W. H. Whall beckons in its brilliant green cover; books on folk ways, and early civilizations, the history of man, untold books on Lincoln, volumes of poetry. Files with tons of clippings, on every conceivable subject, and big metal army record cans loaded with information from the ends of the earth. "I am going to fill up some of those metal cans," said Carl, "and put them in the barn; if ever I need the material I'll know where to get it. An old banjo with a string broken; a guitar, laid carefully on a bookshelf; a battered suitcase. A cot, covered with a navajo blanket. Carl writes here in the quiet of the nighttime, reads, arranges his material; long after the house has quieted down he mulls over his work, and then, tired, he slips into the cot and dozes off. Sometimes he writes until the dawn comes through the little window panes and the meadow larks pipe up just below him. No one disturbs him. Mrs. Sandburg's fine understanding has helped make Carl's married life a song.

Those who have been privileged to cross the Sandburg threshold have never forgotten it; Miss Amy Lowell, among others celebrated her visit to Elmhurst in a poem which she has often read to her audiences, and Carl, after a visit to the Lowell home in Brookline replied in kind. More recently Eugene V. Debs, convalescent in the Lindlahr sanitarium at Elmhurst wrote these eloquent passages to David Karsner, which were printed in Karsner's "Talks with Debs in Terre Haute":

Had a wonderful two hours with Carl Sandburg and his sweet little 11-year old daughter this afternoon, and his visit rested, refreshed, and rejuvenated me. We sat in the shade of the great old elms and poured out our souls to each other. I had not seen him for fourteen years. Since then he has scaled the peaks and written his name among the stars. Carl Sandburg is one of the very few really great poets of our day, and the future will know him to the remotest generation. He lives only three blocks from here and I shall have his three little household gods for playmates and that will be the most vital part of my restorative treatment. . . . Last night (Aug. 23, 1922) I was with Carl Sandburg and Sinclair Lewis at the Sandburg home till midnight and then that beautiful brace brought me home. It was a wonderful occasion—an event in our lives. Mrs. Sandburg had her mother, and the three dear children did the hospitable services for us and we were in paradise after our own hearts. . . . Carl came with his guitar

Saturday evening and gave the patients here a most charming entertainment in folklore. It was a complete conquest and they all love him. Lewis will also entertain them. . . . Lewis and Sandburg are fit companions, genial, fun-loving, whole-hearted and generous, as well as princes of the pen and masters of the literary art. Lewis and Sandburg as distinctively American novelist and poet, with the cosmic understanding of the universal appeal, have already acquitted themselves with enviable distinction and achieved enduring fame, but they are still in their adolescence and have but laid the foundation of the temple that will bear in fadeless letters their deathless names.

He has come by this little house slowly but he has builded well. There is a solidity about all of it, and a wholesomeness. In the community he is respected and loved. Not long ago he added an adjoining lot to his little estate. The owner was a meticulous business man and a discussion developed with the lawyer as to the sort of mortgage that was to be drawn to secure the unpaid part of the purchase price. The owner's comment was revealing: "Since it is Mr. Sandburg who is buying it I won't need a mortgage. His name on a note is good enough for me."

XV

In less than ten years Carl Sandburg has become a figure of national significance. To-day he is invariably named as one of the four or five outstanding poets of America, and his influence toward a liberation from classical bondage and the development of wholesome American themes is felt among a host of followers. He has helped direct our thinking back to the primitive forces of our land; to the soil, human labor, the great industries, the masses of men. No matter what he writes in the future the cumulative effect of his poems will survive and be of great influence in our land.

There are those of us who feel that although he may grow in wisdom, round out his philosophy of life, and perhaps even smooth out his lines, his big contribution to American literature in the future will not be in the field of poetry but in prose. He has a flair for interpretative biography, and a keen interest in the humanness of great historical characters. He sees men with their faults and their virtues; he sees them whole. The years that lie between us and a historical character do not blunt the edges of these figures for him; he thinks of them as men who walked this earth, and not as demigods. He has nothing in common with the tendency of most nations to deify leaders of an older generation, and although he is very partial to friendships, and his judgment is often blurred by sympathy with those close to him, he is able to take a fine disinterested and objective view of leaders dead and gone. His kinship to ward politicians, labor leaders, teamsters, to the lowly ones who toil, is based upon the very qualities that will make him an able interpreter of men and their aims. In delineating other times, in bringing back to us a "homeliness" that has been lost under a veneer of alien culture, in picturing this age as the logical successor of the past, Carl Sandburg has before him a task that calls for all of his powers, and one that he is well equipped to perform.

3. Forgotten Shrines and Episodes

*We talk of the world, but we mean
a very few men and women. . . .
They are the results of the Past;
they are the heralds of the Future.*
                    Emerson.

I

TIME has dealt gently with the landmarks that are associated, however remotely, with the world's fair of 1893, from which Chicago dates its artistic and commercial awakening, and here and there near Jackson Park survive buildings that trace their lineage back thirty years —a long time in a city like Chicago, where the increasing ground values have laid houses low long before their usefulness as habitations was ended. I have wandered along these streets and stood before these houses as I might before an inn of Pickwick's time, wondering what scenes they had beheld and what sort of men and women had passed through their doors. A different generation, surely, from our own, was there in 1893, a generation still engrossed with talk of "home folks," with a love for pies and griddle cakes, with surreys and puff sleeves and antimacassars, a generation which believed that art, both in painting and in literature, meant pictorial representation of innocently beautiful things, and which bought for its education large albums of "art views" containing the sugary, well-modeled and wholly uninspired paintings of contemporary masters. Even now, when we glance toward the park, we get a glimpse through the trees of the very building that housed the original paintings from all over the world—a crumbling ruin of counterfeit stone, imparting, in its glorious decay, something of its forlorn, exotic grandeur; a Greek symphony that turned the thoughts of thousands from rococo and late Victorian to the beauty that lives in simple lines.

But an industrial age demands its tithe; the solid

masonry of a railroad embankment obscures the view; we must pass under its gloomy trestles before the stone pavements of the city yield to the less formal drives of the park. And just before the thoroughfare ends we observe on either hand rows of one-story frame structures that now shelter pop-corn vendors, photographers, and restauranteurs, or have their windows screened with long green curtains that permit a glimpse of studio life within. Just opposite, where clumps of dense shrubbery and iron chains mark the conventional entrance of an American public park stood the flamboyant gate of the exposition, and in that remote day these storerooms were occupied by vendors of all sorts who had not been able to penetrate the sacred enclosure. When the fair ended these Arabs flitted away; the doors of the houses were boarded up and life lapsed as on a desert isle for a period, for the residents who lived nearby did their trading to the westward and no one bothered about these isolated survivors of the great days. Slowly, one by one, artists and writers sought these ancient buildings and found here hospitable and inexpensive shelter. In time a little colony gathered here and friends and fellow craftsmen followed and made these haunts their rendezvous. And so they take their place in the literary history of Chicago and in the story that I tell, and although the years have scattered many of those who once came here as fledglings and whose names have since become widely known, reminiscences of those days flower whenever two or three are gathered together. Most of the time they met in Margery Currey's big rooms, once the habitat of Thornstein Veblen—perhaps they were even called "studio," for in that day, ten years ago, the word had not yet fallen into disfavor through commercialization—and Margery

was the hostess whose gift for hospitality, for friendship, was as genuine and effective as that of Madame
Nodier or Madame Adam or the Marquise du Deffand
in Paris of other days. If you have wandered down
the narrow passage of the Rue Visconti and let your
imagination people it again with Racine and Balzac
and the merry groups that met for controversy or for
mutual laudation in the Café Rochefoucauld, you may
have experienced a regret for the passing of the years;
no less do these ancient store-rooms house a shrine, and
one wishes that time could be turned back and afford us
once more a glimpse of America's younger writers before
they reached maturity. Arthur Davison Ficke and
Witter Bynner came there, engrossed in *vers libre* and
imagist controversies; Maurice Browne and Ellen Van
Volkenburg Browne, deep in plans for the first Little
Theater; Edgar Lee Masters, with the manuscript of a
poem somewhere about him; Sherwood Anderson, always
reading from his unpublished books; Floyd Dell, engaged in gentle disputations with his associates, Charles
T. Hallinan and George Cram Cook; Carl Sandburg,
"just quiet and vast and fine, a wonder to sit beside and
yet never saying anything," Ben Hecht, always in a
spirited controversy with Maxwell Bodenheim over a
play or a poem, and "Bogie" himself, taciturn, ironical,
pulling at a pipe with a long slender stem of bamboo and
obviously happy to have women light the thimbleful of
tobacco in the tiny brass bowl; Theodore Dreiser, too,
and Edna Kenton, and Margaret Anderson in the days
when the "Little Review" was as yet unnamed and unpublished but on every tongue; Michael Carmichael Carr,
rich in reminiscences of Florence and Bordighera like a
new Vasari, and fluent in cockney dialect; Vachel Lind-

say, booming his "Congo" and rattling his "Fireman's Ball," George Burman Foster, wholly preoccupied with Nietzsche and the origins of Christianity and always in argument with Clarence Darrow; Eunice Tietjens, bringing a wealth of delicate lore from the far east; Harriet Monroe, Alfred Kreymborg, Clara Laughlin, Vincent Starrett, Marion Strobel, John Cowper Powys, Llewellyn Jones—these and many, many more.

Glorious days those—rich, tempestuous, capricious, extraordinary. Tremendous days. And unforgettable nights. Out of the past dimly come these pictures:

Long past midnight and silence outside, save for the dull boom of the university bells to the west, marking the hours. Moonlight dimly flooding the walks seen through the half-drawn curtains. Tall candles throwing long, black shadows against the walls. A group sitting in silence, motionless, in easy attitudes. And near the candles Arthur Davison Ficke chants the ancient lines:

How beautiful are thy feet with shoes, O prince's daughter! The joints of thy thighs are like jewels, the work of the hands of a cunning workman.

Thy navel is like a round goblet which wanteth its liquor, thy belly is like an heap of wheat set about with lilies.

Thy two breasts are like two young roes that are twins.

Steps approach without and a shadow falls upon the ivory curtains. The big form of a policeman stands motionless before the window.

Thy neck is as a tower of ivory . . . thy nose is as the tower of Lebanon. . . . How fair and how pleasant art thou, O love, for delights!

The figure moves on. Within, the voice, chanting the ancient melody. Without, the slow, receding footsteps.

And then another picture: of Eunice Tietjens, whose fine understanding of the oriental spirit is brought out so clearly in "Profiles from China," clad in a lovely Japanese robe, moving gracefully, marvelously, through the postures of a No dance, suggesting again and again the prints of the eastern masters. Little men from the orient have sat spellbound before Eunice Tietjens and have spoken generously in praise of the delicate beauty of her poems. Margery Currey told me one day of an incident that provided the poet with a quaint theme for her gift. "It was a hot summer night," she said, "and Eunice was staying with me. We had been unable to sleep and at three in the morning were standing in front of our house looking across the green stretches of the park toward the lake, just tinted with the dawn. A burly workman was sprinkling the grass and turned a big spray on the bushes. Suddenly there was a piercing scream from a child, and then another, and two or three little figures, lightly clad, rushed out from the bushes, flushed from their coveys by the water. They had come from the congested tenement districts and sought sleep in the cool grass. Later Eunice used this for her poem."

And back again in the big high-ceilinged room, and firelight, and a poet reading. His hair sparse and touched with gray, his jaw severely set, his eyes big and contemplative behind his glasses, his voice crisp and direct. It is prose this time, and Edgar Lee Masters is reading the last chapter of "Mitch Miller," which he has just finished writing. That splendid last page, with its note of tragedy, its despair at a philistine civilization, its mourning for the waywardness of a nation the poet dearly loves. He stops and looks about him and none in his audience moves or speaks a word. He tries to scrutinize their faces by the dim firelight. Asleep? No, just spell-bound—mute in admiration before the poet's rendering of a lofty theme.

II

Here then was a shrine of art to which men made their pilgrimage; just friends, they were, come to pass their leisure—the humble, the obscure, the promising, the arrived. Here grew up the Questioners, offshoot of the ancient Vagabond club, meeting in rooms used later by the Player's Workshop. One recalls the latter with elation, an inspired movement it was, and in its short life it gave to the world two or three notable plays; it was founded by Lou Wall Moore, Elizabeth Bingham, and Maxwell Bodenheim, and poets and writers and players were of its cast, and all the south side intellectuals were in its retinue. It was here that Ben Hecht's "Dregs" was first performed before a shocked and horrified world. The portrait of Lou Wall Moore, given me by one who was a player with her, becomes a dithyramb. "Lou Wall Moore—ah, she has the soul of Chicago! She is Bohemia! She is generous, and kind, and truly fine; hospitable always to new things, and learned in the old, leaning to the bizarre and the colorful. She gave us Greek dancing—her toe nails showed from openwork sandals and glistened pink and polished. She studied, she developed others, she inspired them. Truly all who know her love her. . . ." The Questioners were a conglomerate lot, moody at times, determined, wide awake. They held their sessions in dim, eye-straining lights; the air was often bad, the room cold; through the walls came the wailings of a violin to interrupt their pensiveness. A ring of chairs in the far end held those who had come to discuss the problems of their souls. The first three rows held the admirers of the circle and those who had come to worship. And behind them was massed the "slum circle"—silent, observing, curious deadweight—reporters from the newspapers on their evenings off, students from the University of Chicago halting between migrations to Paddy Grimes' thirst parlor; mockers, disputants, and pharisees. Up and down the aisle wanders Stanislaus Szukalski, sculptor and philosopher, in velveteens; a big white collar, a Christopher Columbus haircut—attending principally to the mental occupation of opening and shutting the transom. Within the sacred circle raged the discussions—on whether the artist should paint the tree, or only the treeness of the tree; on whether or not Amy Lowell would sometime become as passé and innocuous as Longfellow; on the art and intention of "Tender Buttons," then just off the press. From the rear benches mild boohoos and rude flouting of the sacredness of art. Sometimes Bodenheim spoke or read. His method was always the same; he would come in slowly, pulling at his long-stemmed pipe and giving the audience a glance of withered scorn. Then seated on the platform he would take his ease, pull out a handkerchief and blow his nose repeatedly with the noise of a trumpeter. They say he always did this, and perhaps it rested him. When he spoke it was with every word enunciated; clearness was one of his qualities. Something of his own attitude toward this group is preserved in certain chap-

ters of his novel, "Blackguard," in which Alexander S.
Kaun, Stanislaus Szukalski, Feyda Ramsey, Margaret
Anderson, Ben Hecht and others of this circle appear
under thin disguises.

When the relicts of these groups gather the question is
often asked: "What is Margaret doing now?" for it was
hither that Margaret Anderson journeyed full of plans
and ideas for the "Little Review"; here it was named,
caressed, reviled, discussed, admired. As a journal of
the arts it was to be different—"making no compromise
with the public taste"—it was to reflect life and dreams
and fantasies and ever to remain open to new creative
spirits. The marvel to-day is not that it actually emerged
out of the hotbed of industrialism in the middle west but
that for nearly ten years it has been loyal to its standards. Magazines, reviews, fugitive sheets, have come and
gone—youth has poured into them its life blood and
passing the meridian of middle age has left them to starve
and die—but the "Little Review" is still young, militant,
and the despair of the generation that sent it into the
world. Seek the answer in the character of its founder,
editor, and nurse; there is energy, resourcefulness,
eternal youth.

Its adherents were tremendously in earnest. Life was
a deadly thing; dreams were the wings of escape; the
heavens reëchoed with the names of Nietzsche, Whitman, Dostoievsky, Ellen Key; movements, tendencies,
philosophies, of the second decade of the nineteenth century lived in its pages. There was much talk of art and
its relation to life. "Appreciation has its outlet in art,"
said Margaret Anderson in her salutatory, in March,
1914, "and art has its source in, owes its whole current to,
appreciation. Close to life is this eager, panting art.

Criticism that is creative—that is our high goal." John Galsworthy, George Burman Foster, Arthur Davison Ficke, Sherwood Anderson, Floyd Dell, Sara Teasdale, Clara E. Laughlin, Edith Franklin Wyatt, Mary Aldis, Amy Lowell—these were among the first to write for its pages. It came into the world when life was complacent and easy and untroubled; when years of peace and secure living had made the world satisfied with mediocre gods; when the novelist's art was stifled and "Pollyanna" and "The Inside of the Cup" were best sellers. It came when the biggest battles were waged by militant suffragists, when women's rights in government and marriage were still violently debated, when the Irish players were spreading the gospel of romantic realism, when Dreiser was suppressed and Rabelais passed furtively under the counter in book stores. It appeared in time to discuss the first poems of Rupert Brooke, the first translations of Tchekoff and Andreyev, the stories of Red Hanrahan by Yeats, the rules for imagist writing by Ezra Pound. It had few friends, and meager resources, and nobody knew when and where it was going to be published next, but it provided inspiration and spiritual sustenance for a large group of men and women whose names have emerged from obscurity into literary fame.

Toward the new art the "Little Review" was hospitable and friendly; toward bourgeois tastes and conventions it was hostile and militant; it scorned smug, self-satisfied writing, commonplace standards, ineffective creation. It found merit in exclusiveness and virtue in minorities. It fought the battle for free verse, for the imagists and vorticists. It "discovered" half a dozen hopefuls, of whom the most promising was Maxwell Bodenheim, the most mourned Sade Iverson.

Let us consider for the moment the strange apparition of Sade Iverson, the milliner poet, whose verses came to light first and only in the "Little Review," blossomed there, and then faded never to be seen again. Sade Iverson's titles reflected her modesty: "Little Flowers from a Milliner's Box," was one. The friends of the "Little Review" met often in the office of that journal in the Fine Arts building at times when all contributors were called to appear. But Sade Iverson mailed her poems without enclosing an address and gave no response to a general invitation. Finally Miss Anderson used the columns of the magazine to direct attention to this new poet whose identity remained obscure. She related how the poems had come with a little note from Sade Iverson reading: "Something about your magazine—perhaps the essential actuality of it—has moved me to make the 'simple confession' which I enclose. Print it if it is good enough— throw it in the waste basket if it is not." "Though we have tried various investigations we have not been able to find out who this remarkable Sade Iverson is," explained Miss Anderson. And then Maxwell Bodenheim indicted a poem reading:

> I wonder if you scooped out your entire melted soul
> With shaking hands and spilled it into this
> Slim-necked but bulging-bodied flagon
> So slim-necked that my sucking lips
> Must fight for wonderful drops.

But Sade Iverson never responded to the appeals and her poems eventually ceased to come. True, it was whispered about with great glee in the vicinity of the "Chicago Tribune" that Mrs. Elia Peattie, whose book reviews in that newspaper were Miss Anderson's particular aver-

sion and the object of her scorn, had indulged in a little
literary masquerade—I do not know.

Some one has said that Margaret Anderson had two
enthusiasms; the "Little Review" and the Mason & Hamlin piano; for both she worked and sacrificed. She gloried
in oriental rugs—it was known that there were always
beautiful objects about her. An intimate sketches this
portrait of her: "She was always exquisite, as if emerging from a scented boudoir, not from a mildewed tent
or a camp where frying bacon was scenting the atmosphere. She was always vivid, is yet, and beautiful to
look upon, and lovely in her mind. There is a sort of
high, wind-blown beauty about her; her fluffy hair blows
marvelously, her eyes are in Lake Michigan's best blue.
And she is valiant, always." One flings roses riotously
in tearful reminiscence; Margaret Anderson to-day is one
of our *emigrées*.

There were tempestuous times when it seemed that the
"Little Review" could not survive the storm; it never carried any advertising worth the name nor drew great sums
from a beneficent patron. No doubt its editor poured
into it all of her meager substance. The story is still
related of the wildest period in the history of the "Little
Review" and its editor, when Margaret Anderson and her
little group lived in tents on the bleak shores of the lake
and thence sent forth inspiring pronouncements that art,
after all, was all that life contained. Margaret, her
sister, and two little boys and their nurse had found the
house rent in Lake Bluff too steep, it seemed; the coffers
were empty, bills for printing had consumed the contents. In the bitter cold of a morning in early April they
determined to emigrate to three tents that they owned
on the shores of the lake. Surely nowhere in the world

is the wind more raw, and the prospect more bleak, than on the western shores of Lake Michigan in April. A rickety wagon was loaded with kitchen and sleeping utensils and started for the lake. The rain fell in sheets. Just outside the village the wagon slid into a mud puddle. While all were struggling to move it creditors got wind of the flight and caught up with the caravan. There were expostulations and explanations—and then the party proceeded. The tents had been pitched on the shore near Ravinia, and several staunch followers of the "Little Review" were on hand to help settle the little family. The first tent held Margaret Anderson and her oriental rugs; the second held her sister and the two little boys, the third was dedicated to the pots and pans and the nurse. The nurse and the children stayed there during the day, with the cold winds blowing and the pitching waves sending their spray high up on the sand, while Margaret Anderson journeyed back and forth to the Fine Arts building to watch for the coming of the literary renaissance. Downhearted? No. "They were always lyric over the beauties of the sunrise, and the bathing and the outdoors, and their exuberance seemed so convincing, even when their hands were blue and the wind took the words out of their mouths."

Once Emma Goldman was there. The episode lives in the memory of a participant. "The picture is a vivid one in my mind—dumpy Emma, in a brown dress, with a tight seamed basque and gored skirt, sitting on a low stool poking at a pot roast that was to be the Sunday dinner, sniffing now one kettle of food, and now another —she was a good cook, in the German fashion, with much dark brown gravy and high seasoning. And talking! Talking! About art! About life! About woman's free-

dom and her place in the world!   Grandmotherly—that's
how she seemed to me."

Out of this atmosphere came the Little Theater of
Chicago—the first Little Theater in America.   Maurice
Browne was responsible for it; he had come west to lecture and had been impressed by the virility, the crude-
ness, the eager attitude toward cultural things in Chicago.   He brought with him the messages of Nietzsche,
Whitman, Hardy, Tolstoi, Strindberg, Ibsen, and all the
moderns; in a few months he had come in contact with
the younger groups and they had caught his enthusiasm.
The Little Theater was a rallying point for those of the
moderns who gloried in revolt, but after a number of
highly artistic successes it failed for want of material
resources.   But to account it a failure would be to ignore
the highly inspirational value of the whole movement;
its work was intensive and spiritual, it carried forward
a whole group of young men and women in the second
decade whose wholesome influence to-day runs like a
golden strand through the cultural movements of all
America.

4. Sherwood Anderson

Corn-Fed Mystic, Historian of the Middle Age of Man

I'll tell you what—sometimes the whole life of this world floats in a human face in my mind. The unconscious face of the world stops and stands still before me. . . . Why do I not say a word out of myself to the others? Already I have written three hundred, four hundred thousand words. Are there no words that lead into life? Some day I shall speak to myself. Some day I shall make a testament unto myself.

Sherwood Anderson.

INTO this alert and colorful atmosphere came Sherwood Anderson, dreamer, philosopher, corn-fed mystic, a man who gathered into himself all the torment of life, who suffered, to some extent voluntarily, all its pangs and ecstasies. He had torn himself loose from the factory that was to remain a dark and fearsome memory all his days and was trying to write in his unemployed hours. Keenly sensitive, brooding much over the ways of men and women, with the conviction that only the artist who is free can find the road to truth, he fitted in well with a group of mentally active people. His habitation was a hall bedroom, and to make both ends meet his body was still in bondage to a commercial pursuit, but he did not resent writing advertising copy and the old feeling that he was responsible for the profit or loss of a corporation was gone. Karl Anderson, the portrait painter, brought him out to the group in the studios on Fifty-seventh street, and from the first it was apparent that he had rarely associated with men and women active in the arts. He sat back in silence, taking things in with black, shining eyes, speaking only when spoken to, and then in a low, gentle drawl and with much hesitation that suggested diffidence. But he became actively interested, and wanted to come back, and finally made a little path of his own to the rendezvous, talking about art, and craftsmanship, and the freedom of the artist, and feminism, and such subjects as were then in the air—getting interested, among other things, in that English periodical of suffrage, "The Free-woman," which carried a priceless message to women in the early days of its appearance—1910 to 1912. And as the discussions opened for him he admitted his own preoccupation with writing and brought a manuscript, which turned out to be "Windy McPherson's Son," and read a great deal of it. A strange jumble it was, bearing, in its story of the rise of a lad from humble beginnings to an influential position in industry, a similarity to the popular "log cabin to mansion" stories of the American magazines, which the group there so thoroughly despised. But the story was more than that—every now and then Anderson read passages that stirred his audience—original bits of psychological reflection, indignant protests at a conventional state of things, disclosures that his hero was a man in whom two natures, that of a vagabond dreamer and of a constructive exploiter, fought for dominance. Anderson wore his hair long and shaggy; his tie was often askew, his trousers bagged at the knees, he wore big, heavy shoes and his hands were large and clumsy; his face had in it powerful masses, rather than lines, but when he read it was with a voice that conveyed gentleness and a great depth of sympathetic feeling. Often he read, with candles placed near him and half a dozen friends sitting back against the wall on the couch or grouped in various attitudes on the floor, parts of "Windy McPherson's Son" and "Marching Men," for it turned out that he had placed many thoughts on paper during years when he was still living an orderly existence with little expectation that he was destined to be included among the influential writers of his generation. Nor could he have guessed, as he read, that in his audience he had captivated men who were to make possible his first public hearing—Theodore Dreiser, at once caught by Sherwood Anderson's revolt against the conventional valuation of sex and social forces; Floyd

Dell, viewing the manuscript with the practised eye of a critic hospitable to new ideas and new forms; Llewellyn Jones, sympathetic and filled with a desire to speed the new message into the world.

As Sherwood Anderson read from his manuscript in the pale light of the candles it became clear to his listeners that mere story-telling was not uppermost in his mind; that he had evolved theories of writing and thinking and was actually trying to apply them, even if clumsily, to his task. And so it was, for in those days of reflection and searching of heart that preceded his coming to Chicago Anderson had reached the conclusion that nothing really mattered except certain fundamentals—truth and honesty —and that if one had to abandon these to make writing profitable authorship was hardly worth doing. Out of this conviction came two or three other basic principles— the author, he felt, must be true to himself, in order to understand men like himself; he must be free alike from the bondage of the old masters, the hampering conventions of his own age and the deadening temptation to listen to new voices crying out new paths. He must be willing to suffer for the sake of his high aim—this Anderson called "craft love."

All this sounds like generalities and platitudes, but in Anderson it became a firm conviction and finally a philosophy. It appeared that some time in his life influences had been at work to make him write stories along the lines of those that were most acceptable to the editors of the popular magazines—all that was needed was an understanding of the tricks of the trade, the art of carpentry and joining, and an audience, and "big money" would follow naturally. This sort of advice conflicted so harshly with Anderson's idea of what he wanted to write that he became convinced that the cards were stacked against him; therefore he became an evangelist for new forms in self-defense. True, many of the authors who practised carpentry were honest—honesty and sincerity are often, after all, only negative virtues, indolent contrivances to escape from the hardship of being oneself—but Anderson's idea of honesty went a little farther. He saw the world as full of deluded authors who deliberately sugar-coated facts, shut their eyes to real conditions and made no attempt to get inside their characters. A lot of puppets walked the stage and cavorted about in the "best" books, authors made reputations and fortunes by manipulating the strings this way and that in attitudes as convention-alized as those of a Japanese drama. Anderson saw all about him men whose lives seemed to have no resemblance to the successful heroes of contemporary fiction and in his big, blundering way he wondered why nobody tried to write down a drama that seemed so much more interesting to alert minds.

The essentials he outlined were to him more powerful than all the weight of tradition, which, truth to tell, rested lightly upon his shoulders; greater than the examples set by the masters in olden times, of which he knew nothing; more important than plot construction, dialogue and simi-lar questions of technique. Often the little group of literary disciples heard him inveigh against commercial-ized writing, against the "money-making magazines," against dishonest cringing before the dictation of literary Brahmins, who judged all writing by their own arbitrary standards and were principally interested in perpetuating the power of their caste. "Truth and honesty is what we need most," he would say, "we must break away from the standards set by the money-making magazines and book

publishers in Europe and America, to older, sweeter standards of the writing craft itself. In proclaiming this we
are not announcing a new doctrine; actually it is as old
as the world; it is merely the voice of the new man come
into a new world, proclaiming his right to speak out of
the body and soul of youth, rather than through the
bodies and souls of the master craftsmen who are gone.
It holds the promise of a perpetual sweet new birth of the
world. But be sure you recognize the new—there will be
thousands of voices crying out that they carry the real
message—do not be led aside by them, for 'temples have
been wrecked before only to be rebuilt.' Be ready to
accept hardship for the sake of your craft in America."

When Sherwood Anderson speaks more directly of aims
and ideals it is to ask that writers depict life as it is,
rather than as the reader would like to have it. Writing
in America, he feels, deals entirely with exteriors—"the
doctor's office, the city street, the vacant lot beside the
factory, are described with an amazing finality and ful-
someness of detail. Into these places people are cast,
wearing the ordinary clothes such as one is accustomed
to see wrapped about the bodies of his friends and neighbors. Having tricked your reader by these purely mechanical details into having faith in the people they are
writing about, you simply make these people do and say
things no human being has ever really been known to do
or say." And so Anderson falls back upon a plea for a
better understanding of people, a deeper inquiry into
their inner selves—the sort of writing that comes only
with an older, introspective civilization. Perhaps he is
asking too much of our times—as if one demanded that
a child should understand the ballot and take part in civil
government. America is still too preoccupied with blazon-

ing a path through pioneer fields to be very introspective;
we are still more interested in seeing a building rise, brick
by brick, and crying "Ah!" when it reaches its full height,
than we are in what thoughts it is likely to house. Sherwood Anderson comes as a pathfinder, a breaker of bonds,
bidding Americans observe what is going on within themselves and give less attention to their clothes and their
possessions.

II

Sherwood Anderson had come to grips with life. He
had lived his life intensely, ecstatically, humbly, sorrow-
fully, arrogantly. He had tasted adversity and misfortune; he had been on the highroad to a certain kind of
middle class success; he had deliberately uprooted himself when surroundings and human contacts became
tedious to him. He had been a manufacturer, and somewhat like John Webster in "Many Marriages" he had
stood at the door of his factory and taken stock of life
and all it contained. Now he was here in new surroundings, seeking new outlets of expression, groping for an
understanding of the elemental facts and motives in life
which were still denied him. He was trying to apply his
philosophy that life is not a mean thing to be tamed and
held to hard and fast canons, but a beautiful, wild thing
of ecstasies and dreams, something that must be lived
deeply to be understood. He holds the same theory
to-day. And so, judged from a sympathetic point of
view, Anderson is the roving artist ever at odds with the
established order, fighting against the standardization of
our emotions, our affections, our thinking; from a hostile
point of view he is a shiftless character, with a fine ability

to turn words into money via the channels of publicity and advertising, and an arrogant and perverse determination to waste this ability in the aimless and desultory writing of unprofitable books. "Sherwood Anderson believes in living every moment of life to the full," said one of his intimates. He has so lived them. To-day, well along in the forties, he is still the irreconcilable artist, shaking his head sadly at the universal desire for conformity. He belongs to the generation of Carl Sandburg; like Carl he is the product of the flat, treeless prairies; like him he feels that nothing under the arching skies is too low, too inconspicuous, too uninteresting, for him to pass it by.

III

Sherwood Anderson's career as a writer falls into three periods. The first, a period of more nearly objective story-telling than the others, began in Ohio and resulted in the writing of four books: "Windy McPherson's Son," "Marching Men," "Talbot Whittingham," and "Mary Cochran." A contract for the publication of three books was signed in 1916, and "Windy McPherson's Son" was published that year. Anderson then rewrote "Marching Men" and it was published in 1917.

Anderson felt that these books were influenced by his reading and so were not wholly himself. But with the publication of the second that period closed and he began to feel growth in his ability to tell a story. A nervous breakdown intervened and he went to the Ozark mountains, where he completed a novel, which he destroyed. He then wrote a book of poems, "Mid-American Chants." This was published as the third book in his contract and introduced the second period of his writing, which includes "Winesburg, Ohio," "Poor White," and "The Triumph of the Egg." These three books were published consecutively.

He then delved much deeper into psychology. He produced another book of poetry, but this he has not yet published, and may never do so. He began another novel, called "Ohio Pagans," and worked on it for the better part of a summer, and then discarded it. He then began "Many Marriages." He feels that it contains the most subtle writing he has ever done, and regards it as the best of his books. He plans to carry the story forward and his next book probably will deal with the career of Jane Webster.

The story of how Anderson obtained publication for his books may well be made a part of this chronicle. If it gets too full of figures and dates at times, let me plead that it has in it a view of the hard steps that must be climbed by an author who refuses to compromise either with the demands of his editors or his readers. His publication grew out of the informal readings that he gave in Chicago. Floyd Dell used to say jocularly, "You, Sherwood, write a big novel, and then I'll come along and write a bigger one." But his enthusiasm for Anderson was unlimited and he hoped for a genuine literary future for this strange, wayward and poetic man who made such fast friends. "But who will publish him?" Dell would ask. "No publisher will care to go against the stream of public approval, and if he gets published no critic will review him favorably."

Ben Hecht, too, fell under the influence of Anderson's powers at these gatherings, and began to spread the news, but with little effect. "I used to say that Sherwood had the making of a great novelist," said Ben. "I wrote Papa Mencken to that effect and Mencken replied that Anderson was merely one of the imitators of Dreiser. I also wrote Mencken about Maxwell Bodenheim at about that time, but Mencken replied that Bodenheim was playing on the ukulele for the ribbon clerks, or something like that. Later he found something to praise in Anderson."

Anderson himself says that his book finally found publication "through the enthusiasm and voluntary help of Floyd Dell." Before Dell actually took hold Sherwood had sent the manuscript to Alfred Harcourt, who had accepted it for Henry Holt and Company, provided certain necessary revisions could be made. When Dell went to New York in the fall he learned from Harcourt that Anderson had agreed to have some of the rough spots smoothed out by a professional writer, but the revision upward proved fatal. "The reviser," said Dell, "seemed to have thoroughly tamed the wild beauty of the book." The revised manuscript went back to Anderson for approval and he became very angry, withdrew it from Holt and placed it in the hands of Dell to submit to other publishers.

It was an entertaining, but disheartening pilgrimage. "I offered it to a number of publishers," said Floyd Dell. "I am sorry to say I cannot remember just which ones, except Macmillan, who were the first to turn it down. My impression is that all the publishers kept it a long time and were reluctant in passing it up. It is true that I talked enthusiastically about Sherwood to every one I met, but I don't think I made very much of an impression at that. Perhaps my way of talking is not convincing. I am talking to everybody about another young writer to-day, without convincing anybody, I fear. But wait. . . . I know that I became discouraged and shipped the manuscript to an English publisher, whose name I forget. The English publisher wrote that he would be glad to publish it except for wartime conditions and asked me what to do with the manuscript, which I told him to hold. This manuscript, I had learned, was the only one in existence, and as ships were being sunk by the German submarines Sherwood had a copy made in London, which was returned to him. The original copy, at my suggestion, was sent to the London office of the John Lane Company. The English reader enthusiastically accepted it. . . ."

The Englishman who picked "Windy McPherson's Son" was the late Frederick Chapman, literary adviser for John Lane, who reported that the author "showed promise." The London office of John Lane wrote Jefferson Jones, then New York manager for the John Lane Company, and said that if Jones would publish the novel the London house would buy an edition in sheets for distribution in England. Jones heard the news with mingled feelings. "That's the man Theodore Dreiser's been telling me about!" he exclaimed. Dreiser had come in contact with Sherwood Anderson in Chicago and was also doing his best to spread the glad news that an original American author was coming into being. Think of it— Floyd Dell carrying the manuscript up and down Manhattan; Llewellyn Jones writing to friends in New York about it; Theodore Dreiser "tipping off" publishers here and there; Alfred Harcourt accepting it and having to give it up, and finally the reader for a London publisher starting in motion the wheels that led to its publication.

Jefferson Jones has made me privy to a good many facts about the publication of Anderson's books, and as

they may have some interest for those who follow the
work of this writer minutely I may be excused for digress-
ing long enough to deal with such practical matters here.
Mr. Jones told me that Sherwood Anderson was always
grateful to Dreiser for his interest in the book and a
long time later wrote an appreciation of Dreiser for the
"Little Review." "It was done out of gratitude," said
Jones, "but it disappointed Dreiser, for there was something in it that hurt his vanity. I finally brought out
Anderson's first book on September 1, 1916, in a first
edition of 2,500 copies, of which 1,000 copies were sent
in sheets to England. The book began to sell, and cheered
by the growing demand we put another edition of 1,000
copies on the press in February, 1917. But the publishing business is a gamble. By the time we had sold a
little over 1,800 copies the demand stopped abruptly.
The reviews of course run all the way from admiration
to abuse. I sent a book to H. L. Mencken and he replied
in a manner that proved he had no use for it."

"Windy McPherson's Son" was followed in a year by
"Marching Men." Mr. Jones had made a contract with
Anderson that called for the first refusal of his next three
full length novels. Anderson was happily situated to
fulfil his part of the contract, for he had with him the
product of his solitary toil over many sheets of white
paper in the Ohio factory. "Marching Men" was published in the autumn of 1917 in a first edition of 2,500
copies. The first book had failed to sell in England so
the London office of John Lane refused to issue an English
edition. "Marching Men" received scant attention; in-
tending purchasers often were misled by the title into
thinking it a war story; finding to their chagrin that it
dealt instead with labor they ignored it. The total sales

reached 1,000 copies. This and "Windy McPherson's Son" were the only novels issued by John Lane, for the third book, "Mid-American Chants," was a volume of poems, published in the spring of 1918, of which less than 200 copies were sold in the United States.

What of the unpublished novels? Will they add to the world's riches in literature or are they only laboratory experiments, such as every writer develops in the quiet of his cloister? Sherwood Anderson takes the latter view; so does Floyd Dell. Anderson said to me: "Those earlier novels really belong to a period of my writing that is past. I couldn't go back to work over material conceived in one mood when my whole writing mood has passed on to something else. The earlier books—before Winesburg—were too deeply influenced by the work of others; my own mood as a writer did not appear clearly enough. For one thing the story in the destroyed books was not clearly put across. I suppose I was not ready to put it across. The books frankly were not good.

"Just before 'Windy McPherson's Son' was published I had a sort of nervous breakdown and went into the Ozarks to lead the simple life. While there I wrote a novel. On my way home I threw it out of the car window. I wrote a novel last year called 'Ohio Pagans' but the swing and rhythm to fit the theme wouldn't come, so I threw that away too, and went to work on 'Many Marriages.' After 'The Triumph of the Egg' I wrote a second book of poetry which I have not had the hardihood to publish. It is always better to throw such work away than to try to fool with it. In fact I have got so now that if a story does not come fairly singing out of me—if it stops dead—I drop it and go out and look at the ships in the river."

I recalled the character of Mary Cochran out of the two remarkable human episodes, "Unlighted Lamps" and "The Door of the Trap" in "The Triumph of the Egg"— Mary, the girl who is seeking fulfilment for herself in life, thinking about herself with an intense curiosity and a courageous determination toward adventure, a favorite theme of Anderson's, which reappears in half a dozen disguises. I asked Anderson whether he had taken the book called "Mary Cochran" and broken it up into short stories. Sherwood said no, the original book had disappeared. "I have never used any part of the old books but the characters," he said. "Some of them did remain living things in the world of my imagination and every now and then one of them pops up and insists on being put into a story, but always into quite a different story than the one in which it figured originally. And that happens to have been Mary Cochran's experience."

Floyd Dell's comment closes the incident of the unfinished books: "Sherwood Anderson used to send me as fast as written the chapters of a new novel upon which he was working called 'Talbot Whittingham' and later the stories which became the 'Winesburg, Ohio' volume. I considered some of these stories to be among his best work, but there were others which marked the onset of a tendency which has become his new manner, the manner of 'Poor White' and 'The Triumph of the Egg.' I didn't like this tendency and told him so and we quarreled over it, genially enough. But eventually Sherwood came to regard me, I gather, as a kind of Brander Matthews or W. D. Howells, trying to reform him. The result is rather funny and also rather sad. I can't help preferring some of his earlier to some of his later work, and he can't help resenting it. So when we meet we talk guardedly about things of no particular consequence. I still have the manuscript of 'Talbot Whittingham,' and I've never dared to give it back to him. . . ."

Picture to yourself, for the moment, a scene in the Missouri bottoms. A farmer turns up with his plow the closely written page of an embryonic novel. He looks it over, hoping to find a new Sears-Roebuck catalog, shakes his head dolefully and throws it back upon the land, and goes on plowing. . . . This didn't happen, but it might have.

IV

Sherwood Anderson's early training could not have fitted him for a writing career any more than did George Meredith's; his father was running a small harness shop in Camden, O., when Sherwood was born there, September 13, 1876. Just what his forebears were like Anderson does not know; his father came from a southern family, probably Scotch-Irish in origin, and there was Italian blood in his mother's veins, but when the editor of the local newspaper at Camden, O., tried recently to trace the lineage he failed. The father must have been a shiftless sort of man, for we hear of his operating a shop in Caledonia and other places, and moving whenever the rent became due. There were seven children in the family, and no two of them were born in the same place. But it is noteworthy that out of this family came two men whose names were to become known nationally, that of Sherwood Anderson, novelist, and Karl Anderson, portrait painter.

Without harboring any illusions about his father's shiftlessness Anderson still found him a "lovable, improvident fellow, inclined to stretch the truth in statement, loving to swagger before his fellow townsmen, not averse to losing an occasional battle with the demon rum—on the whole a dear, lovable, colorful no-account, who should have been a novelist himself." Perhaps he sat for part of the portrait of Windy McPherson, the town braggart, whose reputation, built upon his claims as a bugler, exploded when put to the test in the Decoration Day parade. Anderson's mother lives most tenderly in his memories. She was a woman of fine spirit, with the difficult problem of making both ends meet before her, who died of overwork before she was forty. "My mother was tall and gaunt and silent," said Anderson. In the dedication of "Winesburg, Ohio," he speaks of her with marked affection: "To the memory of my mother, Emma Smith Anderson, whose keen observations on the life about her first awoke in me the hunger to see beneath the surface of lives." And once he told this story about her:

"Lord, but we were poor—too poor. An incident of that time will illustrate how poor we were. In our village the boys celebrated Hallowe'en by creeping along the street in the darkness and throwing heads of cabbages against the doors of the houses. If no one paid any attention to them they went on their way, but if an irate housekeeper came out of the house and ran after them, they returned again and again to the charge. My mother, knowing this, took advantage of it. You get a sense of her tall, gaunt figure crouching in the darkness waiting for the boys. When they had thrown the cabbages she pursued them. The game was sometimes kept up for hours and my mother acquired by this method twenty-five or thirty cabbages, on which we were fed for the next month."

There was manual labor ahead of him. All sorts of odd

jobs—he was not afraid of work and took what was offered. At twelve he was a timekeeper on public construction work. Now and then he attended school, but most of the time he drifted about barrooms, stores, and livery stables, like boys of his kind. He learned wisdom there that no school could have given him—knowledge of men and life, sympathy for humbler folk, and pity for human frailties. He was fourteen when his mother died and an older sister took charge of the household, but as his brother Karl was already in Cleveland Sherwood's meager earnings were badly needed to help support the family. He worked in factories and out-of-doors, but schooling was at an end. When he was nearly seventeen he came to Chicago for the first time in an attempt to get a good job, and for four years he drifted about as a common laborer, with little incentive to pull out of his rut and work into something more congenial. Then came the Spanish-American war and gave him an outlet for his ambitions. Like so many other young men of his generation he enlisted as a volunteer and served in Cuba. He writes of this period: "I enlisted, frankly not through patriotism, but in order to get out of my situation. To my amazement when I returned to my home town to become a soldier I was greeted as a hero—one who had given up a lucrative position in the city in order to fight for his country. My natural shrewdness led me to take advantage of this situation and I enjoyed it thoroughly."

Between 1898 and 1910 comes that time of mental growth and introspection which foreshadows Sherwood Anderson, the novelist. He drifted back to Ohio and married. After several years, through some inadvertence or other, he came into the management of a paint factory. His leaning toward writing was beginning to assert itself;

he had contracted the habit of sitting at odd hours before sheets of white paper and jotting down a thought after long effort. The paint factory involved problems of labor and marketing, and the endless procession of paint pots began to disturb him. He began to regard himself as a cog in American industry, seeking only to speed up the production of paint. There was no release ahead, no vision of writing for the joy of expression, only the deadening routine of commercial life in a little Ohio town, with what social contacts may be guessed. This inquietude of mind gradually approached the proportions of a crisis in his life and left deep scars, and as we go through his books we find frequent reference to it and to the decision that grew out of it. It is recognizable most clearly, perhaps, in Anderson's latest book, "Many Marriages," which deals wholly with the process by which a man breaks with the mental and physical life that has become intolerable to him, the keynote of which may be found in John Webster's remark: "There has been something broken. It is the habit of life in this house." And because so much of what John Webster does is so closely analagous to what we know of Sherwood Anderson's life, and fits in with Anderson's theory that the true artist draws heavily upon his own experiences to depict the life of his characters, I propose to make a short transition here from the actual Sherwood Anderson to the fancied John Webster of "Many Marriages," in an endeavor to picture what might have preceded Anderson's rupture with his Ohio life.

John Webster is a manufacturer of washing machines, who takes stock of his inner life as the story opens and at thirty-eight recognizes for the first time that certain riches within him have been submerged by the press of externals.

"John Webster . . . was rather a quiet man inclined to
have dreams which he tried to crush out of himself in
order that he could function as a washing machine manufacturer. . . . Down within his body something began
to affect him like an illness. It is a little hard to describe
the feeling he had. It was as though something were
being born. . . . Sometimes the feeling of not being himself became so strong in him that he stopped suddenly in
the streets and stood looking and listening. . . . The
whole structure of business, the thing in which all men
and women in America were, like himself, in some way
involved, was an odd affair. Really he had not thought
much about it. . . . He stood in the outer office seeing,
for the first time, all life of modern men as a strange involved thing. 'It wants a lot of understanding and a lot
of thinking about,' he said aloud. . . . John Webster
stood with blinking eyes watching the men unload boards
at his factory door. The little voices within him were
saying strange, joyous things. One could not just be a
manufacturer of washing machines in a Wisconsin town.
In spite of oneself one became, at odd moments, something
else too. One became a part of something as broad as
the land in which one lived. . . . One might easily become
involved in small things when there were big rich things
to be thought about."

And then this passage, which has little relation to the
development of John Webster of the story, but may well
have come from the stirrings within Sherwood Anderson:

For a time he had read a good many books. At one time
he had thought he might like to be a writer of books. And
no doubt a great many of the writers of books had been visited by just such thoughts as he was having now. Within the

pages of some books one found a kind of refuge from the tangle of things in daily life. Perhaps, as they wrote, these men felt, as he felt now, exhilarated, carried out of themselves.

Sherwood Anderson passed through much the same mental experience as did John Webster. I have from his own lips the story of how, dismayed, confused, he sat at his desk in the factory wondering how to reconcile his outer and his inner life. There was no Natalie Swartz in his life as in the life of John Webster, but like Webster he was puzzled by the hopelessness, stodginess, and drudgery of so-called normal living, and wondered whether he or his neighbors were abnormal. It came to him that if ever he was to write and acquire peace through self-expression he would have to uproot himself from the life he was living and reach out for what now seemed intangible, afar off. But he knew that no orderly explanation was possible, that the world which accepted duties and responsibilities had not time for dreamers and mystics and men who sought for vague, intangible things that could not be turned to practical account. One day his feelings reached a climax. He had called his stenographer and was dictating a business letter. It occurred to him that unless he stopped at that moment he would go on dictating countless letters, placing orders for raw material, acknowledging orders for the products of his factory. It was an endless round. He stopped in the middle of the letter and turning to the girl, said: "I am walking in the bed of a river." The girl stopped and looked up, puzzled. Anderson felt that he had given the effect he intended. He rose, put on his hat and walked out of the office. Without speaking to any one he left the town.

The manœuver had the desired result. Men incapable of understanding a clear, plausible explanation of the artist soul could easily excuse Anderson on the grounds of aberration. The report spread that he had suffered from some sort of hallucination and had wandered away. When he reached Cleveland he called on friends and found that his associates at home had tried to locate him. It was suggested that he talk things over with a mutual friend, a physician, the intimation of course being that Anderson was mentally unbalanced. Anderson readily consented, took the man into his confidence, told him of his plans, and asked him to convey the information as best he could to his Ohio associates. The physician thereupon reported that he felt convinced that it was best for Anderson to get out of his Ohio environment, go to Chicago as he wished, and try writing. Anderson thereupon went to Chicago, located a hall bedroom, and through the influence of his brother Karl, who had become a magazine illustrator, obtained work with an advertising agency. This work appears to have been sufficient to keep him in clothes and not binding enough to interfere with his writing. For a long time, naturally, his books paid him very little, so that he was dependent upon several advertising accounts for subsistence. Until very recently—a year or two ago—he still maintained his association with the Critchfield advertising agency of Chicago.

So we have stumbled upon an American writer to whom revolt is not an empty phrase but an actuality, lived through in suffering and silence. Sherwood Anderson had taken his freedom where he found it; no army of applauding aspirants had cheered him on, nor did any one bother much about what he intended to do. There followed him the criticism and abuse that a conventional, standardized society always visits upon those who have the temerity to break from its accustomed grooves and thereby cause other men to fear for the security of the social structure they have so painfully built. He had a lonely life ahead of him both in the world of men and of books; his knowledge of books was negligible; he knew nothing of literary traditions or current literary movements; he expressed himself clumsily and with a disregard for the rules of grammar. He had read desultorily of course, and once told me that the construction of "Windy McPherson's Son" and "Marching Men" was due to his study of other examples and hence of no great value as an expression of himself. But in view of the utmost simplicity of his style, his use of plain Saxon words and the Biblical ring of many of his best passages it is significant that he credits the Old Testament with being the most important influence in his writings. Anderson once said to me: "Oddly enough, if I were to name the books I have read most consistently, it would not be the Russians. I suppose that the reason the Russian influence has been spoken of so often in connection with my work is that my own approach to writing is very similar to the Russian writers, but for just this reason I perhaps admire most something not quite so much like my own work. I have always been a great admirer of George Borrow and I suppose I have read all of his books twenty-five times. And without any pose in the matter I think I can honestly say that I have had a tremendous lot of joy out of the Old Testament. When I traveled around the country as an advertising writer I used to take my knife and cut books out of Gideon's Bibles in hotels and carry them in my pocket."

Anderson acquired a profound admiration for Borrow's

"L'Avengro" and "The Bible in Spain" and often referred to them; among other authors he admired Balzac, Mark Twain and Fielding, but he had never read them exhaustively. Whitman and Tolstoi interested him, particularly when Tolstoi was widely talked about ten or fifteen years ago. His style, which has often been compared to that of the Russians, actually owed nothing to them; until Ben Hecht gave him "The Idiot" about five years ago he had not read Dostoievsky. In Chicago he met Theodore Dreiser and became sympathetic toward his books. After "Winesburg, Ohio" appeared he read "Sons and Lovers" and became enthusiastic over D. H. Lawrence, yet his reading of this author, with whom he has more in common than most, has been limited to a few books. When in Paris and London in 1921 Anderson came in touch with Jacques Copeau, Ezra Pound and James Joyce—Copeau had previously visited him in Chicago and both Pound and Anderson had written for the "Little Review" when first it appeared, but he had never read Joyce. In London Anderson saw very few of the English authors. It is significant that although friends in America gave him all sorts of letters of introduction he refused to present them unless for cause. "I don't know these men or their work," he would say, "so I see no reason why I should waste their time."

In Paris Anderson gained much satisfaction in the friendship of Gertrude Stein, whose experiments in words he had always taken seriously. In fact Anderson had been one of the first to see unusual merit and penetration in her "Three Lives," and "Tender Buttons," which was generally accepted as lunacy by many intelligent workers in the arts, found in him a spirited defender. Anderson had, all his life, had a feeling for words; he often mused about their connotations and pondered over the relation of sound and meaning. In Gertrude Stein's work he immediately recognized an experiment that he himself might, under other circumstances, have made. He saw that words to her were in reality only vocal symbols, and that she was using these symbols to express only her own intimate feeling; that the word then came to signify not the fact found in the dictionary, but stood for something inside the consciousness of Madame Stein which she was trying vaguely to express. She possessed moreover magnificent courage in boldly traveling against the current of all possible intelligent opinion; he was rather proud to stand out as one of her defenders. In Paris he found her a cultured and spirited woman with a prodigious capacity for work—very much in these respects like Miss Amy Lowell. He there agreed to write a sympathetic introduction to her new book, "Geography and Plays," which was published in 1923. (Four Seas.) In this he said: "Every artist working with words as his medium must at times be profoundly irritated by what seems the limitations of his medium. He would like to create in the reader's mind a whole new world of sensations. One works with words, and one would like words that have a taste on the lips, that have a perfume to the nostrils, rattling words one can throw into a box, and shake, making a sharp jingling sound; words that, when seen on the printed page, have a distinct arresting effect upon the eye; words that, when they jump out from under the pen, one may feel with the fingers as one might caress the cheeks of his beloved. I think that these books of Gertrude Stein's do in a very real sense recreate life in words."

To offset his apparent lack of literary culture Ander-

son had definite theories about novel-writing and a determination to express them. He also thought that he should
become a subjective writer, and that a wide experience of
men and women was necessary for understanding them.
He felt that when one discovered a writer with a true
note one felt that he had lived life deeply, wholly, and
was giving the world chapters of self-revelation. "How
can I love my neighbor if I do not understand him?"
asked Anderson. "I know from my own experience how
baffling it is constantly to be coming upon good, well-done
work that is false. It is the most delicate and the most
unbelievably difficult task to catch, understand and record
your own mood. The thing must be done simply and
without pretense or windiness, for the moment these creep
in your record is no longer a record but a mere mass of
words meaning nothing. The value of such a record is
not in the facts caught and recorded but in the fact of
your having been able truthfully to make the record.
Something within yourself will tell you when you have
not done it truthfully. I myself believe that when a man
can thus stand aside from himself, recording simply and
truthfully the inner workings of his own mind, he will be
prepared to record truthfully the workings of other minds.
In every man or woman dwell dozens of men and women
and the highly imaginative individual will lead fifty lives.
Surely this can be said if it is said that the unimaginative
individual has led one life.

"So whenever the writer finds himself baffled in drawing
a character or in judging one drawn by another let him
turn thus in upon himself, trusting with childlike simplicity and honesty the truth that lives in his own mind.
Indeed one of the great rewards of living with small children is to watch their faith in themselves and to try to

emulate them in this art. This practice has been such a help and delight to me."

V

Somewhere in his notebooks Samuel Butler has recorded: "It is with books, music, painting and all the arts as with children—only those live that have drained much of their author's own life into them." We get the impression that the books of Sherwood Anderson, even aside from technical defects, are warm and alive for the very reason that into them the author has poured his life blood. And so, conversely, we can read Sherwood Anderson through his books. If every man uncovers himself in his work surely a writer is the most easily understood of all men, for he deals with tools that are much more generally a medium of expression than those of the painter, sculptor or composer. And no writer ever gets very far away from himself; objectivity is after all only a relative term, and even the most objective writer of all betrays himself by his selection of material, his narrative processes, his choice of words. It is not solely because these writers of whom I speak have put so much of themselves into their writings that I dwell so much on the personal side, but more because the outcroppings of their own individuality is to me the most fascinating part of the examination. Whether or not this is a form of emotional criticism that is abhorrent to the student of esthetics is to me a matter of indifference; a book built primarily upon friendships and memories can afford to leave to the more scholarly inquirer problems of technical skill, the more subtle balancing of literary values and the relation of these men to the literature of all time. And so when

"Windy McPherson's Son" comes to me, and I find in the story a certain immature craftsmanship, a hodge-podge of unrelated incidents strung on the thread of one man's life, I overlook those blemishes and turn to the more absorbing subjects of: "What has Sherwood Anderson tried to express?" and "How much of this book represents the result of his thinking and his experience?" And those topics, you will admit, are more absorbing. In fact we are still applying the same test to Dickens and Nietzsche and Flaubert; we are tracing the effects of intellectual revolt, royal patronage, popular applause and affluence in the themes of the Wagner music dramas; we are discovering with heightened interest that whole pages of "Maria Chapdelaine" are like leaves from the book of life of Louis Hémon on the Peribonka. And so when we consider "Windy McPherson's Son" we are apt to wonder in how far the narrative of this impulsive character dovetails with the story of Sherwood Anderson's own life. Sam was raised in a small Iowa town, close by the farming country; his father was a shiftless character—in this case the town braggart—and the lad helped support the family with his meager earnings. Sam was just a lad in his teens when his mother died, and her death made a deep impression upon him. Sam was more than a village lad without ambitions; dreams surged within him, and the talk of success in other fields made him long to go to the big city and conquer, too. There was a certain dualism in his character; underneath he was apt to be the timid, dreamy, emotional lad to whom monetary success was only a means and not an end; on the surface he became at times hard, shrewd and grasping, fighting the world with the weapons it gave him; pitting his wits against its own craftiness and succumbing to the conditions that his environment made.

Over and over again the hidden side of his character broke forth and made him do unexplained things; moods of contemplation and reflection sent him away from his kind and out on long walks, or into strange, forlorn corners of the city where no man on the way to become a financial giant was likely to go. It made him wonder about life and the laws that humankind had imposed; it made him see stultified, groping, futile lives with eyes of wonder and sympathy; it caused him to regard sex as something beautiful before God, in spite of the fact that it was frowned upon in public by his kind as something abhorrent and disturbing. It made him feel that there was something to be gained in life besides the accumulation of wealth; what, he did not know, no, not even at the end of the book could he define what it was that he wanted save in terms of what he did not want. How much of Sherwood Anderson's life lies hidden in these gropings I shall not endeavor to disclose, but that the externals of Sam's career follow to some extent that of Anderson is apparent. When, later on, we find this same autobiographical parallel reappearing in successive books—in "Marching Men," in "Winesburg, Ohio," in "Poor White," in isolated stories in "The Triumph of the Egg," in "Many Marriages," we may say, without attempting to make a judgment on superficial evidence, that Sherwood Anderson has at least lived very close to the main theme of all his tales.

It is always a question how far one can put himself back into the days when a new writer first appeared on the horizon, especially when that writer has since produced much work that obscures his first effort. That is what makes it so difficult to determine what men saw, and did not see in "Windy McPherson's Son" when it was given to a cold and critical world. Most of the men who had spoken in favor of its fine qualities had read it in manuscript, and for the most part had heard it read by Anderson himself, and had discussed it with him. In this way Floyd Dell had fallen in love with its youthfulness, its independence, its rebellious spirit; and Theodore Dreiser had become impressed with Anderson's contempt for the popular American conception of financial success. Some early critics had agreed that it needed rewriting— in fact there was much comment on technical faults, and there was some rewriting. After the book appeared various critics looked at it coldly and pointed out certain glaring errors of construction. And it is true that it lacks style, that there is no appeal to the ear in cadence or prose rhythm, that the conversation between characters is often stilted, that Anderson loses his theme in a jumble of conflicting emotions. So many incidents are piled up that the story moves along clumsily. But looking at the book now, with our knowledge of what has come after, we see that Anderson has incorporated many of the characteristics and the mannerisms that were to become distinctly his in later books. There is, for instance, that attitude of puzzled contemplation, of patiently pondering over the lives and actions of men and women, which always leads me to think of Anderson as sitting in the position of Rodin's Thinker. There is his way of using darkness and the rain as a background for the mood of a character, usually leading up to certain reflections upon life itself. It is always a light rain; often the pattering of drops upon the roof, or down the spouts, creates that atmosphere that lends itself easily to quiet reflection and contemplation. There is his way of wondering why the stirrings of sex should be considered vile, and of making his characters walk out into the night when thoughts of sex disturb them, much as in the following characteristic picture, which he draws again and again in the course of his books: "One night, when the sex call kept him awake he got up and dressed, and went and stood in the rain by the creek in Miller's pasture. The wind swept the rain across the face of the water and a sentence flashed through his mind: 'The little feet of the rain run on the water.' There was a quality of almost lyrical beauty in the Iowa boy." Then there is Anderson's contemplation of the lives of tired, helpless individuals hopelessly caught in the social fabric, pictured objectively and suggesting to a slight extent the sympathy and commiseration with which he was to treat such themes later on, themes of which this fragment is an example, with the pattering of a light rain in the dark as incidental to a contemplative mood for his character. One finds here also that understanding of tired, helpless individuals, and appreciation of distorted lives that later on becomes so prominent a characteristic in Anderson's stories. The note of sympathy and commiseration is not yet so clear as later, but the objective picture is there. "In every city and in every village there is a class of women the thought of whom paralyzes the mind. They live their lives in small, unaired, unsanitary houses, and go on year after year washing dishes and clothes—only their fingers occupied. They read no good books, think no clean thoughts, are made love to with kisses in a darkened room by a shamefaced yokel, and after marrying some such yokel, live lives of unspeakable blankness. . . . In these women is no light, no vision. They have instead certain fixed ideas to which they cling with a persistent, touching heroism. To the man they have snatched from society they cling also with a tenacity to be measured only by their love of a roof over their heads and a craving for food to put into their stomachs. . . . A fierce animalism in them makes them cling to the babe at their breast and in the days of its softness and loveliness they close their eyes to try to catch again an old fleeting dream of their girlhood, a something, vague, shadowy, no longer a part of them, brought with the babe out of the infinite. . . . Something touching the lives of such as walk in the clean air, dream dreams, and have the audacity to be beautiful beyond the beauty of animal youth maddens them, and they cry out, running from kitchen door to kitchen door and tearing at the prize like a starved beast who has found a carcass. . . . In them is all of femininity—and none of it." And finally Anderson's study of industrialism, which seems to have been with him from his Ohio days, and which is the principal theme in "Poor White" and in certain short stories. Here, in the body of the novel, he is intent on describing the methods by which industry and big business achieve their ends, and although he has not yet developed the ironical touch that he uses later he makes it clear that he has no sympathy for a nation drunk with "a blind grappling for gain." These are among the more apparent characteristics that are hallmarks of Sherwood Anderson, the novelist.

There are other incidents which are straws that show the direction of Sherwood Anderson's thinking. His love of life could almost be said to be the basis of Telfer's impassioned cry: "Here in this western village I stand and fling my challenge to the world: 'On the lips of not the greatest of you,' I cry, 'has life been more sweet.'" And it is easy to follow his sympathies in the incident of the evangelist who misunderstands the fine avowal of the youth, innocently responding to an emotional awakening that has its origin in adolescent growth. The lad is plainly puzzled by the denunciation of vice by the preacher, but when called upon to testify he rises and speaks a sentence that is a simple indication of his innocence and poetic detachment. But he is laughed at for his openness, and lecherous old age reads into his words meanings that are foreign to the boy, so that he turns and runs out of the church. That is an incident that shows Anderson's ability to understand the psychology underlying the whole subject and points the way to "Winesburg, Ohio." And this leads directly to the episode of Mike McCarthy, murderer, indicting the morals of the town of Caxton from his cell in the county jail on the same night that the hypocritical evangelist had failed to move Sam in the church. "In the midst of the blasphemy of Mike McCarthy he had sensed a deep and abiding love of life. Where the church had failed the bold sensualist succeeded," concludes the author.

I have spoken of his attitude of brooding over the actions of men and women. We meet this for the first time in Sam McPherson's interview with Mary Underwood, in which Anderson depicts his hero watching Mary and analyzing her thoughts and motives as she performs her simple, household acts. This incident, which reappears often and later becomes the basis for his studies of subconscious motives—as in "Unlighted Lamps" in "The Triumph of the Egg"—leads me to recall that in "Windy McPherson's Son" as well as in other sustained narratives there are episodes that stand rather alone and have no direct relation to the story as they are strung on the thread of the hero's life. They help the impression that Anderson has never mastered the technical difficulties of the novel and that his field is the short story and the essay—in fact, upon careful examination, we may conclude that it is in the short story that he has won his most marked success.

Anderson has pictured America as a land with two classes of men: those who piled up their gains and those who piled up power and used it for a wholesome purpose. It was the men who said "I will get what I can" against those who said "I will do what I can." And in his mind Sam McPherson was an example of the second class who was being swayed by his surroundings and the competitive element in business to crush out the dreamer and the thinker and develop only the acquisitive instinct. "The sense of equity in Sam fought an unequal battle," is the way Anderson expresses it. All through the book Sam fights—his material success is as ashes in his mouth and finally he turns deliberately from his success and gropes for things in life that count. What they are we do not discover. Anderson feels that in the tremendous battle for success men bolster up their courage by declaring to themselves that they will not fail; after a certain point they grow weary; "tight brains have loosed a little. Strong convictions have become weak. Old gods are dying. . . . We Americans have believed that life must have point and purpose. We have called ourselves Christians but the sweet Christian philosophy of failure has been unknown among us. To say of one of us that he has failed is to take life and courage away." Sam McPherson, no longer a slave to manufacturing, becomes interested instead in certain helpless children that he adopts. After trying to run away from life and all its entanglements, he finds that he must face life now. Perhaps in building for the coming generation he can also build for his inner self. " 'I cannot run away from life. I must face it. I must begin to try to understand these other lives, to live!' The buried inner thing in him thrust itself up." Such is the story of Sam McPherson.

In spite of all its deficiencies "Windy McPherson's Son" disclosed a writer with a note of protest in his voice; a man in revolt against the accepted standards of success in the United States, not a novelist with ready made propaganda, with a remedy for the evils, for at the end of the book Anderson can only leave Sam McPherson to grope further.

VI

Sherwood Anderson's first novel left much to be desired, but our detailed examination reveals that it contained the main currents of his thinking. When we come to "Marching Men," we observe immediately a similarity of plot and idea, although Anderson had made progress in the interval between the two books. "Marching Men" points the way to "Winesburg, Ohio," and "Poor White"; it is written with a greater economy of words and incidents than "Windy McPherson's Son." It is also the story of a boy of imagination who rebels against his environment, whose father was "a bit off his head," who breaks with the crude village life to enter the battle for existence and power in a great city, and who longs for some form of undefined individual expression. Strangely enough "Beaut" McGregor's expression lay in the direction of order; his observations crystallized into the idea that workingmen must learn to march, shoulder to shoulder, in orderly ranks, and thus demonstrate their solidarity and gain confidence in themselves. There was a certain spiritual exaltation about McGregor as he developed his theory. . . . "The very soul of the marching men was a sense of order. That was the message of it, the thing that the world has not come up to yet. Men have not learned that we must come to understand the impulse toward order, have that burned into our consciousness before we move on to other things. There is in us this madness for individual expression. For each of us the little moment of running forward and lifting our thin childish voices in the midst of the great silence. We have not learned that out of us all, walking shoulder to shoulder, there might arise a greater voice, something to make the waters of the very seas to tremble." . . . Eventually McGregor marshals his men and parades them through the streets—"the song of labor expressed in the threshing of feet." The book appears to have a definite social object, inspired by Anderson's thinking about labor and his resentment against exploitation of human material in American industries. But the author stood alone with his program, which was not allied with the political propaganda of any labor or radical group. Anderson's remedy was purely hypothetical, and even if feasible appeared without aim and unlikely to bring about any specific benefit. "Beaut" McGregor in his harangue to the men unlimbered all the guns of the soapbox orator:

This talk of brotherhood. The words mean nothing. Man cannot love man. We do not know what they mean by such love. They hurt us and underpay us. Sometimes one of us gets an arm torn off. Are we to lie in our beds loving the man who gets rich from the iron machine that ripped the arm from the shoulder?

. . . We have given them automobiles and wives with soft clinging dresses. When they have cried we have cared for them. . . . They speak with pity of us—Labor—their father.

And now we will show them their father in his might. The little machines they have in their factories are toys we have given them and that for the time we leave in their hands. . . . We make of ourselves a mighty army, a marching army going along shoulder to shoulder. We can love that.

When they see us, hundreds of thousands of us, marching into their minds and into their consciousness, then will they be afraid. . . . They have forgotten our power. Let us re-awaken it. . . . You are the arms and legs and the hands and the eyes of Labor. You have thought yourself small.

When you have marched until you are one giant body then will happen a miracle. A brain will grow in the giant you have made.

In contrast to "Beaut" McGregor stands David Ormsby, who represents the factory and is the father of Margaret Ormsby, the last girl in McGregor's life. David is the representative of the aristocracy, who has no confidence in the brains of the mob. He thinks McGregor has thrown away a brilliant career. But he is perturbed because his daughter is fired with a feeling of sympathy for McGregor. His aim must be to win his daughter back at all hazards. "If I can take her from him," he muses, "I and my kind can take the world from him also. It will be another victory for the aristocracy in the never-ending battle with the mob." It is his conviction that he knows the true road to beauty—that McGregor, the dreamer, is following the false road. For the moment he wins his daughter away. But at the end of the story doubt enters his mind. What if McGregor were right?

This development does not seem to have been clearly conceived in Anderson's mind. Anderson had attempted to give McGregor a concrete answer to his dreams, but the reader remains unconvinced. It is worth noting that Anderson has reintroduced his favorite triangle—the hero with his dreams and his desire to change his environment, coming into close relationship with a talented, high-spirited, aristocratic girl and being pitted against her father, who always represents the materialistic class. The last chapter brings forward the germs of "Many Marriages." The father is fighting to hold his daughter, and his narrative of his marriage and its spiritual failure foreshadows John Webster's redundant explanation to his daughter Jane. David Ormsby's wife also did not keep pace with him, but he speaks of her more tenderly than John Webster does of his wife. When he pleads for his daughter's interest she responds very much as does Jane Webster: "I love you," she said. "Some day I may have a lover but always I shall love you. I shall try to be what you want of me."

"Marching Men" disclosed that Anderson was becoming more occupied with the problems of American industrialism. The early chapters, dealing with life in a mining town, possess power, keen observation and pity. When the book was published Anderson was accepted as "significant" by one or two daring critics but there was no general recognition of his abilities. Nor did his next book do much to increase his audience. This happened to be "Mid-American Chants," musings, rather than poems, which Anderson had set down at odd moments through a series of years. They are appropriately named, for they are actually chants, or monologues in rhythmic prose, and many of them attain great dignity and forcefulness. Here we find a deep concern with industrial America. In a number of the poems the author celebrates the crude strength of Chicago, and in spite of the mud, the tur-

moil and the confusion, he finds songs waiting to be sung
and a great life renewing itself. "My mouth is dirty,"
he writes of Chicago, "my feet are sunk in the black
swampy land, but I am a lover. I love life. In the end
love shall save me." Some of the poems remind one of
Sandburg:

> Back of Chicago the open fields—were you ever there?
> Trains coming toward you out of the west—
> Streaks of light on the long grey plains? Many a song—
> Aching to sing.

The publisher considered "Mid-American Chants"
highly important and hoped that the unexpected welcome
given "The Spoon River Anthology" in spite of its
radical form, might lead the public to accept this book.
Some critics thought Anderson had spread his sails to
catch part of the breeze that was bearing Edgar Lee
Masters on to fame and fortune, but this was an error.
The sale of the book was less than two hundred copies
and Anderson did not feel encouraged thereby to give
any more poems to the world, although he continued to
write them.

"Winesburg, Ohio" is a primer of the heart and mind,
the emotions and the method of Sherwood Anderson. It
is the most compact, the most unified, the most revealing
of all his books. It is his most successful effort technically, for in it he has told the story of one community in
terms of isolated short stories. Certain tales in "The
Triumph of the Egg" rank higher in workmanship, but
"Winesburg, Ohio" stands higher as a whole. The telling
is almost primitive and elementary and has the qualities
of the simple annals of the poor. The author presents
the impression that he is discovering for the first time

the situations that he reveals to the reader, consequently he leads up to them as haltingly, as slowly, as a child opening a door and entering an old, unused room. In the end the effect is cumulative and powerful. It is "Winesburg, Ohio" that permits us to link Sherwood Anderson's name with that of Tchekov.

Although the stories are supposed to deal with an Ohio town most of them were written in Chicago; many of the types portrayed were drawn from men and women with whom Anderson came in contact in Chicago, and some of them lived in his boarding house. Their universality, for that matter, is distinct; they are types to be found in any community. But the narcissus character of most individuals, who look into a mirror and thereupon pronounce all the world beautiful, will not let them acknowledge the typical character of Anderson's people. These critics apply the terms abnormal, subnormal, delinquent, vicious, and other epithets that are in current use to designate a variation from the normal and the average. In reality their criticism should have been directed against the author's selective process. It was not that the mythical Winesburg abounded with more low types than the ordinary American town but simply that the author had written entirely about such types to the exclusion of others. He had omitted no doubt many "good" people whose goodness was not hypocrisy but a positive virtue, but who did not happen to come under his observation. After all, he was entitled to the right of selection.

We find in "Winesburg, Ohio" a series of most convincing portraits. Take the book and observe how simply the author places his puppets before you. He is writing almost with the simplicity of colloquial speech. "Doctor Reefy was a tall man who had worn one suit of clothes ten years. It was frayed at the sleeves and little holes had appeared at the knees and elbows. In the office he wore also a linen duster with huge pockets into which he continually stuffed scraps of paper." . . . "Elizabeth Willard was tall and gaunt and her face was marked with smallpox scars. Although she was but forty-five some obscure disease had taken the fire out of her figure. Listlessly she went about the disorderly old hotel, looking at the faded wallpaper and the ragged carpets." . . . "Doctor Parcival was a large man with a drooping mouth covered by a yellow mustache. He always wore a dirty white waistcoat out of the pockets of which protruded a number of the kind of black cigars known as stogies. His teeth were black and irregular and there was something strange about his eyes. The lid of the left eye twitched."

The stories are told just as simply and deal with the sort of men and women that you might expect to meet on the street. They pay no tribute to the short story formula of the successful magazine. The words these people speak come naturally out of their mouths and not one seems to have the gift of epigram and wit that distinguishes Americans solely in books. The troubles they brood over seem to be the troubles many persons have, so that our words "realistic" and "romantic" need to be defined anew. On the critical horizon the appearance of these stories created a sensation. H. L. Mencken recognized their power and truth at once and spoke of "Winesburg, Ohio," as "a brilliant procession of little tragedies, a vivid and moving picture, Dreiserian in its fidelity and almost Conradian in its irony of the insoluble riddle at the heart of human existence. He gets into the minds and souls of his remote and unregarded yokels and what he finds there is not the mere sordid farce that one glimpses from the train windows but the eternal tragedy of man." Even the conservative and literal "Boston Transcript" was moved to admit that there was nothing commonplace about it "but the material."

"Winesburg, Ohio" was the boldest writing Anderson had done up to this time. He applied his canons of honesty and truth and wrote down what he found went on in the hearts of men. The picture was not always cheerful and romantic. Avarice, lust, strange broodings over sex, repressions, selfishness—all these seemed to have a hold deep down in the hearts of his characters. Naturally many readers objected to having their mental sleep thus rudely disturbed by a hawker of human frailties. Far from admitting that the people of Winesburg were real, many so-called rational persons insisted that they were grotesques, as did the old man in the first story of the book. This old character had written, as you will recall, a volume which he named "The Book of the Grotesque." . . . "The old man had listed hundreds of the truths in his book. There was the truth of virginity and the truth of passion, the truth of wealth and of poverty, of thrift and of profligacy, of carelessness and abandon. Hundreds and hundreds were the truths and they were all beautiful. And then the people came along. Each as he appeared snatched up one of the truths and some who were quite strong snatched up a dozen of them. It was the truths that made the people grotesques."

The drastic criticism to which Anderson was subjected because of his revelations in this book made a deep impression on his sensitive nature. When he was attacked as perverse, ignorant, uncouth, and even immoral he went about the streets wondering by what turn of fate the stories that he had written with loving hands and which represented people living round about him had become contemptuous and vile. His vindication came in the course of time and "Winesburg, Ohio" is now regarded with respect and admiration. It has done much to help liberate the writers of America from the bondage of the formula short story. Ernest Boyd wrote in his introduction to the edition in the Modern Library: "The stories are written out of the depths of imagination and intuition . . . the impression of surface realism is reinforced by that deeper realism which sees beyond and beneath the exterior world to the hidden reality which is the essence of things." It was Winesburg that brought Anderson the approval of discerning critics in Europe and widened his audience of thinking people in America, bringing about his appearance in magazines like the "New Republic" and the "Nation," which could afford to encourage a pioneer in the short story.

VII

"Poor White," the next book, would have been hailed as a most auspicious first novel had its author presented it to the world in place of "Windy McPherson's Son" and "Marching Men." Here Anderson again took up rural Ohio as his theme and in Hugh McVey projected a character that had in him something of a barbaric giant groping toward a spiritual rebirth. Again Anderson gave much attention to the sex stirrings in his principal characters, and to the rise of industrialism in a rural community, and we observe with interest the place that the harness shop takes in the story, recalling his father's occupation. There were passages of great strength, especially those describing rural manners, but the "drive" of the novel was dissipated toward the end and one came to the conclusion that here, as in other instances, Anderson had not mastered a coherent form for a continued story.

"The Triumph of the Egg" contains the best isolated examples of Sherwood Anderson's art. It is not the most coherent book—"Winesburg, Ohio" is that—nor is it intended to be coherent, for it is made up of sketches assembled from half a dozen magazines. At first glance a puzzling book, it proves, upon closer acquaintance, a very simple one. Some of the sketches go back to Sherwood Anderson's earliest days in Chicago; others are the result of more recent cogitation. But in its essentials the book displays a singular unity in this, that the author has here set down his reflections on life as it appears to his characters and each one is a lonely figure, groping toward the light. And over and over again he masquerades in the guise of these characters. Sherwood Anderson is meditating on the perverseness, the aimlessness, the futility of life in a spirit of humbleness and pity; pity for the strange, distorted creatures over which he toils with the care of a scientist struggling toward the light in a crying need to be understood.

Groping, deluded youth, baffled middle age, defeated senility—all have their place in this piteous cry for light. In the first of the stories the plea comes from the heart of a boy who has met his first harsh rebuff from life— "I Want to Know Why." The story has unity and atmosphere; its message rings true. The lad who tells it follows the races, makes his own estimate of the sports, the touts, the jockeys, the camp followers of Saratoga. He is brother to white and black; life has not yet planted the seeds of prejudice in his heart; he loves all who love horses and hates the man who is not as clean as the gelding Middlestride. "Often when I think about it, this always going all season to the races and working in the livery barn in the winter where the horses are and where men like to come and talk about horses, I wish I was a nigger. It's a foolish thing to say, but that's the way I am about being around horses, just crazy. I can't help it. . . ." The pitch of the story is admirable; the adolescent observations have a forcefulness, a genuineness; they carry conviction. "At the tracks you sit on the fence with men, white and niggers, and they chew tobacco and talk and then the colts are brought out. It's early and the grass is covered with shiny dew and in another field a man is plowing and they are frying things in a shed where the track niggers sleep, and you know how a nigger can giggle and laugh and say things that make you laugh. A white man can't do it and some niggers can't but a track nigger can every time. . . ."

Anderson himself places great store by the tale called "The Egg" which gives the title to the book and which demonstrates, in concrete form, the victory of trivial matter over ambition. Nevertheless next to "I Want to Know Why" the most important story is "Out of Nowhere Into Nothing," in which we encounter a favorite Andersonian theme, the spiritual awakening of a young woman of twenty-seven, told with all of Anderson's capacity for catching overtones and the subtle influences of the subconscious, for Anderson is one of the few authors in America who comprehends how closely the physical and the spiritual are allied. This story has perhaps more external movement than most of his, and yet the preoccupation of the author is entirely with what goes on in the mind of Rosalind Westcott. . . . "Brothers" is a powerful story, the tale of a broken man whose life is circumscribed in the routine of existence and who seeks release in fanciful dreams; groping feebly toward some form of beauty that shall satisfy his longing he becomes by force of circumstances a murderer. His brother tries to tell the tale. "The whole story of mankind's loneliness, of the effort to reach out to unattainable beauty tried to get itself expressed from the lips of a mumbling old man, crazed with loneliness, who stood by the side of a country road on a foggy morning holding a little dog in his arms."

The prose is clear—slowly put together, but concise, moving. The exalted style that becomes the most distinguishing characteristic of "Many Marriages" will be found emerging here and there in the stories that make up "The Triumph of the Egg." In the preface Sherwood Anderson has put into words the feeling that so often overpowers him—the urge to write what is struggling for utterance. He says: "Tales are people who sit on the doorstep of the house of my mind. Many tales come to sit for a few moments on the doorstep and then go away. They murmur and cry out they are dying of cold and hunger. I am a helpless man—my hands tremble. I feel in the darkness but cannot find the door-knob. I look out at a window. Many tales are dying in the street before the house of my mind." Anderson has here expressed poetically the groping, the seeking for hidden impulses and overtones that is never absent in these tales.

Anderson writes with great industry and in addition to his novels has produced a large number of short stories and articles which have appeared in magazines, but have not yet been collected in book form. A great mass of extraneous writing Anderson has lately been

doing in what he calls "A New Testament," which consists of a series of notes and observations, often filled
with subconscious elements, set down during the years
that he has been writing. Some day he hopes to publish
the latter in a book; in the meantime it exists in the form
of random notes, in articles contributed from time to time
to magazines like the "Little Review" and the "Double
Dealer," and in unwritten observations often repeated in
conversation by their author. Anderson's habit of speaking of his body as a house, and carrying on the metaphor
to include garden walls, ruined paths, doors open and
shut, windows lighted or dark, crops up in the testament;
often long passages are entirely in metaphor and then
again he indulges in direct comment on literature and
affairs. He sees again and again that men are encom-
passed by a shell, that the true man rarely appears because we have so thoroughly buried him under human
conventions and restrictions. This is typical of his
method:

I am building me a house slowly. Take this key. Go in.
At noon, and in a glare of light, God brought me death to
hang over the door of my house. God put the key in the
sun-washed fork of a tree.
I am building me a house slowly. It has many rooms.
There is a house building itself for me slowly. Brick by brick
the walls go up. Stone by stone the walls go up.
Take the key of my house. Go in. Walk slowly through
my house. Go into the rooms. Go into the great room. The
sills at the doors have been washed. Go in. . . .

The writings of "A New Testament" are plainly experimentation, just as the books of Gertrude Stein are
experiments with words, and so Anderson regards them.

He thus described them to me: "Prose always opens new vistas to one working in it. Hardly any one cares to work long and patiently, I suppose, because they are after results, praise, fame or something of the sort. One who writes, however, out of the pure sensual delight in white paper, the smell of ink, sentence forms, etc., might try all sorts of purely experimental things. Why not think of 'The New Testament,' therefore, as pretty much the prose writer's experiment in rhythm of words, emotions, thoughts. I believe it to be just that. You see I have never given it book publication, although there is a great deal of it. I go back to it now and then, trying to break it into new rhythms, new freedom of imagery. Will it achieve form of its own? Will it sometimes break into real poetry? That I should say is on the knees of the gods and for the present I am content to let it lie there."

VIII

"Many Marriages" marks the peak of Anderson's attempts to interpret the subconscious elements in life, and is a study in various phases of sex expression and their effect on the unconscious. Four characters bear the principal burden of his investigations: John Webster, a middle-aged manufacturer, who, after wrestling with his repressions, attempts to liberate himself, soul and body, from the bondage that inhibits his spirit; Jane Webster, his daughter, an unformed rather than unliberated spirit, whose repressions have not yet taken rigid shape and whom Webster imagines he can "save" from an inhibited life of distorted values; Mrs. Webster, his wife and the mother of the girl, an example of a repressed, useless woman who can no longer respond to outside stimuli and, having nothing within herself to liberate her, is therefore useless in this scheme of things; and finally Natalie Schwartz, the stenographer, who is the willing and placid object of John Webster's new affection. The tale is a reflection of what goes on in the mind of John Webster, and he and his daughter Jane are actually the only two living characters in it; the mother is a foil who can only work out her destiny through suicide, a logical elimination, and Natalie merely serves as the symbol of John Webster's newer life and does not emerge fully from the limbo of unformed characters.

In his book on the Russian Art Theater Oliver M. Sayler describes the "mono drama" theory of Yevreynoff, the Russian, who, accepting the premise that the members of an audience always identify themselves with certain characters in a play and "live" the rôles with them, has decided to create a principal character, into whom the spectators will be able to project themselves, and then present all the other players as they are seen through the eyes and the understanding of that principal character. In "Many Marriages" we have a book in which only one character really lives and in which we practically see all the other characters solely through the eyes of John Webster. Preoccupied with the moods of John Webster, Sherwood Anderson fails to realize for us wholly the facets of the other characters that are not turned toward him, but which we know must exist. This gives the book the air of a monologue.

As a story "Many Marriages" has been variously interpreted, and the favorite method of literalists, to place it on a Procrustean bed and hack and tear until it fits, has been applied only too severely to this work. Judged wholly as a tale it has certain defects that are characteristic of Sherwood Anderson; it is to a certain extent autobiographical; it is largely a monologue, an expanded discourse in the informal manner of which Anderson is fond; it bears evidence of much preoccupation with sex disturbances, wholly out of proportion, perhaps, to the actual cause of John Webster's trouble, which Ben Hecht has aptly characterized as "the masculine menopause."

It is fully two-thirds too long; as an episode, shorn of much of the repetitious musing of John Webster, it would gain in forcefulness and effect; it fails in the end to bring a convincing solution to the situation or to sum up a philosophy of conduct; it focuses the reader's attention on certain incidents, largely symbolical and yet told so literally that they appear vulgar. The essential touch of the artist, who can gain the reader's comprehension of an idea by a word, a hint of direction, is here lacking.

Despite these defects it gives a clear, courageous picture—redundancy and all—of what goes on in the mind of one man of middle age who refuses to compromise with his surroundings and to repress his subconscious sex urge. It is actually a confessional wrung out of the soul of a man, and so forcefully done that it either antagonizes or converts the reader. It is couched in plain, homely prose—prose that recalls the hours Anderson devoted to poring over the King James version of the Old Testament,—hours of patient toil with nouns and adjectives and a few verbs.

The plot development is simple; in brief, a man approaching middle age finds his married life and his occupation burdensome and prepares to desert both. He is in love with another woman and wishes to leave with her.

The accomplishment of his purpose is preceded by a great deal of cogitation on his part, by soliloquies on the state of his mind, and by attempts to acquaint his daughter with his reason for going. Such is the bare external framework. It is stated perhaps more clearly in the foreword, in which Anderson says that "if one seek love and go towards it directly, or as directly as one may in the midst of the perplexities of modern life, one is perhaps insane. Have you not known a moment when to do what would seem at other times and under somewhat different circumstances the most trivial of acts becomes suddenly a gigantic undertaking? You are in the hallway of a house. Before you is a closed door and beyond the door, sitting in a chair by a window, is a man or woman. It is late in the afternoon of a summer day and your purpose is to step to the door, open it and say, 'It is not my intention to continue living in this house. My trunk is packed and in an hour a man, to whom I have already spoken, will come for it. I have only come to say that I will not be able to live near you any longer.' . . . Why has it become so difficult for you to take the three steps towards the door? Why are your feet so heavy? Why do your hands tremble like the hands of an old man?"

There are certain passages of great beauty. There are lines and paragraphs that sing themselves. There are other passages that reflect a deep study of human motives through many years on the part of Sherwood Anderson. Certain incidents have been severely criticized. The charge of repetition may well be made against Anderson on the ground that he refers too often to the body as a house, made to go in and out of, and that he needlessly repeats the idea in Webster's head that by taking off his clothes he is taking new hold on his real self and shedding the superficial, hemming garments of civilized life.

Standing alone, both metaphors are justified. "Down in the office he had thought of her body as a house within which she lived. Why could not more than one person live within such a house? . . .

"There was the thought about Natalie being a house kept clean and sweet for living, a house into which one might go gladly and joyfully. Could he, a washing machine manufacturer of a Wisconsin town, stop on the street a college professor and say, 'I want to know, Mr. College Professor, if your house is clean and sweet for living so that people may come into it and, if it is so, I want you to tell me how you went about it to cleanse your house.' The notion was absurd. It made one laugh to even think of any such thing. There would have to be new figures of speech, a new way of looking at things. For one thing people would have to be more truly aware of themselves than they had ever been before. . . ."

There has also been violent criticisms of the passages wherein Anderson causes John Webster to undress and lie naked, or parade naked before the statue of the virgin. Again metaphor and symbolism clash with realistic treatment. The regenerative effect produced by the removal of clothes and the resultant exultation in a clean, unhampered body, is a psychological fact that needs no explanation. The episode of the virgin is distasteful to many because of the religious connotations that have been built around that figure. Yet if we take Anderson seriously it will be seen that he put before John Webster the perfect symbol of absolute purity, in order to drive home the idea of a rebirth. This situation, as so many others, is not a new one with Anderson. We find a precursor of it in the story "Out of Nowhere into Nothing" in "The Triumph of the Egg." In that also occurs a reference to the virgin, suggesting that the idea has long been dormant in the author's mind. The virgin is being carried through the streets in a religious procession. This is witnessed by Rosalind Westcott. The story goes on:

In her bed at night Rosalind put down the book she had been reading. "The worship of the virgin is a form of sex expression," she read.

"Well, what of it? If it be true what does it matter?"

She got out of bed and took off her nightgown. She was herself a virgin. What did that matter? She turned herself slowly about, looking at her strong young woman's body. It was a thing in which sex lived. It was a thing upon which sex in others might express itself. What did it matter? . . . She made an odd and lovely figure standing nude before the glass in her room there in Chicago.

But the spectacle of a middle-aged man, no longer an Apollo Belvedere, parading in the nude, proved distasteful to many readers.

Similarly there is a medieval symbolism in the incident wherein John Webster, after his harangues with his daughter Jane, gives her a little stone which he calls "the jewel of life" and bids her keep it as the concrete realization of the abstractions he has been propounding to her. But whether Anderson was aware of its historical symbolism is doubtful. In his psychological ramblings he has probably discovered much more truth than he is himself aware of.

His prose has been described as "liturgical"—one gains at times a sense of exaltation, of a lofty feeling that goes with a theme simply and beautifully rendered. Whole episodes out of "Many Marriages" might be detached from the tale and cited as examples of nobility in writing. There is the boyhood reminiscence that John Webster calls up (pages 44 and 45), in which Anderson conveys a sense of the wholesomeness, the richness of the farm through "the rich smell of things, fragrant and strong smells" from the bins where the apples, pumpkins, and squashes were piled up. There is the picture of the house that had been laid bare to all the world by a fire (pages 76 and 77), which comes to symbolize John Webster's mood and his ability to strip houses of their walls and to look within. There is the narrative of the episode with the little girl in the forest, where the mental mood of Webster and the girl is conveyed to their surroundings and they behold in a half-decayed stump the figure of a kindly old man (pages 141-143). There is that triumphant passage where Webster ascends the hill with the woman (pages 177-181), a passage again strongly tinctured with the smells of the wood, the soil, the grass.

We find in "Many Marriages" a recurrence of certain ideas, certain philosophical conclusions, that appear from time to time in Anderson's earlier books. As we are primarily interested in the man, and regard his work as an indication of his mental processes and his crystallizing viewpoints, we may find these passages to be relevant:

Loving Natalie did not preclude the possibility of his loving another, perhaps many others. A rich man might have many marriages, he thought. It was certain that the possibility of human relationship had not even been tapped yet. Something had stood in the way of a sufficiently broad acceptance of life. One had to accept oneself and the others before one could love. . . .

What he wanted, more than anything else, was to give way to the impulses within himself.

Everywhere lives are lived without purpose. Men and women either spend their lives going in and out of the doors of houses and factories or they own houses and factories and they live their lives and find themselves at last facing death and the end of life without having lived at all.

It is a trick one practices, this lying to oneself about oneself. . . . He had created a world of unrealities. Would he and the woman be able to live together in that world?

In every human body there is a great well of silent thinking always going on. Outwardly certain words are said, but there are other words being said at the same time down in the deep, hidden places. There is a deposit of thoughts, of unexpressed emotions. How many things are hidden away in the deep well!

If one kept the lid off the well of thinking within oneself, let the well empty itself, let the mind consciously think any thoughts that came to it, accepted all thinking, all imaginings, as one accepted the flesh of people, animals, birds, trees, plains, one might live a hundred or a thousand lives in one life.

All the art of life perhaps consisted in just letting the fancy wash over and color the facts of life.

The book, tremendously significant of one man's psychological strivings, fails in its ultimate effect because of a faulty technique, of which the principal example is redundancy and a certain aimlessness. After John Webster has cleared up all the cobwebs in his consciousness he walks out into the night with Natalie Schwartz, and one gets the distinct impression that he has found, not the ultimate solution that will bring contentment through unhampered self-expression, but merely another amorous episode. There is no evidence in the sketchy character of Natalie that she can "stir any fires in him" other than those of the physical. One seems to feel that the problem voiced by Rosalind Westcott in "Out of the Nowhere into Nothing" applies equally to John Webster, with the same result: "If the sex impulse within it (the body) had been gratified in what way would my problem be solved? I am lonely now. It is evident that after that had happened I would still be lonely."

IX

So thoroughly convinced is Sherwood Anderson that the artist must express himself that he is apt to regard technique with a certain disdain. This in spite of the fact that his own style is a thing apart and has been arrived at by careful attention to the sound and meaning of words and the cadence of sentences. Years ago, when he was more than ever convinced that the message was greater than the interpreter, he would express scorn for technical perfection, and one of his favorite remarks was: "Some day, when the spirit moves me, I am going to that piano and play for you, and I won't need a knowledge of the piano to express myself. I will play what is in me." This artistic impulse has moved other men; it is the basis for an observation by Havelock Ellis in "Affirmations": "Just as Goethe found in poetry an expression for the painter's vocation he had missed, so Wagner utilized in music his dramatic instinct." What sort of music Anderson would have produced had he made good his threat may be divined from the paintings that he produced when, ignorant of the painter's art, he tried to place on canvas the colors of Mobile Bay a few years ago. His attempt to paint was due to his amazement at the riot of color in Alabama—the contrasting shades in the clay soil, the yellow mud running down hill after a rain, the heightened tints in the waters, the sky and the foliage. He regretted that he had not mastered painting in his lifetime, but as representative art meant nothing to him he put down his ideas and impulses in colors—and as ideas purely his paintings are to be regarded. When they were exhibited in the Walden book shop in Chicago they drew a stream of amazed, disgusted, exhilarated, and sometimes enthusiastic friends; nothing exactly like them had ever been seen, even in the most radical exhibitions. Painters stood back in dismay, yet several canvases were sold, and when the exhibition was shown later on at the Sunwise Turn bookshop in New York City four more paintings were purchased and an excellent price was paid. To accuse Anderson of attempting to trick the public was unkind; the paintings fairly reeked of sincerity and no one but a man deeply stirred would have permitted them to be shown. Anderson's explanation of the paintings was simple. He related how deeply the interplay of colors on Mobile Bay stirred him. The paintings were his internal reactions before the things he saw about him. Technical questions dropped away before the mighty artistic impulse, the impulse to express. The technique, in Anderson's mind, would have destroyed the clear impression here conveyed. He felt that the pictures might be pleasing or insignificant or distasteful to different observers, just as his intimate thoughts and impulses might be. . . . At the Walden book shop Anderson met Ben Hecht and asked him what he thought of the paintings. "They look to me like the sort of thing a drunken man might paint while asleep," said Hecht. Later Hecht told me that he felt they expressed Anderson's inhibitions. "There are several negro heads that come close to the anthropological specimens of primitive man," said Hecht. "I have watched women stand before them fascinated in terror and revulsion, and finally buy them."

X

A hard fight is going on within Sherwood Anderson to-day, a fight between the artist who demands isolation, and the man who seeks social contact with his fellows. To some extent this has been going on all during his manhood, and he has hied himself away at intervals to cleanse his mind of the small talk of the day and get back to essentials in thinking. "Once in a while I like to go to a little rural community where nobody knows me and do my work there," Anderson told me. "If I go to a hotel where people might look me up I change my name; it gives me a rest from too much aimless talking. One of the most profitable trips I ever had was down into the Ozarks. It occurred after I had become established in Chicago but just before "Windy" was published, and the real reason for my going was to recuperate from a nervous breakdown. I had heard about the little cabins that are scattered around the mountains and decided that if I could rent a shack and stay there I'd get my strength back. I got to a little bit of a village on the railroad and a Missouri farmer picked me up in his buckboard. "Whay're yuh going?" he asked, and I told him I wanted a shack in the mountains. "Guess I kin take yuh, stranger," he said, "but you'll be darned lonely out there by yerself this time o' year." We drove miles into the woods and finally he pointed out a shack on a hill. "Guess that's yer place ef yer kin make yerself comfortable," he said, and dropped me and my bag. "Where's the man that owns this?" I yelled. "Oh, he'll come along some time," the farmer shouted over his shoulder. So I took my bag and moved in. It was winter but I made things easy for myself. There was a little town nearby and I used to go in to get supplies, and sit around with the men and talk. They had never seen a big town and talked about St. Louis and Kansas City as if they were in another world. They were suspicious of me at first but not for long. Their lives were circumscribed and I suppose we would call them downright ignorant, but I found that they had just as good a grip on life as we think we have, perhaps better, and that they had good hearts, and a genuine feeling for human beings. I lived around there a month without finding out who to pay my rent to. One day a farmer came by and stood looking into my shack. "Howdy," he said. I said: "Howdy, Friend, who are you?" "I'm the man who owns this place," he said. "Well, I've been looking for you for a long time," I said. He smiled and we talked about other matters and finally I said: "Well, pardner, what's the rent for this shack?" He looked around the landscape and then turned back and said: "Oh, ten dollars." "For how long?" I asked. "For as long as you care to stay, stranger," he replied. Then came Christmas, and Michael Carmichael Carr, who was teaching art in the University of Missouri at Columbia, came down to see me. He brought a couple of great big juicy steaks and we roasted them at my fire. He stayed during the holidays and we had a bully time. I wrote a novel there, but it was worthless and I threw it away. I enjoyed being down there for the time, but after all, Harry, I am convinced that you and I are city men. We can't remain away long from our kind."

At another time Anderson went to New Orleans and there found much to interest him. He obtained a quiet little room in an old house with a balcony and when unable to write he would pace up and down the balcony and take the air. This was in the winter of 1921-1922. He worked all morning at his table and in the afternoons often wandered about the city. There he found many pleasant social contacts, especially with Basil Thompson and the alert minds of the Double Dealer group. New Orleans made a lasting impression on him and he has written of it in generous praise. During that winter he completed "Many Marriages."

But it was his trip abroad that made the deepest impression on Anderson. This took place in the summer of 1921. Anderson had no knowledge of old world cultures and Paul Rosenfeld, whose interest in Anderson was that of a devoted admirer and interpreter, arranged the trip for him and Mrs. Anderson and accompanied them. Anderson found a haven in the Rue Jacob in Paris and for the first time came in touch with the old world. One anecdote that reveals much of Sherwood's nature survives. When he saw the Louvre he sat down and wept. "I was thinking of the beauty of that old building and of all the tradition behind it," he said. The trip opened his eyes to the great lack of background in America. But he agreed with the French authors whom he met that Europe has lost much more than its best minds—that much of its spirit is gone and that the world must look to America for new forms and new expressions in literature. And he felt unmistakably that America was the country for his own work. But he could not down a certain dissatisfaction and uneasiness upon his return, and when he reached Chicago he was more dissatisfied than ever and declared that the city no longer afforded him any reason for remaining. His exultation in the crude strength of Chicago, in its virginity, its fertility, which he had sung in his chants, passed in his hunger for new cultural contacts. "Great projects arise within me," he had written of Chicago; "I have a brain and it is cunning and shrewd. I want leisure to become beautiful, but there is no leisure." Europe had shown him that there was something besides strength and power that made life sweet. Chicago, it now seemed, was a barren field for him. He thought to find this new life in New York City and thither he went to live, late in 1922.

XI

Sherwood Anderson is not vain, but self-confident; he has confidence in himself, a resolute determination to express his ideas, and the will to work. He likes to talk about his books, but only in terms of what he is trying to accomplish; self-glorification is beyond him. He never seeks publicity; he rarely reads the reviews of his books. He knows where he has failed and he has probably thrown away more sheets of paper filled with laborious writing than any author living in America. When he refers to these unpublished books it is without a pang; he chuckles over them and laughs at the thought that they might have contained anything worth retaining. An invitation out is to him always an embarrassment unless he can romp round and play as much as he likes, and I have seen him at homes of mutual friends cavorting like a youngster and having a fine time dancing and joking. One memorable evening survives: Burton Rascoe, not yet won away by New York, had gathered about him in his north side apartment all the writing folk the place would hold and there was the usual children's hour for grown-ups. Sherwood had devoted part of the evening to a discussion of D. H. Lawrence and an attempt to find out just why certain women guests did not care for "Women in Love." There was of course a definite attempt on his part to penetrate their psychological processes indirectly. He was then prevailed upon to tell his famous story of "Mama Geigen," and after much coaxing agreed to do so. This famous tale will probably be told wherever Sherwood goes, but it has never appeared in print and it is to be hoped it never will, for the printed page would be a poor medium to convey Sherwood's inimitable manner of story telling. "Mama Geigen" was an underworld character who had raised herself to the position of owner of a summer resort on the banks of a Wisconsin lake, and the story deals with Sherwood's arrival in her locality on a fishing tour and what befell. The story has rich touches of Boccaccian humor. Sinclair Lewis was there that night, and indulging in his own unsurpassed talent for mimicry he made up as a clergyman with a Roman collar and gave a sermon on "Mama Geigen; Pollyanna grown to womanhood. . . ." The playboy was uppermost in Sherwood, and leaning forward on the piano bench with his eyes aglow and his lips wreathed in smiles Sherwood had as much fun over the choice morsels he told as his audience. The evening proved long and colorful, with the usual divertissements —it closed, we believe, with Sherwood falling asleep and being put to bed with the Rascoe children, who had lately had chicken-pox. . . .

And public honors embarrass him. He has rarely spoken in public, and then only informally when pressed to do so, and the only real occasion of this kind remains in his memory as a nightmare. He had been awarded, in 1921, the Dial prize of $2,000 for the best original work by an American published in that magazine during the year, and its editors had asked him to come to New York to receive the prize at a dinner. He was to be called upon to speak, so he prepared a few notes, but they seemed inadequate. When Anderson finally rose he stammered like a school boy; he, who had written voluminously about art and the aims of the artist and had often talked about his theories of writing among friends, was tongue-tied. He made a point of the fact that he had kept his work as an advertising writer going because he could not make a living as an artist; that it was impossible for an artist to exist independently in America. Then, as if from the height of many years, he looked back on his career—"he talked," said a friend, "like a civil war veteran"—and Gilbert Seldes was perturbed at this venerable attitude because the prize had been announced as for a young and promising writer—ostensibly one who still had to win his spurs. . . . The only other occasion on which Anderson spoke in public of which I have knowledge was at a dinner of the promoters of the negro art theater in Chicago, sponsored by Raymond O'Neil, in which Anderson has always had a direct interest. The negroes present were bent on self-expression and the development of a native drama in America; Sherwood, harking back to his old theory that the artist is misunderstood in America, declared that the kinship between the negro and the artist rested on isolation. "The negro is an outcast in America; so is the artist," said Anderson; "we must get together." But this was hardly the reason that animated the founding of the theater.

But in more intimate contacts he is a delightful talker, an excellent companion, and he appreciates fully the right sort of praise. Perhaps the most significant moment in his life came when he was asked to go to the Drake hotel to meet Abraham Cahan at lunch. Anderson found that Cahan had asked a number of delegates to a meeting of the Amalgamated Clothing Workers of America. They ate at different tables but from time to time men at the table where Anderson sat would yield their places to others and these would come and talk to him. He discovered that although these men were not primarily readers of books they had read practically everything he had written, and understood his characters and his themes. To him the incident was a revelation of the interest he had aroused in groups remote from him and stood in strong contrast to meetings with uninformed gushing women who crowd about an author whenever he shows signs of becoming a popular lion.

"It's an odd business, this novel or story writing with me," said Anderson. "For example, I went home the other evening and on the way home the form of a longish short story I've been waiting for years to write came to me clearly. When I got home I sat down and wrote until three in the morning, then went to bed, slept until seven, and got up and went to the house of a friend. I was tired and he had some good whiskey.

"At his house I sat down and wrote in a heat until about three that afternoon—that is to say, almost seven hours more. It was a curious experience. When I got through most of his flask was gone but the story was fixed as I wanted it. Perhaps I had written from twelve to fifteen thousand words. I was perfectly awake until I had written the last word. Then suddenly I fell into bed and slept for several hours like a dead man.

"As to that story, I've tried to write it a dozen times and it wouldn't come; that is to say, just the swing and rhythm of the lines to fit the theme wouldn't come. That happens in novel writing sometimes. And when it does I throw the manuscript away. All this might sound discouraging if it were not for the fact that I love passionately the mechanics of writing, the blank sheets before me, the smell of ink.

"Where most writers fail—and this is not clearly enough understood—is because they are not, at bottom, story tellers. They have theories about writing, notions about style, often some writing ability, but they do not tell the story straight out. You see, after all, style is like the dress worn by the actor, the way he walks across the stage and all that—important enough, to be sure. But if a man thinks too much of these things, and does not feel within himself the part he has to play, well then. Style should naturally grow out of the content of the thing itself."

XII

Sherwood Anderson, who reads women's souls, who knows psychology and psycho-analysis as if he had studied under William James and Sigmund Freud, acquired all his knowledge honestly without the aid of books. He dug it out with his own superb technique for

getting at the root of things and many a woman who has
talked with him in an idle hour has given up rich secrets
from her own inner self without knowledge or intention.
As a result his motivation in his stories is rarely wrong;
his understanding of subconscious factors in our lives is
often uncanny. A woman once said: "I can withhold
nothing from Sherwood Anderson; when I have talked
with him I feel as if I have been with my father con-
fessor." And since all his life he has been preoccupied
with the inner life of men and women one gets the feeling
that he is everlastingly eager to add to his store of knowledge; that he is always ready to improve an opening.
Once he had a glorious opportunity. It was at a camp
for rhythmic dancing conducted by Miss Alys Bentley
in the Adirondacks, where Miss Tennessee Mitchell had
been a pupil when Anderson married her. For several
weeks during a number of summers they went back to
the camp as a sort of honeymoon anniversary and a
mutual friend has pictured the scene to me. "Imagine,"
she said, "this lovely camp of the nymphs out in the
open, girls dressed in lovely flowing Greek draperies,
dancing in the grass with their feet twinkling in the sun,
and Sherwood the only faun in the camp, dancing with
them, spinning long yarns in the drowsy days under the
old trees, and asking volumes of questions. It was all
as it should be, he being Sherwood. Joyous, and boyish,
and full of fun, and quiet and contemplative, and inquiring. Mostly the latter. He learned volumes about
women's souls in the sunlight and what Sherwood could
not discover by casual inspection he asked about. He
did the trimming on one woman's hair (other novelists
too have discovered the value of that as an emotional
experiment) and his word was golden with many. If

any one asks me where Sherwood Anderson learned about women I answer: 'From themselves.' "

It was at this camp Sherwood Anderson found Tennessee Mitchell when he came east to marry her—and this event throws additional light upon the romantic side of the novelist's nature. Miss Mitchell was a member of the camp. As it was located several miles from any railway station Anderson had to travel there by a farmer's wagon, and his appearance in Lincoln green, wearing a huntsman's cap with a feather in it, is still described by those who were privy to this colorful episode. Miss Mitchell was wearing the costume of the rhythmic dancers—a short smock dress, with her hair in long braids down her back and her feet bare. With Miss Alys Bentley, the high priestess of the dance, they climbed into a wagon and an old man drove them many miles over the colorful hillsides to a rural justice of the peace. The office was mid-nineteenth century; the old man himself, with side beards, seemed to have stepped out of a tintype of civil war days. After he had performed the ceremony he said he "hoped he had done a good job." And then, in an old deserted cabin on a placid lake in the Adirondacks, they passed their honeymoon.

Nor let us overlook those other romantic play-days in and around Chicago, when the writing group learned to know Sherwood Anderson as a dancer, a faun, a boy who had never really grown up, an alert, happy character always bubbling over with fun, ready to play practical jokes or to join in any fantastic undertaking. During the hot summer months the colony of which Sherwood Anderson became a part often spent week-ends and vacations at Union Pier, Mich., where a little shack hanging on the side of a big sand cliff overlooking Lake Michigan was the headquarters where gathered Anderson, Ben Hecht, Alexander Kaun, Michael Carr, Tennessee Mitchell, Cloyd Head, Robert Titus, Fedya Ramsey, Margaret Allen, Margery Currey—ever so many more. One occasion that stirs an ancient fund of reminiscence was Anderson's birthday, when a barbaric dance was staged out in the open to the great hilarity of the more staid and conventional citizenry which made Union Pier its rendezvous. Anderson clad himself in two vivid oriental hangings from a curtain pole in the shack, entwined oak leaves in his hair; the others vied with him in attiring themselves in wisps of grass, vari-colored garments, odds and ends of pillow cases and bed spreads. There were sacrificial dances in the sand; one maiden was buried alive; over all the fantastic rites presided Sherwood Anderson, whom we know as the calm, brooding, suffering spirit of his books.

XIII

Let us say this for Sherwood Anderson: he is one of the few native novelists in America whose field is the human mind; where writers of thirty years ago concerned themselves wholly with the external happenings in the life of a character, Sherwood Anderson is concerned almost wholly with their mental life. His appearance is not on the highroad of American literature, but marks a deflection from the main currents, a variation. That he will become the founder of a school is doubtful; that he will have followers is certain; that he will profoundly affect American writing along the lines he first preached about—simplicity and honesty—is assured. His influence exerts itself in two ways—in theme, and in treatment; in subject-matter and in technique. One may read him for one or both, and be assuaged. His pre-occupation with sex stirrings as the basis for many simple human acts may obscure some of his better qualities, and make an approach to the real Anderson harder for those who find themselves nauseated by his ever recurrent adumbration of this subject, but it cannot wholly eclipse his simple prose, his exalted approach to a lofty theme, his candor, and his knowledge of lonely people—who were practically neglected by American novelists before he came.

He is an original writer, and wholly native. He possesses traits that are likened to those of Europeans, but they are not derived from Europeans. This singular fact has escaped his orthodox critics. He is as thoroughly an American of our day as the old New Englanders were in their time—and despite Brander Matthews, Paul Elmer More, and other spokesmen for the puritan tradition, he has the right, as an American, to speak for his generation. He has made articulate a whole social stratum that had no spokesman at the high court of American letters. The fact that he writes differently from the old household gods whose engraved portraits hang on schoolhouse walls has often been held against him by the very men whose advice to young writers should be: "Take nothing from others, but dig deep into your own native soil with the implements God has given you." Like his deep black eyes certain tendencies in his writing may be the fulfilment of generations of Italian culture inherited through his mother, but I do not think so; even if this could be ascertained it would prove nothing against his American origin, no more than the thoroughly Anglican strain could be held against the

Concord group. As a writer he is wholly self-made. He owes nothing to any influence, to any other mind. In his technical triumphs as well as in his failures, in his subconscious elements, in his psychoanalytical turn of mind, in his psychology, in his mysticism, in his plot construction or lack of it, he is thoroughly himself. If you should ask me where he got this or that, I should have to reply: "Out of the air, perhaps, or out of the soil, he took it with bare hands."

Those who seek for the traits of an older writer in the work of a contemporary—and to our shame, only too often find them—assert that Sherwood Anderson is derivative of the Russians, of D. H. Lawrence, but a close examination will disprove their contention and leave Anderson in possession of his own gifts. That two men may reach the same goal simultaneously without ever having heard of each other is a common occurrence in mechanical invention, in chemistry, in many fields other than that of writing. Sherwood Anderson took nothing from the Russians, for in his formative period he knew nothing about them. In fact he knew so few writers that sophisticated persons, after talking with him about books, described him as unread. They failed to appreciate the fact that Anderson represented a variation badly needed in America, where we had come to feel the superfluity of men who could not think clearly because their minds were cluttered up with all the hoary literary truck of the ages, and where we needed men who had the courage to write and think without awaiting the approbation of condescending deans of literature. Sherwood Anderson is a naïve product of our soil who owes little to our deeply-rooted Anglo-Saxon culture, nor derives from "immigrant sources," or more recognized continental influences. In spite of that he more nearly approaches the homely Saxon speech than many carefully trained writers, and often invests it with a deep spiritual significance that gives new power to the plain, belabored words. He is a mystic and a dreamer, a groper after truth, deluded at times by his childlike faith in his own dreams and imaginings, and yet, like a child, a little nearer truth by reason of his dreams.

5. Three Million Marching Men

*Forgive us if the monotonous
houses go mile on mile*
*Along monotonous streets out to
the prairies.*

Carl Sandburg.

I

"You know my city—Chicago triumphant," sings Sherwood Anderson in "Mid-American Chants": "Factories and marts and the roar of machines—horrible, terrible, ugly, and brutal. Can a singer arise and sing in this smoke and grime? Can he keep his throat clear? Can his courage survive?"

Let us contemplate the spectacle, not in the manner of Narcissus, but rather in the spirit of the searcher in his laboratory, for men (of the East, truly) have pointed fingers at us, admonitory often, contemptuously sometimes, and, on rare occasions, to mark a distinguishing trait. Here, to paraphrase Anderson's theme, are three million marching men, marching with dinner pails and shovels, with tool kits and hampers, with brief cases and portfolios, save such as belong to the more favored trades of the carpenter and the mason, who progress by motors —marching, marching, marching, on and on and on. One asks: "Whither bound?" One knows not where.

"Can a singer arise and sing in this smoke and grime? Can he keep his throat clear? Can his courage survive?"

The makers of Chicago are the toilers, the men of brute strength, and the great square hulks that house other men are their handiwork. Sprawling out over the prairie lies my city, an agglomeration of workshops and dwellings; heterogeneous, utilitarian; its factories designed for capacity production, its houses intended solely for shelter against wind and rain. Its colors what the winds and the smoke and the soot have made it; its streets, the paths that the marching men have cut; here and there in the barren waste an oasis, a spire, a clean shaft of marble like an exquisite gem in a tarnished setting; but for one block of houses that manifests an attempt to grasp spiritual values and to attain architectural harmonies in accord with an enriched inner life there are hundreds of forlorn, orphaned streets, dedicated only to the meager shelter of the body, forgetting the soul and the spirit, and owned and maintained no doubt by the very men who in their better hours feel drawn toward a spiritual awakening.

In Chicago, close to the natural resources of our land, one looks in vain for a conspicuous art contribution from the people themselves. Wherever beauty has set its shrine an intellectual aristocracy, assisted by wealth two or three stages removed from primitive greed, has provided the incentive. The great university with its magnificent material equipment owes its development to the benefactions of a wealthy few. To the great mass it is a privately endowed institution which exists without any drain on their purses, and which has no direct relation to their lives save in the football season. Even the contributions of its alumni have been so niggardly as to pass almost unobserved among the great sums provided for its maintenance. Truly the Art Institute, the Chicago Symphony Orchestra, the Civic Grand Opera, the Field Museum, the St. Gaudens Lincoln, the Chicago Historical Society, the Newberry Library, the John Crerar Library, the "Poetry" magazine, have not come into being in answer to popular clamor. All are monuments to the patience, the culture, the tolerance, or the wealth of certain individuals who could dream in a stifling atmosphere. Even the great Public Library, with its many branches reaching into the heart of the city, and always more or less insufficiently supported from the public purse, has had to rely on the leadership of men like Henry E. Legler and Carl B. Roden for its rise and influence. The mass of Chicago is typified in the toiler, bending over his workbench throughout the day, boarding stuffy, overcrowded street cars at night, giving the few leisure hours of the evening to the movies or the newspapers. The mass comes in unwittingly; it is meek and patient; it thinks of Chicago as a boarding house, a place where one sleeps and receives one's mail without bothering much about the landlady's problems; it suffers unspeakable civic abuses, tolerates the most lamentable housing conditions, lets its alleys be overrun with filth and dirt, jostles along on the worst transportation in the world. One wonders how far Chicago's development of good roads and streets would have progressed if politicians had not sensed the advantage of big fat contracts for "improvements" as part of the unselfish scheme of a body of men for a city beautiful.

Like a great Golem Chicago strides forward, crushing beauty in its path unless guided by men of superior intelligence. As a democratic government Chicago exhibits probably the most colossal failure of our time. None of its material and esthetic achievements are the product of mass intelligence or mass action. The great groping giant has failed to accomplish anything except grow to gargantuan proportions. External embellishment of the city has taken place under auspices similar to that of the old world, where capitals owe most of their beauty to emperors and kings—and to successful trading corporations. In the middle of the nineteenth century Chicago was a slough of mud and Lincoln's supporters had to drive over plank roads to his nominating convention. The great architectural awakening came with the World's Fair in 1893, and of the small group of men who impressed their personality upon that event one name reaches up to the zenith—Daniel H. Burnham. The first attempt to unite beauty with the utilitarian demands of the skyscraper elevates the name of Louis H. Sullivan. The first movement to weld a college group into a harmonious whole by the use of a uniform architecture distinguishes the name of William Rainey Harper. And of leaders like these there are many more.

II

The literary foundations of Chicago go back to pioneer times, but it is of the present we would speak, and the present seems singularly out of joint with the past. Chicago has progressed in periods, and none of these has knit up with its successor. Political history, chaotic as it is here, is nevertheless more continuous and easily traced than schools of thought and writing. Actually there is no Chicago school, in spite of the fact that it is the fashion in the east to group together writers with certain western characteristics and give them this name. These traits are often spoken of in the cultured east as uncouth, vulgar, coarse, unpolished, unrefined, and in the self-conscious west as forceful, honest, naïve, true, virile, and close-to-the-soil. If these traits can actually be distinguished they imply a lack of veneer, or gloss, or delicately nurtured refinement; a preoccupation with primitive themes and emotions. That is all that one finds common among these men and women, who work in isolation, coming together now and then for social contact, but neither recognizing a community of ideas nor striving to create one.

It is criticism that Chicago has needed most, yet in this it has been served but niggardly. Brilliant men have come out of the prairies, out of the productive hinterland, seized for a space the opportunity for constructive building, and passed on. In the arts Chicago too often has been but a way station, a place where trains stopped of necessity, where passengers alighted, spent a few hours unwillingly, and went on. Examine the list of outstanding names that Chicago often includes in its galaxy and you will find that half the men who bear them came through at an impecunious moment in their career, struggled and suffered in an illy ventilated hall bedroom, wrote one or two books, and then answered the call of the east. More novels have been written about Chicago by men no longer of Chicago than about any other city. Theodore Dreiser, Frank Norris, Hamlin Garland, Rex Beach, Ernest Poole, Samuel Merwin, Will Payne, Edna Ferber, Upton Sinclair, Brand Whitlock, George Horace Lorimer, George Barr McCutcheon, Ray Stannard Baker, George Ade, Finley P. Dunne, George Harvey, Harold MacGrath, these are but a few of those who came in on a freight and left on a Pullman at a convenient time in their careers.

Chicago recognizes two kinds of authors as peculiarly her own; those who draw upon her own deep elemental life for their themes and so become interpreters of her hopes and fears, and those who have been hers geographically, although they have gone elsewhere for their themes. Both have been cultural factors; both have exerted an influence on writers and readers. Of the first group the outstanding example is Theodore Dreiser, and despite his long residence as an editor in the east this province must claim him because he represents a stage in its cultural growth. It was from this locale that he drew his first stories—"Sister Carrie" walked these streets and "The Titan" and "The Financier" came out of the web of Chicago life. He served his apprenticeship on Chicago newspapers in the early nineties, days when Melville E. Stone, Eugene Field, George Ade, Brand Whitlock, George Harvey, Frank A. Vanderlip and Joseph Medill were still active in Chicago newspaper life; when David B. Hill, Bourke Cochran and Adlai E. Stevenson were squabbling over democratic politics in the corridors of the old Richelieu hotel; when reporters still wrote stories in long hand and ran after fire wagons; when all the wastrels, race track touts and toughs of the west congregated in Chicago and gamblers ran roulette and faro openly in its most crowded streets. Dreiser has told about those days in plain, unromantic fashion in "A Book About Myself," and his portrait runs true to the tradition of that time.

So Sherwood Anderson's question: "Can a singer arise and sing in this smoke and grime?" is easily answered in the affirmative, and although it may be difficult for birds to live in a smoky atmosphere writers have not been deterred by it. But his question: "Can his courage survive?" is more difficult, for there are many examples at our elbow of men whose courage for one reason or another has not survived, and perhaps their case is stated most succinctly by Hamlin Garland. Chicago claims Hamlin Garland because, despite his aspirations to an eastern culture, he remains of it, and his best work is that in which the autobiographical note is most marked, and his identity with our soil is most apparent. And a decade or two ago it was in Chicago that he exerted his capacity for leadership and organization, and then, that task accomplished, and finding nothing more to satisfy his appetite, it was to New York he went to begin anew. To-day he is one of our most regretted *emigrés*. Instead of living among us as a patriarch, guiding the footsteps of the young with a ready sympathy, he passes his time among groups in the east and in London of which he is not truly a part, regretting the wayward habits of our literary youth, complaining about the lack of culture, seeking, by embalming an older method of writing and living in a marble mausoleum of the arts, to perpetuate a civilization that has been dead these twenty years. In "A Daughter of the Middle Border," that fine autobiography that tells so much of his hope and despair in Chicago, and of his desire for wings, we read of his growing discontent with Chicago because of its slow recognition of the finer elements in our native culture. And in a way he paints a portrait of the man to whom the amenities of literary life are a crying need. "In Chicago," he writes, "I was a perversity, a man of misdirected energy. In New York I was at least respected as a writer. In short, New York allured me as London allures the writers of England and as Paris attracts the artists of Europe. It was my literary capital. Theoretically I belonged to Wisconsin, as Hardy belonged to Wessex or Barrie to Scotland, actually my happiest home was adjacent to Madison Square. Only as I neared the publishing centers did I feel the slightest confidence in the future. . . ."

And again he writes of our "literary sterility":

"Meanwhile Chicago, rushing toward its two million mark, had not, alas! lived up to its literary promise of '94. In music, in painting, in sculpture, and architecture it was no longer negligible, but each year its authors appeared more and more like a group of esthetic pioneers heroically maintaining themselves in the midst of an increasing tumult of material upbuilding. One by one its hopeful young publishing houses had failed, and one by one its aspiring periodicals had withered in the keen wind of eastern competition. 'The Dial' alone held on, pathetically solitary, one might almost say alien and solitary. . . . Against all this misfortune even my besotted optimism could not prevail. My pioneering spirit, subdued by years of penury and rough usage, yielded more and more to the honor and intellectual companionship which the east offered. To Fuller I privately remarked: 'As soon as I can afford it I intend to establish a home in New York.' . . . It was a very significant fact that Chicago contained in 1903 but a handful of writers, while St. Louis, Cleveland, Cincinnati, Detroit, and Kansas City had fewer yet. 'What is the reason for this literary sterility?' I asked of my companions. Why should not these powerful cities produce authors? Boston, when she had less than three hundred thousand citizens, had Lowell, Longfellow, Emerson, and Holmes. The answer was (and still is): 'Because there are few supporters of workers in the fine arts. Western men do not think in terms of art. There are no literary periodicals in these cities to invite (and pay for) the work of the author and the illustrator, and there is moreover a tendency on the part of our builders to give the eastern sculptor, painter, or architect the jobs which might be done by local men. Until Chicago has at least one magazine founded like a university, and publishing houses like Scribner's and Macmillan's, our authors and artists must go to New York. . . .'"

It was this feeling that Chicago had nothing around

which men active in the arts could rally that led Hamlin
Garland to found the Cliff Dwellers in 1908.   It was to
be "a meeting place for artists and writers, a rallying
point for Midland arts."   He comments on Henry B.
Fuller's lack of enthusiasm for the plan: "Fuller, who
refused, characteristically, to endorse my plan, was
openly discouraging.   To him the town was a pestilential
slough in which he, at any rate, was inextricably mired,
and although he was not quite so definite with me, he
said to others: 'Garland's idea is sure to fail.' "

But one wonders whether any club has ever been, or
can ever be, a "rallying point for the arts."   No doubt,
in the essentials, Fuller was right.   The Cliff Dwellers
to-day is a place where artists may meet, but only after
they have achieved a certain badge of distinction, and
nothing creative has come out of Mr. Garland's idea, no
more than will come out of his American Institute of
Arts and Letters.   A group easier of access is the Society
of Midland Authors, founded several years ago by John
M. Stahl, which makes up in indiscriminate welcoming
of any and all persons who write with pen or typewriter
what the Cliff Dwellers lose by their aloofness from the
creative spirit of our times, but one cannot say that either
of the organizations has been of influence on the literary and cultural development of Chicago, from the
creative side.   Organizations like the latter have proved
more effective in another field—that of creating readers
and a healthy interest in books.   That is the work performed by the Friends of American Writers, organized
a little over a year ago by Mrs. John H. Bohr and already
exerting a wide influence on the reading of clubwomen.
Effective work in this direction has also been accomplished by the Bookfellows, who have increased their

membership to more than 3,000 and who also publish every year several books written by their members, and by the Greater English Club, which began with teachers of English in the high schools and is gradually widening its scope.

What Mr. Garland overlooked, even in his analysis of his own work, was that the great creative spirit works in isolation, far from men of his profession, that the best work of an author is never inspired by lunch table gossip. When the desire for the social amenities becomes greater to a writer than that overpowering urge to express his own mood and interpret his own times on white paper he rises as a social factor and at the same time slips downward as a cultural force. And that will be the verdict of posterity on Hamlin Garland.

It is indeed remarkable that at the moment when Hamlin Garland was lamenting over Chicago's "literary sterility," men and women were working on books that made it possible for H. L. Mencken, ten years later, to call the city "the literary capital of the United States." The appellation was a misnomer; we have often blushed for it since and explained to our eastern friends that it was conferred by an *Ausländer* who was surfeited with New York and who, wishing to bestow an honorary degree, singled out Chicago without first asking whether we would care to receive it. Yet his choice indicates that this tract of land has not been entirely barren. "Go back twenty or thirty years," says Mencken, "and you will scarcely find an American literary movement that did not originate under the shadow of the stockyards." Many men whose names have since been regarded with esteem must have been active in the arts in Chicago when Mr. Garland decided to emigrate, and soon after his departure the desert blossomed like a garden. And in most cases the writers came from everywhere and nowhere; no one group could claim them, no club or movement gave them shelter. Edgar Lee Masters, Sherwood Anderson, Carl Sandburg, Henry B. Fuller, George Ade, Finley Peter Dunne, Ernest Poole, William Hard, Edwin Herbert Lewis, Francis Hackett, Will Payne, Henry Kitchell Webster, Samuel Merwin, Joseph Medill Patterson, Emerson Hough, Edith Franklin Wyatt, Robert Morss Lovett, William Vaughn Moody, Robert Herrick, Charles D. Stewart, Earl Reed, I. K. Friedman, Ernest McGaffey, Stanley Waterloo, Opie Read, Edwin Balmer, Rex Beach, William MacHarg, Floyd Dell, Clarence Darrow, Ben Hecht, Maude Radford Warren, Eunice Tietjens, Clara Louise Burnham,—these and many more were sharpening their pencils and working honestly and earnestly, making more or less of a dent in the literary sphere, running the gamut of romance, sentiment, realism and naturalism, in this atmosphere of smoke and grime.

III

The window at which I work looks out on a court—a forlorn, ramshackle court that still bears traces of the whitewash periodically applied to its walls. It is one of the few ancient light wells left in Chicago, for the building opposite hails from 1872 and so becomes identified at once as a venerable landmark erected just after the big fire. Up this well on warm summer days floats the strong, invigorating smell of printer's ink and the dull, grinding whirr of ponderous presses. Sometimes the gray and blue street pigeons whirl down into the court in fantastic parabolas, and once a pigeon hatched her eggs on a window ledge and two squabs sprouted their first pin feathers in the security of a half closed iron shutter. Out of a court like that, with a patch of sky above, one can draw quaint, Dickensian romances; no doubt other men have done so, on this very spot. One thinks of the lanky Eugene Field, one of the first columnists, who elevated his feet on a desk not far from my own and littered the walls with clippings of his verse. Men still tell strange tales of the eccentric forms in which his surplus energy found outlet. That was in the early nineties, and Field died soon after the World's Fair and long before his time. George Ade began his writing career near at hand and pictured the humble life of Chicago in stories that were incorporated later in "In Babel," and John T. McCutcheon drew sketches to embellish his writing. Not far away George Barr McCutcheon began his career by writing "funny ads with drawings." Here Melville E. Stone wrote his big time interviews, here Ray Stannard Baker turned in his first efforts at reporting; innumerable others whose names have been written large in our national letters and in our newspaper life passed through these corridors and here served an humble apprenticeship. To those of us who love the flavor of old times this building with its awkward wings, its rooms inside courts, its floors three steps up and two steps down, its reluctant elevator, its crowded nooks and corners, is a hallowed shrine. Some day, no doubt, bowing to the inevitable laws of decay, it must give way to the white-tiled, alabaster-lined corridors and symmetrical rooms of an imperial America, and when that day comes it will lose, for many of us, something of its warmth and reality. . . . If these writers of old had left their portraits here after the manner of scholars the halls would be lined with them. But perhaps even more comforting is the fact that here we touch hands daily with the living who are active in the arts. The roster is long. Keith Preston of "Types of Pan" and "Splinters," Henry Justin Smith of "Deadlines" and "The Other Side of the Wall," Robert J. Casey, observing history abroad as a captain of artillery and coming back to write "The Haunted Castles of Luxemburg," and "The Lost Kingdom of Burgundy"; Carl Sandburg, and, until recently, Ben Hecht; T. K. Hedrick of "The Meditations of Ho-hen," Hiram K. Moderwell of "The Theater of Today," Paul Scott Mowrer, alternating between politics in "Balkanized Europe" and poetry in "Hours of France," Edgar Ansel Mowrer and his monumental "Immortal Italy," John F. Bass of "The Peace Treaty," Victor S. Yarros and his studies in social progress, Amy Leslie and her reminiscences of stage stars, now a collector's item. Not so long ago Wallace Smith of "The Little Tigress," was there, and Vincent Starrett, who carried our colors into Mexico; Henry Blackman Sell of "Good Taste in House Furnishing" set the pace in books and haberdashery, and even more recently Woodward Boyd of "The Love Legend" had her desk in the spacious local room. And in happy reminiscence we recall that it was in these rooms, as one of us, that John V. A. Weaver developed his vocabulary for "In American" only a few years ago.

IV

Bookselling as a cultural factor cannot fail to interest any one who observes the literary habits of a community like Chicago. Chicago has always had bookstores that have been the rendezvous of collectors, connoisseurs, men of strong enthusiasms about books. The position held through many years by the retail department of A. C. McClurg & Co., by Frank N. Morris and Walter E. Hill is sufficient to prove their importance. The proudest boast of McClurg's has been its "amen corner"—where gathered writers and thinkers of twenty years ago like Eugene Field and Frank W. Gunsaulus—and many influential men of the middle west found its rare book section as important a place to visit on a trip to Chicago as the stockyards. But that was in the eighteen-nineties, and the "amen corner" did not perpetuate itself beyond its generation. The store continued as a great distributor of books and with the coming in 1923 of Brentano's, as its successor, its usefulness is likely to be enhanced to a great degree. But it is the individual bookseller who has been the greatest force in shaping the reading taste of Chicago. Can a bookseller actually influence the taste of a community? Most assuredly he can when he brings imagination into his business methods and becomes more than a mere vendor of books. And singularly enough, the moment he does so, his material returns increase and prosperity stares him in the face. Bookselling is an occupation to which men may bring high hopes and enthusiasms, and once an audience is gained they may realize in it some of their finest aspirations. The book buyer is pliable; he can be led meekly into new pastures or absolutely discouraged in his reading; once his interest is obtained he becomes a firm friend. In Chicago this has been proved conclusively by the success of A. A. Kroch. His store, which grew from a little hole in the wall on Monroe street ten years ago to its present proportions, holds an enviable place in the minds of the booksellers of America.

When its profits are discussed booksellers invariably try to explain its success in terms of its location (on Michigan avenue, the broad highway of Chicago), its owner's foresight in buying and his ability to keep his stock moving. But an actual study of his methods would show that his influence as a cultural factor has been mainly responsible for his position. To Mr. Kroch books are not like so many crates of eggs or sacks of coffee—they are friends, and in the quiet of his home he reads as diligently as a reviewer. He then studies the men and women who enter his store and is able to lead them to books that they will enjoy. The personal gift of the owner has been communicated to Will H. Solle, Jerald W. Bigelow and half a dozen of his associates, with the result that one is constantly discovering new friends in the Kroch store. He has discovered that many good books are not announced by the publisher's tom-toms, and that when a book is really satisfying to readers it does not have to die in six short months. Again and again he comes back to old favorites, and publishers sometimes have been astonished to find a continuing sale for some obscure book of poems or essays to which they gave little attention and which they considered "dead" months before. The virtue of knowing good books and then finding readers for them is similar to that which makes good editors, good architects, good musicians; it can be expressed in terms of salesmanship or inspiration. To-day Mr. Kroch touches hands with an innumerable company of readers, many of whom ascribe their reading habit to his personal interest in them. What in an ordinary inventory of a business house would be described as good will may be translated here into the terms "confidence in his judgment," and this is the biggest asset in the Kroch organization.

Another big factor in extending the influence of books in Chicago has been the retail book section of Marshall Field & Co. Here the problem was different—a department store is an impersonal affair and the buyer faces vendors with whom he is not acquainted and who have but little interest in him. The success of a store of this kind lies in perfecting an organization capable of enthusiasm and energetic work. When the time came to establish the section Marshall Field & Co. selected as manager a little Irish girl who had sold fiction at McClurg's and whose dynamic personality had made her an important influence there. Marcella Burns was always delving into the possibilities in her occupation; her mind was agile and likely to be occupied with a new idea every minute; she had energy, poise, boundless optimism and an easy, informal approach. Her task at Field's was to take a body of women, potential readers, and lead them by easy steps into the realm of good books. Here again the soil was fallow but untouched; great numbers of women cared not at all for books because they had never been thrust under their noses. The Field book section was strategically placed near the women's waiting rooms and the candy department; some of the davenports even appeared to have been placed informally among the book aisles. The story of the success of Field's is again the story of finding a new audience and developing new readers. But even here, in a book section that in December employs nearly 100 clerks, and which is moving toward a million-dollar turnover, personal contact has not been lost. Marcella Burns Hahner, as she is known now, has carried with her the ability to keep in touch with many readers. Her gift for showmanship has resulted in book fairs, exhibits of special groups of books, lectures, and arrangements with publishers by which the making of books, from manuscript to printing and binding, has been shown on her floor. It has become generally known that there is always something going on at Field's and the interest in books has been heightened thereby.

In the smaller bookstores of Chicago the personal equation is most important and the size of their following may be an index to the influence of their owners. Miss Fanny Butcher has developed an interesting bookshop within the last few years; her reviews of books, which appear regularly every Saturday in the Chicago "Tribune" have gained her a wide following, and as her judgments are most often conservative she has become an important influence on the reading of many women. At the Public Library it has been said: "When Fanny Butcher recommends a book we get many inquiries for it from shop girls." There are half a dozen bookstores in Chicago that are building up patronage out of nowhere, showing that there is a potential audience which needs but be invited in. Silbermann and Sayers, on East Monroe street; the Economy bookshops in the heart of the "loop"; Alexander Green on Cass street; the Radical bookshop on North Clark street,—these are a few of the more recent additions to the book world of Chicago that have to be considered as exceptionally promising.

Then there is Covici-McGee, "three steps down," a small bookshop, too, but one is interested principally in the publishing venture established there. There have been a good many small publishers in Chicago since Kimball & Stone blazed a meteoric path across the skies in the nineties, but none other seems to have departed from safe, conventional bookmaking until the coming of Pasquale Covici and Billy McGee. Many of the publications of Kimball & Stone were in their day considered revolutionary; some are now choice items on collectors' lists. Covici-McGee already have published half a dozen books that call for spirited praise or antagonism; the very air of the place is combative and iconoclastic. Their entrance into publishing may be credited to the inspiration of Ben Hecht, who has guided most of their decisions, although he is not responsible for their entire list of books. It was Ben who enlisted the interest of Wallace Smith and Herman Rosse, who have illustrated several of these books in an unconventional manner, and suggested the publication of the works by Maxwell Bodenheim and Stanislaus Szukalski. He was also the inspiration of the Chicago "Literary Times" and its editor.

v

To-day Chicago is becoming aware of itself, and of its relations to its neighbors. A New York man may casually extol the advantages of his city as a place to live in, but a Chicago writer will name his city with a note of boastfulness and resentment in his voice. Everywhere there is a tremendous activity in the arts. One learns of small gatherings here and there to further a literary object. Especially active are the poets, and the inspiration of the "Poetry" magazine has extended to half a dozen groups that acknowledge no kinship with it. Steen Hinrichsen, deft in printing, in wood cut engraving, in his patronage of the arts, opens a print shop and a number of small magazines issue from it. Of these "The Wave," edited by Vincent Starrett, gives expression to many writers of the younger generation while drawing its principal inspiration from the eighteen-nineties. "The Circle" at the

University of Chicago gives that institution for the first time an unorthodox literary magazine. Walter E. Hill issues privately from time to time stately monographs compiled by men like Vincent Starrett and Christian Bay; Will Ransom has put into attractive form the poems of at least three Chicago poets of the young groups in "A Prayer Rug" by Jessica Nelson North, "Fringe" by Pearl Andelson and "Orioles and Blackbirds" by Hi Simons. Sam Putnam, critic, and Mark Turbyfill, poet of the metaphysical moods, find a new expression for their energies in "Evaporation," a theory of poetry, and when a city evolves a poetic theory its literary consciousness is assured. To this group also belong John Drury, often mentioned as a follower of the Sandburg influence, and Virgil Geddes, and to some extent Jun Fugita. The pages of the national magazines are filled with evidence of the activity of the poets and the new edition of "The New Poetry," an anthology by Harriet Monroe and Alice Corbin Henderson, bears witness to their numbers and the quality of their verse—for here are included: Mary Aldis, Sherwood Anderson, Emanuel Carnevali, Alice Corbin, Florence Kiper Frank, Fenton Johnson, Maurice Leseman, Edgar Lee Masters, Harriet Monroe, Carl Sandburg, Lew Sarett, Frances Shaw, Marion Strobel, Eunice Tietjens, Mark Turbyfill, Glenway Wescott, Yvor Winters, and Edith Wyatt.

But it is to the novelists that one looks for an expression of the character of Chicago. And in their books we find it. Protest, resentment, revolt against the damnation of the commonplace, are characteristics prominent in most of the outstanding novels that have a Chicago origin or background. And in nearly all of these a realistic or naturalistic method predominates. The city, dealing with the elementals of our lives, inspires men to a realistic mood. Theodore Dreiser in "Sister Carrie" and "The Financier"; Robert Herrick in "The Web," "The Common Lot," and "The Memoirs of an American Citizen"; Edgar Lee Masters in "Children of the Market Place" and "Skeeters Kirby"; Henry Kitchell Webster in "An American Family"; Joseph Medill Patterson in "Rebellion" and "A Little Brother of the Rich"; Sherwood Anderson in "Marching Men" and "Winesburg, Ohio"— the latter, despite its locale, a story of Chicago origin and types—Ben Hecht in "Erik Dorn," I. K. Friedman in "By Bread Alone," Hamlin Garland in "Rose of Dutcher's Coolly" and "A Daughter of the Middle Border," Frank Norris in "The Pit"—these and many more betray evidence of the influence that the primitive and elemental strength of the city exercises on novelists.

The best thing about many of these men is their forcefulness, their freshness, their naïveté; what they lack most is a cultural background. And although, for our own purpose, we recognize the validity of strength, power, vitality in spite of crudities; although, in our American way, we exalt the voice from the soil and brush aside the learning of the ages, yet it is the latter that proves such a tremendous asset to writers of foreign countries when they essay literature; which gives them poise, coherence, a firm hold on their art. Like the American skyscraper the American novel rises out of the soil—uneven, utilitarian, often formless, appealing to the eye rather than to the intellect; bizarre, striving for novelty of expression, incongruous, with little relation to the site on which it stands or to its surroundings. Often its outer ornamentation is copied flatly from old world models; sometimes there is an attempt at adaptation; more often the object of the builder is to crowd into the structure all that it will hold. The great forceful writer of the future will assimilate the cultural background of the ages and with his equipment transmute it into gold in interpreting the spirit of his own times. And the experiments of to-day are but steps to that future accomplishment.

6. Of Critics and Cynics Full Is This Buke

> *Life is an experience which packs its increasing load of memories and finds itself in the pack it carries; nothing in the present, nothing certain in the prospect, everything in the past. What it remembers it has. The burden it carries is itself. The way that it has gone is the only way it knows.*
>
> Clifford Raymond, "Almanac."

I

THOSE twinkling eyes set in a rotund mask belong to Llewellyn Jones, who nods approval as the stories fall; he is himself an excellent raconteur, prolonging the anecdote until your appetite has been properly whetted and driving home the point in an outburst of provocative chuckles. Llewellyn Jones talks even better than he writes, which is saying much, for his reviews are among the first in the land and he wields a calm, dispassionate style freighted with much clear thinking and shrewd analysis. His product has the ring of conservatism, but in truth he is often as advanced as the most noisy of our expressionists, and a decade of editorial work during an age when men now forty are looked on as mossbacks and lads in the early twenties carry the banners of half a dozen new schools, has not tamed his enthusiasm nor blighted his thinking. When he writes on prosody his reasoning is almost as intensive as that of Einstein and it is often said that there are not more than twelve men who fully comprehend. Certainly Miss Amy Lowell was not aware how well her antagonist was equipped when Jones wrote her that he was sending her an article in the "Sewanee Review" in which he had declared her ignorant of prosody, and Miss Lowell replied, in effect: "I shall read your article when it comes but I do not expect to find anything I do not already know." But leaving his scholarship wholly aside, I like to think of Llewellyn as a brother in an order of friars, who carries beneath the scholar's robe the heart of a man who loves the world and everything in it as much as his books. The place he fills is an honored one; as literary editor of the Chicago "Evening Post" he upholds the critical tradition of Henry B. Fuller, Francis Hackett, Floyd Dell, Julian Mason, George Cram Cook and Lucian and Augusta Cary. Associated with him is his wife, Susan Wilbur. The reviews in the "Post" bear the stamp of one mind perhaps more than those of any other literary journal in America and as such attain a unity in point of view that is invaluable. The files of the "Post" alone are a part of our literary history.

Henry B. Fuller is to-day the veteran of the group; the writer whose reputation is most secure, and whose books, though highly prized, are the least known; ask at random the next writer you meet whether he has read "The Chevalier of Pensieri-Vani" and like as not he will shake his head sadly. There is a tradition that when Francis Hackett first came to Chicago from the old sod he obtained a job in Field's at $6 a week—humble surroundings are good beginnings for critics. But the name that occurs to us most often is that of Floyd Dell, partly because his name must come up in any discussion of the younger writers of America, partly because of the notable leadership he exercised, when little more than a youth, through the pages of this literary supplement.

II

Soon after Floyd Dell came to Chicago Francis Hackett began editing the literary supplement of the "Post" in a spirited, liberal vein to which Floyd, with his socialist sympathies, was readily attracted. It might be profitable to tell of Floyd's beginnings had he not described them, thinly disguised, in the adventures of Felix Fay, the

sensitive, diffident, romantic hero of "Moon Calf." Floyd
Dell was born in Barry, Ill.—which he calls Maple—and
lived at Quincy, Ill.—which he calls Vickly—and then
proceeded to Port Royal, where most of the action of the
story takes place, and which may be easily recognized as
Davenport, Ia. Davenport was then a picturesque river
town with rare historical associations and literary
promises that have been richly fulfilled. When Floyd
Dell lived there and attended the high school Arthur
Davison Ficke was writing his first book of lyrics; Susan
Glaspell was toiling under the midnight lamp over short
stories for the "Black Cat" and attempting musical comedies; George Cram Cook was living on a farm in the river
lowlands to the south and basking in the sunshine of a
local reputation won from writing with Charles Eugene
Banks; Octave Thanet had been popular for years with
the readers of "Scribner's" and "Harper's" as a writer of
short stories and was about to emerge as a best seller with
"The Man of the Hour." George Randolph Chester had
slipped away; Charles Edward Russell and his son, John
Russell, who was later to write "The Red Mark" and
other tales, had gone on to Chicago, but something of their
influence remained in the newspaper offices. Floyd Dell
was in high school when I first heard of him; the story
was that the high school had a freak poet, who actually
sold verses to "McClure's" but who was eternally damned
because he was a Socialist. Those who have read "Moon
Calf" know to-day that Floyd's socialistic activity was
largely due to a lad's hunger for new intellectual contacts,
a reaching out for new friendships to replace the inade-
quacy of association with mere schoolboys. I remember
Floyd Dell of those days as a slight, diffident lad, who
walked as if he were treading on eggs and who smiled

faintly and deferentially at whatever was said, especially when he did not believe it, and then would disturb a gathering of callow high school youths by opening a serious debate on whether the chicken or the egg came first. It was but natural that in seeking for knowledge and beauty he had to turn to men and women much older than he, and so arose his friendship with "Wheels," and "Rabbi Nathan," and other well-remembered characters in "Moon Calf." He was doing high school notes when I first heard of him and tried to bag him for my newspaper; later, however, we became colleagues on "The Daily Times." Floyd was working on the Moline and Rock Island section, for the most part; capturing "personal" items by watching the railway stations for arrivals and departures; chasing anything from a fire in a barn to a murder in a low resort, doing odds and ends of footwork in police courts, fire stations and steamboat offices from early till late. It is possible that he has worked more intensely since then; it is unlikely that he has worked harder from the standpoint of physical labor. The lot of a cub there, or anywhere, was not an easy one. It was because of this early glimpse of his beginnings that my review of "Moon Calf," when it came to be written, turned out to be more of a reminiscence than an appraisement, in spite of the fact that even had no name been attached I would have been equally under the spell of this first distinguished autobiographical novel of an adolescent. And because this review tells something about the Floyd Dell of those days I have incorporated most of it in the following section.

III

If a friend had come to me months ago and said, "Floyd Dell is writing a novel about a town on the river called Port Royal and about certain characters called Hastings and Madison and J. G.," I should have leaped into the breach and given him the actual name of Port Royal, and the real names of Hastings, and Madison, and J. G., and told him where he could find them, sitting to-day in practically the same occupations they had when Dell first met them thirteen or so years ago. And I should have identified for him Tom Alden, the novelist, whose eyes were on Chicago, and Clavering, the poet, who went there with his work. But to-day, when I had read the book, these men needed no other identification. I do not think of Floyd Dell moving through these scenes of his youth in the middle west, but of Felix Fay, the character he has created—a character so clearly limned, so living, so intense, that one seeks no human counterpart. Felix Fay lives in the book, the first characterization of the youth of searching mind and groping mentality, the lad who questions all things, ponders over all things; the beginnings of the American intellectual radical who refuses to accept what comes down to him from other ages and other times, but only that which his own judgment tells him is good. Frank, outspoken, but never rude; hesitant, yet sure of his own capacity for seeing true; a ready listener, but often better informed than his elders; malleable to advice, yet never a blind follower of doctrine or creed, and, finally, determined that the dictates of his heart shall not overcome the carefully considered judgment arrived at through concise, desperate reasoning—that is the Felix Fay whom Dell has created for us and into whose creation he has put the best of his own adolescent experiences.

In the days of which he writes and in which I knew him Floyd Dell was a lean lad with a bit of fuzz on his cheeks; rather negligent of his clothes and somewhat diffident in his manner; unobtrusive in a group, with a sort of smile that might be half interest, half disdain. And yet he was the best and most fluent talker of all if you hit his subject —though his subjects were hardly those that the average adolescent cares or knows anything about. Strange comment on philosophy; quotations from poets with unfamiliar names; stories from books with unconventional foreign titles. I remember a walk with Floyd Dell to that Vandervelde park of which he speaks in "Moon Calf"—a walk that yielded my first acquaintance with Huneker, and through him with the dramatists who played so large a part in the early reading of Felix Fay; a walk that brought me my first glimpse of "A Shropshire Lad"—quoted for the most part by Dell, to be read later with much searching of heart from his own little copy. Nobody really understood the boy save the few kindred souls he has enshrined in "Moon Calf"—most of his schoolmates thought him a poet, hence a dreamer—and when they called him a socialist they felt they had accounted for any eccentricities he might possess.

What is "Moon Calf" all about? Principally about the growth of a lad in several Mississippi river towns—but the sort of lad who becomes an intellectual radical in later life. Not the plodder but the dreamer—a type new to American literature. To tell the story of Felix Fay Dell goes back to Fay's beginnings and the beginnings of his family; to his father's service in the civil war, to his parents' courtship, to the environment that early molded the youth, and to the things that attracted him. Three towns figure in the process: Maple, an Illinois town; Vickly, a town of 30,000 on the river; finally Port Royal, a larger city, lying across the stream from two other cities and the place where his principal intellectual and emotional experiences take place. Into his life come a number of girls—and some touch him as lightly as the butterfly touches the flowers it skims over. With one he works out the whole emotional conflict of independence and marriage, of that freedom inside the marriage bond that has taken so strong a hold on the thinkers of our generation. And in less than a hundred pages he has covered the whole ground of that argument—has pictured the mental struggle, the clash of wills, the motives that sway two people caught in the web of ideas. Therein lies mastery.

Floyd Dell's style is smooth, suave, ingratiating. In the hands of a less skilled writer his topics might be dynamite; with infinite skill he builds up a bond of sympathy between the reader and Felix Fay. I tried to detect mannerisms; tricks of style—there are few. Just English that is pure and chaste, serving the practised worker in words and ideas. A pertinent comment, this, on the writer who must resort to the practices of the harlequin and the acrobat to bring an audience to its knees. And an inspiration to all plodders who detest chicanery. Floyd Dell's book is in the best tradition and in the best manner.

IV

For aspiring writers in the corn belt Chicago is the first goal. Floyd Dell reached out for Chicago when Davenport no longer held him. Chicago! Only a man who has thought of Chicago as Felix Fay thought of it can speak that word as Floyd Dell has written it down in his novel. You of the east, secure in your traditions, confident of your aims, cannot comprehend the spirit of exultation that moves youths when first they speed across the plains toward this sprawling, awkward city. The west is just coming to understand the cultural influences that were your heritage early in the nineteenth century. With your cities close together, each rich in literary lore; with your colleges, large and small, each with a roll of alumni extending back over one hundred years; with your libraries and foundations, your youths have an advantage over the sons of laborers and pioneers whose life on the western soil goes back only a generation or two. To the western lad Chicago is the city of great cultural advantages and Floyd Dell has caught this mood in the last few pages of "Moon Calf"—he has picked it up again in his second novel, "The Briary Bush."

Readers will recall with what joy he turned to Hull House, of which he had heard much in Davenport—he calls it "Community House" in the book; it is there that he meets Rose-Ann. And the story goes on to tell how he tramped about Chicago for a modest apartment. . . . "One evening, on Canal street, in a dingy building which had apparently once been a residence and was now rented out, room by room, he found a tiny hall room on the third floor which he had not the excuse of not being able to afford. It was a room about eight by eleven feet, hardly holding the cot-bed, table and chair, which constituted its furnishing. He improvised a shelf above the tiny radiator in the corner for his half-dozen books. . . . And for one evening he was happy, in being away from Community House, in being in a place of his own, in

having in some way established his independence." And
then, a little farther on, he tells about the men he meets
there. "His kindly neighbors, who lived in the big room
at the back next to his own, were Roger Sully and Don
Carew, so he learned from the inscription on their mailbox
in the entrance. He went in that evening after dinner to
thank them. He was surprised to find, in this dingy
building, so charming a room—striking in contrast to his
own bare and cheerless one. Across one wall a blazing
splash of color—some kind of foreign-looking dyed-stuff
—and a few brilliant cushions on the couch, warmed the
place and made him forget what seemed the bleak chill of
all the rest of the world. Roger, it appeared, was the fat
little man with the air of distinction, who was making
coffee in a glass bulb over an alcohol lamp. Don, a long
and bony youth, was stretched at case in a big chair . . ."
So runs the tale.

Perhaps the actual surroundings were even more picturesque than Floyd has made them in this transcription.
For the friend who brings up again the picture of Floyd
Dell's first days in Chicago recalls that he came with a
letter of introduction to Dr. James Russell Price, a vast,
glossy-mustachioed doctor who was a Rosicrucian among
other matters, and who helped Floyd locate the Canal
street flat. "There were two others there," goes on our
veracious chronicler, a postman, who was a socialist, with
leanings toward economics, who had an immense stack of
newspaper clippings reaching almost to the ceiling. From
this he expected to compile a work on the coöperative
commonwealth. All his noon hours and spare moments
were spent at the John Crerar library in pursuit of this
ambition. The other man was an inventor, who had put
a great deal of money into a whirling ventilator, without

so far having won an adequate return. In the midst of this Floyd had his room—a funny little post, with a lot of dust and disorder about. It was sparsely furnished, but attractively, and on the chiffonier and at those Canal street windows (imagine—of all places!) were Japanese runners, dug up from some basement bazaar and put to a use that was to become popular later. And, of course, lots of books about. For in those days, you know, Floyd had a class in literature at Hull House. . . ."

v

In one of my rambles along the quays of the Seine I came upon an authentic program of the coronation of Louis XVI, a most remarkable book, giving the ritual of the various church services, the non-religious ceremonies and the observances of court etiquette. Most important historically is the order used in the court procession, in which the rank in line of all the nobles is set forth, and it has often been my fancy to run down this list and see what sport fate has had with this august entourage— after the names of generals and admirals and captains, dukes and lords one might place such designations as "guillotined in '93," "banished," "emigrated by choice." A startling document . . . Sometimes when I think of the nobility of letters that Chicago has lost I am led to compare it with this tragic list out of the old document. Again and again men of mark have come to Chicago to make it the fountain-head of their cultural work—again and again they have gone down in their efforts or passed on, mostly to the east. The list of *emigrés* grows larger year by year.

Francis Hackett has passed on now, to New York and

to Ireland; when he returns to Chicago it is as an oracle
out of the east, with words of wisdom; Floyd Dell has
passed on now, a legendary figure in Greenwich Village,
a bourgeois *pater familias* at Croton-on-Hudson; Lucian
and Augusta Cary have passed on, lost to us in turbulent
Manhattan, and Burton Rascoe, who for a short space
sent men into the bookstores for the new and old lumi-
naries, and made pulses beat faster at mention of a
writer's name, he too has passed on and is numbered
among the *emigrés*. Henry Blackman Sell, with an innate
capacity for showmanship and understanding of the popular appeal and the gift of making friends, endeared himself to us and passed on to become the editor of "Harper's
Bazar." It was Henry Sell who conspired with John B.
Woodward to give the Chicago "Daily News" a "book
page"—meager enough that boon, when compared with
the exhaustive reviews of books published in New York
City, and yet, through the agency of Henry's catching
enthusiasm, ever a source for the replenishment of one's
mental stimuli. In the field of literature and literary
criticism great have been our losses, and ever greater wax
our needs. Of the literary editors who have sparkled
for a little period on the Chicago firmament and then gone
on we like to recall the turbulent pontificate of Burton
Rascoe. His influence in Chicago was brief, but formidable. Even when at the university he began to be talked
about. He read English and French into the small hours
to the accompaniment of much black coffee. His impetu-
osity, his insatiable curiosity about literature, his militant modernism, attracted followers among the less daring. When the Chicago "Tribune" extended him the
privilege of reviewing books in the wake of the gentle
Mrs. Elia W. Peattie he unsheathed his sword, buckled

on his armor, and fell to. He had definite opinions about French moderns; he detested books that fitted with Victorian interiors; he deprecated smugness, hypocrisy, puritanism. In his haste he often forgot to buckle tight his armor, yet when an antagonist cried *touché* Burton gave no ground but started such a terrific counter attack with slingshots, arquebuses and catapults that the controversy invariably disturbed the serenity in the "Tribune" directors' room. Readers questioned his taste and his judgment, never his learning—it took too long to hunt up his references in the encyclopedia. One determined and cocksure man can lead a regiment even into a thicket of gooseberry bushes; Burton Rascoe, by the very vigor of his attack, became a most effective agent for bringing people into the bookstores, which was at that time a most difficult feat. Men and women who had done no more than scan the bright jackets in bookstore windows for a generation now actually crossed the threshold and inquired for novels far removed from the New England tradition. A new cultural force had been let loose in Chicago.

It seemed at times that Burton was itching to find a subject on which to let fling his unbridled vocabulary; his enthusiasm, if not vented in the columns of his newspaper, turned into the channels of conversation and deluged an assembly. Burton was always a man with an ebullient flow of speech; like a victrola record he could produce music, but the auricular faculty was denied him. In conversation Burton would lean back in his chair, look at you with a sort of appraising expression and talk at length on whatever topic happened to engage his sympathies at the moment. At one time this topic would invariably be related to psychiatry; somewhere in the

conversation Burton would discover the inevitable switch
and lead his auditors gently into the realms of the subconscious, the unconscious and the repressed. His auditor
would interpose a remark that ordinarily would call for
comment, rejection or acceptance; Burton, with his eyes
on the distant hills, would continue as before, unconscious
of interruption.

It was thus in his reviews. Will any of us forget the
trumpet notes of the first great blast for James Branch
Cabell, that brought us from our beds early one Saturday morning? Burton had been reading Cabell apace
and had become one of his greatest admirers. When
"Jurgen" came he was jubilant. It was dedicated to him
—but we know that this had nothing to do with Burton's
violent defense of this book. It was wholly in keeping
with his character, with his convictions, to become the
spokesman for "Jurgen." And he did. Gentle and un-
assuming Guy Holt, attempting to sell the book for the
publisher, could not, in his wildest moments, have conceived a "blurb" that would stand up beside Burton's
effective championship of James Branch Cabell. From
this allegiance he has never swerved. Burton Rascoe was
not one of those who were persuaded into the Cabell camp.
From the first he was an apostle of the master. For him
Cabell is sacrosanct and all his critics are anathema.

Ben Hecht reviewed "Jurgen" for the book page of the
"Daily News"; the review was put in type but never
printed. Henry Blackman Sell, with his ability to foretell
rain from the look of the sky, felt that Ben's unfavorable
verdict might bring about the investigation that later
actually did result from a letter in a New York newspaper
—so he put the review in type, sent a proof of it to Cabell,
and then threw it into the hellbox. Now that the whole

matter has been thrashed out in controversy Ben Hecht's comment may or may not have a historical value. "It is," said Ben, "the most obscene book I have ever read." But the courts, it will be remembered, freed it from all blame.

Throughout the long and acrimonious controversy over "Jurgen" Burton's loyalty never wavered. He gloried in a fight and his disgust at puritanism and comstockery was voiced freely and without restraint. There were times when the editors of the Chicago "Tribune" must have wondered what it was all about, but they gave him free rein until he had trod upon half a dozen journalistic taboos. Burton eventually felt his liberty of expression impinged upon and resigned. New York beckoned and he went, and Chicago lost again a young man who might have been a profound influence in the development of our culture had he remained beyond his formative years.

His influence made booksellers scramble for books that had long stood undusted on the top shelves. It made them look up catalogs of foreign publishers whose wares they had never felt impelled to investigate. A. A. Kroch summarized the situation once in a memorable line:

"Yes, Mr. Rascoe's recommendations always made people buy books. I have very few calls now for books he was most fond of. Seems to me I have sold very few of Rémy de Gourmont lately. Come to think of it, I believe he bought nearly all of them himself. . . ."

VI

But not all of the men and women who have been effective agents in extending a literary culture in Chicago have been literary critics. Gene Markey is, in a way of speaking, a critic who has led readers to books—his medium of expression is in caricature and in a friendly and generous fashion he hits off the foibles of contemporary writers. The first collection of his sketches, "Literary Lights" (Alfred A. Knopf, Inc., 1923), is a book both of promise and performance, and the artist's sketches in the Chicago "Daily News," and the New York "Tribune," show that he is growing more accomplished in piquancy and wit and satire. This wholly aside from the fact that Markey is actually a writer of tales, and has a leaning toward becoming a playwright.

Nor can we afford to overlook the conspicuous contribution by those gentle cynics and ironists, Tubman K. Hedrick and Clifford Raymond, whose principal work has been done through the newspapers, although both have published books. For a number of years Hedrick's writings appeared in the columns of the Chicago "Daily News," for the mantle of Eugene Field fell upon his shoulders before it descended upon Keith Preston and it was incumbent upon him to discuss the day's events and write his opinions of mankind in prose and verse. In this mood he developed a philosophical character called Ho-Hen, who spoke through the Japanese *hokku* and indulged in meditations in an oriental manner. Hedrick was the first writer to use this verse method; later he saw it adopted with dexterity by half a dozen other writers, notably Christopher Morley, who has written some inimitable humor in this form. Ho-Hen is happily not lost to posterity even though Hedrick has carried his gifts into the advertising department, for an attractive book, "The Meditations of Ho-Hen" (Bobbs-Merrill Co., 1921), makes him accessible for those who seek his wisdom. Some of it is in the form of proverbs, some of it observa-

tions and crisp comment on passing events and on human
frailties. For instance:

> "All things were made for me,"
>   Said the man.
> "Nay, for me," said the earthworm,
>   And the man could not reply.

> The monkeys, having established
>   a dictatorship in the jungle
>   decreed that all animals
>   must sleep, suspended by the tail,
>   in trees.
> It went pretty hard with the elephants.

Hedrick's literary career has been closely identified
with the middle west, but his own work has been obscured
because early in his life he came under the influence of
William Marion Reedy and threw all his efforts into
anonymous editorial work for the St. Louis "Mirror."
A singular unenviable distinction is his—he may be said
to be the originator of the ouija board movement in literature. Down in St. Louis they still tell how Hedrick
introduced this diversion with a great show of formality
one evening at the home of Caspar Yost, editor of the
"Globe-Democrat." Later when Mrs. Curran and Emily
Grant Hutchins discovered "Patience Worth" and began
to receive messages from her via the ouija board Reedy
and Yost became enthusiastic supporters of the movement. "Patience Worth" was ostensibly a medieval
maiden who dictated novels and poems and who became
the inspiration of many similar spook writers. Hedrick
takes an ironist's view of the whole manifestation by saying: "Happily the spook drive lessened in intensity and
appeal, else how could we who subsist on porterhouse and

near beer provide for our material wants against competition requiring no material upkeep whatever?"

Between writing *hokku* and meditations Hedrick used to lean over the desk now used by Keith Preston and discourse on the influence wielded on writers by the "Mirror" school. Reedy was a carefree spirit of considerable power and acumen, who could easily have become a great figure in the east had his quiet, phlegmatic temperament not anchored him to St. Louis. When he first founded the "Mirror" the writers of the middle west had few avenues of expression. Poets were still starving; those were lean years for literature. Reedy helped many aspirants escape complete eclipse not only by printing their verses but by building up an appreciation for poetry in his community. His stewardship goes back to the dawn of time, as moderns measure it. As far back as 1900 he encouraged the writing of Ernest McGaffey's book, "Sonnets to a Wife," which became widely known, and thereby lost considerable money.

"But who cares for those ancient days?" Hedrick said one day, when we were indulging in reminiscence. "The outstanding figure of Reedy's 'Mirror' school is, in modern terms, Edgar Lee Masters, who proudly acknowledges his debt to 'Bill.' Fannie Hurst's first story came to the 'Mirror' in 1905. I was sitting in for 'Bill' then and I accepted her story. Orrick Johns, Zoe Aiken and Sara Teasdale found quick encouragement in the 'Mirror' and I fancy they are pleased to acknowledge Reedy's influence and help. Much of Louis Dodge's able early work was published there. Henley's most famous poem, 'Invictus,' was first published in the 'Mirror' and given its title by Reedy."

Hedrick then spoke of an interesting episode. "In a

strange sort of double play," he said, "Carl Sandburg discovered Clifford Raymond to the world in Reedy's 'Mirror.' Raymond was writing an almanac anonymously in the Chicago 'Tribune' which had attracted the attention of Carl, who was quick to see unusual merit in it."

Happily the Almanac, or choice parts of it, is now available in book form, known as "Clifford and John's Almanac," by Clifford Raymond, illustrated by John T. McCutcheon (Reilly & Lee, Chicago, 1922). To those who have possessed themselves of a copy it is a source of perennial joy. Irony, poetry, cynicism, color, flit through its pages; there is a fragrance of ancient lore about it, tempered with modern wit. Between the paragraphs run lines of sage observations which form a whole philosophy of life.

Happiness is content in a comfortable and kindly mediocrity.

Life is a code of manners by which we present ourselves as what we want to be and deny ourselves as what we know we are.

Life is a sum of experiences; to judge it by its background is tragic; to esteem it for its future is pathetic. It must be valuable in the perceived conditions of its present or it has no value.

Contentment is best talked of by such as have it without effort. Thus it represents the perfection of circumstances for self and not the conciliation of self to imperfect or unpleasant circumstances.

Nearly all virtue is tranquillity or stolidity unvexed by desire.

He cut a reed at the water's edge and found he could play one note.

In order to live optimistically, which is happily, we must attribute to others emotions which they do not feel and ascribe to them acts which they do not do.

7. Robert Herrick and Edgar Lee Masters
Interpreters of Our Modern World

*We chatter of the curse of Castle
Garden, unmindful that in the
dumb, animal hordes, who labor
and breed children, lies the future.
For theirs will be the land when
the blond hunter of the market
and his pampered female are
swept into the dustheap.*

Robert Herrick, "Together."

I

Two men of mark stand out sharply against the gray background of the middle western scene—Robert Herrick and Edgar Lee Masters; the first a calm, unemotional analyst, a representative of New England culture transplanted into the heart of the west; the second a disillusioned, sometimes cynical observer of the passing throng, warm-blooded, closely attached to the soil and yet not identifiable with the western clan. I think of the two men as standing aloof, conforming only rarely to the social demands of our literary movement, and not at all to its methods and style. Widely dissimilar, they have in common certain external traits that lead me to bracket them in this estimate of their place in our western culture.

When I picture Robert Herrick I think of him as sitting before his classes as an arbiter, his right hand clasping a book, his left hand upraised as if rendering a decision, and a halo about his head as in the portraits of the bishops and dignitaries of the church in ancient frescoes. Immovable, too, as they, examining the world with blue eyes that seem cold and distant, his features expressing firmness and determination and giving no hint of the glow of human understanding in the heart of the man. When I picture Edgar Lee Masters I invariably think of him as slumped down a bit in his chair, saying little, smiling now and then a bit wryly, at best flinging a challenge across the table in the form of a poem that expresses a serious reflection on life in relation to our national ideals.

Both Robert Herrick and Edgar Lee Masters were born in the same year—1868—and both are descended from an Anglo-Saxon ancestry. The families of both men have been long in America; but Herrick's forebears were always resident in New England until he came west, whereas Master's grandfather came north from Kentucky and settled in what was later to become the Lincoln country of Illinois in 1825. Both were sons of lawyers; both were from the first contemptuous of a smug, self-satisfied Americanism; both made no concessions to the prevailing taste in books, and both have achieved an outstanding success by following their own convictions in their own way. But here the similarity ends; for in the field of writing they have very little in common. Herrick became a factor in American letters almost from the first; his scholarship was well-balanced, he had his literary backgrounds well in hand; he was always dignified, technically correct, and reserved in his work. Edgar Lee Masters exhibits a growth that marks him as an interesting personal study; his field was the law, and for a long time he practised it actively; both reading and writing were done as an avocation, and so through his books we are able to trace a gradual growth and development and also a widely divergent experimentation with literary styles. To-day Robert Herrick is an established novelist from whom one may expect matured, well-rounded work but few surprises, whereas Masters, having gained a wide audience with the *tour de force* of the "Spoon River Anthology," is writing prose that marks him as still among the authors whose future cannot be accurately charted and whose ultimate place in our letters cannot be foretold.

II

My knowledge of the personal side of Robert Herrick deals almost wholly with externals, and the picture that I formed of him over a decade ago has never been stripped of its frame. He remains to me a fixed star of a superior magnitude, apart from the thousand scintillations of the literary milky way, unaffected by the meteors and comets that flash across his sky. Externally he has changed very little. Robert Herrick in his early forties would walk across the grounds of the University of Chicago with that detached, ruminating air that was characteristic of the sexagenarian Ibsen strolling down the *Karl Johan's-gade* of Christiania for his daily coffee. He was the picture of health then, with a boyish face, blond hair, and ruddy cheeks; to-day he is much the same, save that his face is a bit more full, his lips are more firmly compressed and a glint of silver has touched his hair. His manner was always deliberate. At extramural lectures he would stand gravely and unmoved and read essays of polished English and sound thinking that made no concessions to the more diffused attention and the lower level of intelligence of his non-college audience. In the classroom he was never emotional in speech or in gesture, but we were always startled into attention by his crisp comment on men and affairs, his irony, his unerring judgment. College tradition credited him with most of the biting and acerbic comment on student brains that has come down to us via Goettingen, the Sorbonne, and Oxford; as a matter of fact he rarely courted the risibilities of his students and never tried for clever and devastating epigram. In the course of the

years that I have read his books his position has remained unchanged. In America he is a singular figure;
one might almost say that he is unique. For in a nation
and an age when self-advertisement is regarded as so-
cially correct, Robert Herrick is content to follow a
course of self-effacement that he must have laid out for
himself back in college days. He seeks no publicity,
courts no distinction, wears no badges; behind his name
on the rolls of the University of Chicago stands the
simple baccalaureate degree that came from Harvard in
1890. He has observed life coldly, calmly, and with an
inquiring air; he has not followed the tides nor trimmed
his sails to the winds. That he should, at one time in
his career, have become the author of a "best selling"
novel was due to the fact that his theme in "Together"
and the appetite of the public coincided, and to no
manœuver on his part to win a wide hearing.

Robert Herrick is not typical of the middle west at all
in the sense that Hamlin Garland is typical. Place Mr.
Garland anywhere and there will still be wisps of straw
in his hair, but Mr. Herrick, even after his thirty years
of intermittent residence in Chicago, remains a representative of eastern culture. One cannot picture Robert
Herrick as standing in the killing pen of the stockyards
watching Carl Sandburg's hunky sweep blood off the
floor with a broom—although the first chapters of
"Homely Lilla" prove that there is nothing devitalized
about his writing. One cannot even think of him as
jostling victims of our social laws at the Morals court,
or dangling his feet off a half-drowned pier to listen to
the lingo of yeggs and bindlestiffs in a biscuit-box jungle.
Yet much of what he writes he has observed and no
doubt lived at first hand, and only a little has been ex-

perienced vicariously. He is the outstanding New England writer who has pioneered into the middle west. His American ancestry goes back to 1632 and all his traditions are Anglo-Saxon. His father was a lawyer in Boston and he was born in Cambridge, Mass., April 26, 1868. He was educated in the Cambridge public schools and in Harvard College, where he was graduated in 1890. In Harvard he attended courses in English and literature; he was an editor of the "Harvard Advocate," and later, with Norman Hapgood, of the "Harvard Monthly." Both during college and immediately afterward he traveled widely, touching Alaska, the Caribbean, and Europe, and in 1895 he wrote in Paris and Florence. His first work as an instructor in English immediately after his graduation from Harvard, was done at Massachusetts Institute of Technology, where Prof. George R. Carpenter was then in charge. In 1893 he became one of the numerous gifted young men that William Rainey Harper gathered from the ends of America to build the new University of Chicago, and although he has been in residence only about six months of the year ever since, and has had opportunity for travel and living elsewhere, this connection has never been broken. Although never the head of his department his name is one of wide influence in the university, and the department, which includes such outstanding men as Robert Morss Lovett, James Weber Linn, and John Matthews Manly, regards him as a source of strength. He stands aloof from faculty politics, gives little attention to the social affairs of the university, and is regarded as the last word in courses in English composition, where his influence has always been thrown to the cause of clear writing, breadth of view, and good taste. With his New England background he represents the best that the puritan tradition has left behind. His tastes have nothing provincial about them and his viewpoints are based on long observation and study. In his classes he opens the minds of his students to the essentials in writing; the great authors of the world are at his elbow. He places emphasis on "Anna Karenina" and "War and Peace," on "Henry Esmond," on "Madame Bovary," on "Vanity Fair," on all the masterpieces of realism of the Nineteenth Century. He is friendly to new themes and tolerant of a wide latitude of views among his pupils. Figuratively and actually he never steps down from his platform to mingle with his pupils; he remains the arbiter, the path-finder, but never the companion in literary adventures. Similarly his influence on the culture of Chicago is in-direct. He has never taken part in a popular movement, or spoken in a popular forum; his membership in clubs has been limited to a few organizations where he is able to meet men of his type, and his attendance there is rare.

All this savors of the aristocrat in letters, and yet this man could write, in 1905, a straightforward, unembel-lished account of a raw youth who comes to Chicago from Indiana honest but poor, begins life little better than a tramp, sees that fortune is to be achieved by taking advantage of opportunities, both devious and above-board, and, playing the game neither better nor worse than his fellows, finally lands in the United States Senate. Herein is contained not only the memoir of an entire career but the summary of a whole era and a mode of life. When "The Memoirs of an American Citizen" was written America had reached the peak of its op-portunist philosophy of optimism and monetary success; labor had yet to wring a tithe of its earnings from a

swollen and swaggering industrialism, become a giant
under the Republican administrations; men talked of
national greatness and of the extension of the nation's
boundaries beyond the seas, and the field of art showed
the same lack of understanding of relative values. In
Chicago men who had raised themselves to political
power through spoils politics and open graft were often
welcomed in good society, and dominant opinion held
that what is, is right. The statue that commemorated
the death of the policemen in the Haymarket riot of
1886—an incident in the book—still stood, although it
had been removed from the site of the catastrophe to
the less obtrusive surroundings of a public park, and no
one attempted publicly to question the righteousness of
the verdict by means of which the men adjudged guilty
of inciting to violence and murder were hung and im-
prisoned. Under conditions such as these it was but
natural that the public should demand not actualities
but romance in its books, and men who took an unfair
advantage of their fellows in their business practices
during the day, at night could read glowing accounts of
humble lads rising to fame and fortune by the exercise
of all the virtues, and so, by projecting themselves into
the character of the hero, they could achieve immunity
from the twinge of conscience. This was, therefore,
hardly the time when a book that treated business life
realistically was likely to be welcome.

Perhaps in writing it Robert Herrick's New England
aloofness came into play. He had already lived ten years
in the western scene, but he viewed the development of
the story from the outside, and by no means could he personally have experienced all that he told. The story is
therefore all the more a credit to his imaginative faculty,

for the facts had to be obtained by reading, by observation, and by talks with public men. Those who believe that the protest against America's complacent acceptance of tawdry ideals began with Theodore Dreiser's thunderous adumbrations in the second decade of the century may turn with profit to this earlier book by Robert Herrick. Herrick differed from Theodore Dreiser in this: he could write English, and so he saw events in their proper relation to each other; Dreiser's incidents were frequently out of focus, enlarged, overemphasized. As a result Herrick's book paid the penalty that an author always incurs in a tasteless age when he strives for normality in treatment; he had chosen to tell his story smoothly, naturally, letting events fall as they do in life, and therefore a public avid for headlines could find little on which to feed. All the theatrical trappings of the romantic novel had been discarded and for once a young man portrayed a rôle very much like that of his readers; he came to Chicago eager and honest, like men who walked these very streets; he lived in a plain boarding house on West Van Buren Street, got interested in the packing business as a teamster and rose by his own ingenuity in the field of buying and selling, made sausages, took part in civic affairs, toyed with courts and political offices and eventually became powerful by playing the game with a shrewd hand. He gave up his life for monetary success just as so many thousands of young Americans were doing. Into his mouth Herrick puts reflections such as these:

I remember Grace saying sentimentally to Slocum that Sunday:
"You fellows keep thinkin' of nothin' but money and how

you're goin' to make it. Perhaps rich folks ain't the only happy ones in the world."

"Yes," Hillary chimed in, "there's such a thing as being too greedy to eat."

"What else are we here for except to make money?" Slocum demanded more bitterly than usual.

He raised his long arm in explanation and swept it to and fro over the straggling prairie city, with its rough, patched look. I didn't see what there was in the city to object to: it was just a place like any other—to work, eat, and sleep in. Later, however, when I saw the little towns back east, the pleasant hills, the old homes in the valleys, and the redbrick house on the elm-shaded street in Portland, then I knew what Slocum meant. Whatever was there in Chicago in 1877 to live for but Success?

The novel flows forward like a record of daily adventure in the seventies and eighties of the last century; Van Harrington, who carries the tale, relates it so simply that one scarcely realizes that through him the author is summarizing the philosophy of several decades. Van Harrington is so clearly visualized that he becomes a part of the mosaic of his own time—and that is a characteristic of Herrick, for although one thinks of his novels in terms of their strongly individualized characters, yet these are always a part of their time and never step out of focus. The interplay of incident and episode is continuous; a whole social structure is built up before our eyes. The episode of the bomb-throwing in the Haymarket in 1886 touches Van Harrington as it touches the class of employers and, although he is inclined to view it from two sides, his rôle in life is to be one of the owners and masters, and so he explains the situation thus:

The hatred and rage of all kinds of men during these months while the anarchists were on our hands before they were finally hanged or sent to prison, is hard to understand now at this distance from the event. . . . That bomb in its murderous course had stirred our people to the depths of terror and hate; even easy-going hustlers like myself seemed to look at that time in the face of an awful fate. The pity of it all was—that our one motive was hate!

When the arrested men come up for trial Van Harrington is urged by his employer to sit on the jury, and he does so. He knows that it will work to his advantage, but although he has "made money in the scheme of things as they are" he is not entirely at ease. Into his mouth Herrick places his impeachment of the trial: "From the start it seemed plain that the state could not show who threw that fatal bomb, nor who made it, nor anything about it; the best the state could do would be to prove conspiracy. The only connection the lawyers could establish between those eight men and the mischief of that night was a lot of loose talk. His Honor made the law—afterward he boasted of it—as he went along. He showed us what sedition was, and that was all we needed to know. Then we could administer the lesson. Now that eighteen years have passed that looks to me like mighty dangerous law. Then I was quick enough to accept it."

Van Harrington performs his duty to society by returning the expected verdict of guilty. He is widely congratulated and becomes immensely pleased with himself. But somehow his doubt never leaves him. When he sees the prisoners brought up for sentence he is moved to remark: "No one pled for mercy. I was sorry for them. 'The world is for the strong,' I said to myself, as

I left the court, 'and I am one of them.'" Deftly the author continues to explain his own opinion of an action by the doubts and reflections that are voiced by Van Harrington. One sees the philosophy of his social group gradually being developed by this man who was once a simple, honest Indiana boy with no feeling of responsibility for the daily business of the world. The scene at the Metropolitan club when announcement is made that Harrington has been elected senator is a subtle satire; over fifteen years later Sinclair Lewis incorporated the same motive in "Babbitt," and made his derision so plain that even the simple-minded could grasp it; Herrick's method is one of greater subtlety, the Babbitts of the nineties are there, acting much like the Babbitts of 1921, but it is Van Harrington who records these memoirs and in his eyes the bombastic speeches, the references to "our broad prairies, our great forests, our vast mines" are not wholly out of place. So, too, the concluding chapters, giving the inner thoughts of the man who has been elected senator from Illinois and who knows that his life has been one of compromises, yet who cannot find much to blame himself for, stand apart for their superior satire and irony. The reader may find Van Harrington a pitiful figure, with his power, his office, his simple-minded desire to convert his Illinois farm home into a reform school "to take boys to who hadn't a fair chance in life," but Harrington himself, moving uncomprehending through the scene, contemplates his material achievements with worldly pride—"my plants, my car line, my railroads, my elevators, my lands—all good tools in the infinite work of the world," and concludes that by another scale, a grander one, he may not be found wholly wanting.

III

Both Robert Herrick and Edgar Lee Masters are inter-preters of our modern world, but how differently! In Robert Herrick one is conscious only of highly indi-vidualized types, and as one follows the development of his characters one realizes only gradually that he is dis-secting a whole society. Thus his major contribution is an analysis of the American woman, and far from por-traying the romantic type so dear to the American magazine, Herrick shows a living being not devoid of faults or blemishes; a woman, who, as the product of our American environment, may be both mistress and parasite and only occasionally boon companion and the embodiment of an ideal. But this woman cannot help be a part of her times, and so this author has invariably made her environment an important aid in estimating her character. Take Nell Goodnow in "The Healer," a book that begins with an idyllic love story between Doctor Holden and Nell—the girl is unable in spite of her re-sponse to his romantic temperament to forget the world around her: "Dimly it appears to her woman's heart that this wild one of hers is building into those stone walls not merely their love: he is building up his will, his man-hood,—purpose, the hope blazoned in that last dawn upon the mountains. She cannot fully understand what it means, bewildered as she is by the social flutter of her wandering life, confusing voices all about, possible lovers, idlers, Vera's young diplomat, her mother, all the com-plex triviality of her leisured life. . . ." It is this "com-plex triviality of her leisured life" which later wrecks the marriage, for far from sinking her identity in the aims and hermit personality of her husband Nell must go back to the environment that has so strong a pull upon her—to the demoralization of her married life. When we finish the book we have not only the woman clearly in mind but her social group is admirably limned. Similarly Herrick has portrayed a very human sort of girl in Adelle Clark of "Clark's Field," who is at first a dull and uninteresting school girl, and later, through contact with the sharp corners of life, grows in wisdom and experience. In thus portraying the effect of great wealth on a girl, Herrick shows us no siren lolling on the sands at Palm Beach or posing on horseback for the photographers at Newport, but a simple unambitious girl who is more a victim of conditions than a free agent. But the inherent spark of honesty with which she and so many other women of Herrick's repertory are endowed enables her to rise above the legal make-shifts which would enable her to remain the possessor of great wealth that was technically not her own. In painting in the background Herrick takes a fling at half a dozen of our illusions—for instance, that girls' schools shelter their inmates with the mantle of innocence, that money can buy anything but boredom and that its possessors are always free and contented, that our laws governing inheritance and private property are just and humane. In "Together," easily Herrick's outstanding study of women in America, and one of the notable books of the first decade, half a dozen portraits demand our attention; here as in "The Memoirs of an American Citizen" the women seem to stand for a much sterner sense of business honesty than the men, yet extravagance has them in its grasp, and matrimony, once interpreted as a partnership in which two are joined together till God puts them asunder, becomes an interplay of wills, a jockeying for advantages and a game of spurring the husband on to greater efforts at moneymaking to meet the extravagant demands of the society in which he lives. When the Faulkners go on the rocks because Bessie would persist in building a house that cost far more than they could pay, Isabelle Lane comments to herself that it is "the old difficulty—not enough money." It is an American situation: "So few of her friends, even the wealthy ones, seemed to have enough money for their necessities or desires. If they had four servants they needed six; if they had one motor, they must have two; and the new idea of country houses had simply doubled or trebled domestic budgets. It wasn't merely in the homes of ambitious middle-class folk that the cry went up: 'We must have more!' . . . Even with her skilful management and John's excellent salary, there was so much they could not do that seemed highly desirable to do. 'Everything costs so these days! And to live meant to spend— to live!'" And later on, in "Together" when John Lane's devious practices in giving rebates are exposed in court and he is branded a thief and a grafter Herrick shows his continued faith in the puritan strain that runs through the American woman. Extravagant she may be, but Isabelle is also inherently righteous. When Isabelle interrogates John Lane about the verdict, we discover a situation similar to the one in "The Memoirs of an American Citizen," wherein Harrington tries to gloss over his attempt to bribe a judge, and in which his wife, confused at this quirk in the masculine mind, stands sharply on the side of honesty. Isabelle Lane, too, is worried about "the cloudy places in her husband's soul," and it is her sobering wisdom, acquired in ten years of battle with life, that eventually paves the way toward their spiritual rebirth. In the characters of Margaret Pole, of Isabelle Lane, of Bessie Faulkner, and of Alice Johnston, Herrick has portrayed a whole generation of American women with a realism and a sureness of psychology that make "Together" the book that ranks him as the peer of Galsworthy.

Through half a dozen books these women of Herrick's are no pale pastels but breathing, vibrant creatures, essential to the plot development. The latest of his heroines is Lilla of "Homely Lilla," a novel that first appeared serially as "Her Own Life," and was published in book form early in 1923. It was his first long novel since "Clark's Field," of 1914, although in the interval he had published a short sketch called "The Conscript Mother," and had written many reviews, and some war sketches from France. Lilla's history is fundamentally that of a woman of independent traits who tries to compromise with the demands of the social group in which her life is cast and fails, eventually regaining her spiritual and physical independence after a long period of suffering and indecision. In this case the author portrays a clash between two temperaments—that of her mother, who is stern, repressed, and puritanical, and who regards any reference to sex as obscene, and that of Lilla who inherits from her liberal and misunderstood father a keen zest for living and a hatred of pretenses, but is constantly bowing to a discipline which acknowledgement of her mother's authority inculcates in her. The tremendous capacities in the girl are suggested by the opening episode, in which her father is injured to the death by a saw and in which she drags his body from the saw and attempts to stay the flow of blood. Cast, after his death, into the company of her mother she permits herself to drift, despite her own strong individuality, into a marriage with a man who plays a rôle of sex hypocrisy and eventually, after much cruelty due to his own egotism, becomes unfaithful to her. Her emancipation comes slowly and only after she has fled the city and sought new life and new thoughts on a farm in Arizona. In the final pages Herrick foreshadows her marriage with another man from the wide prairies—a man who is as free from the restraints of conventional society as she herself. The two types of women in this book are revelatory of Herrick's opinions—the mother is clean, but repressed and insincere to the point of indecency; the daughter, seeing nothing anti-social in the pure expression of life in its proper place, is just as clean and infinitely more wholesome. Although presenting what in some quarters is still regarded as a radical view —that sex experience does not contaminate—Herrick's book gleams but palely beside those highly colored romances of sex passion with which our youngest writers announce their emancipation from a conventional world. And therein lies his strength—for Lilla, in the hands of our Fitzgeralds and Elliot Pauls might have become a girl who threw down the gauntlet to convention with every movement she made, whereas by the careful craftsmanship of Robert Herrick she seems almost decorous and dignified. He is always able to see the relation of an incident to the whole; his novels are developed as entities, and no part is ever out of proportion; his characters are visualized not as abnormal beings with one profound aberration obscuring all other traits, but as human beings who live their lives very much as we live ours, and who meet the problems and fight the influences that we also meet and fight in our modern world.

IV

Edgar Lee Masters came into literature by a side door
—that is, by way of the law, like so many gifted men
before him. In 1892 he came to Chicago, just a year before
Robert Herrick was summoned to the University of Chicago. Ever since, save for time devoted to travel, he has
practised law here, has taken part in political fights and
has been a close observer of the city's complicated life.
But he has not become the chronicler of the city; for his
most effective themes he turns back to the experiences
of the days before he reached Chicago, and to the atmosphere of "the Lincoln country" in the farming lands of
Illinois, where he spent his boyhood. The reason for
his preoccupation with these subjects becomes more clear
when we consider these early years.

Masters' grandfather was a native of Virginia and
reached Illinois from Tennessee in 1825. In 1847 he
settled near the town of Petersburg, in Minard County,
on the Sangamon river. Masters was born in Kansas,
where his father was practising law, but when he was
one year old his parents returned to Illinois, and as a boy
he attended the public schools in Petersburg. This is
only two miles from the site of New Salem, the village
which Abraham Lincoln reached in April, 1831, when he
was engaged in taking a flatboat from Beardstown, Ill.,
to New Orleans. The flatboat stuck on the dam at New
Salem, and Lincoln's efforts to get it off first introduced
him to the villagers, who were to become well acquainted
with him later on. In July, 1831, he was again at New
Salem, becoming a clerk in a general store opened by
Denton Offutt. It was at New Salem that Lincoln did
his first reading, decided to become a candidate for the

state assembly of Illinois and enlisted in the Black Hawk war. It was here, too, that Lincoln met Ann Rutledge, for in 1832 he boarded at the Rutledge tavern. Ann, of whom Masters later wrote in "The Spoon River Anthology": "beloved in life of Abraham Lincoln, wedded to him, not through union, but through separation," was buried at Concord cemetery, seven miles northwest of New Salem. As a surveyor Lincoln became a familiar figure in this country and when campaigning for the legislature he made many new friends there. This part of Illinois therefore became prolific in Lincoln anecdotes and Masters, as a boy, heard many of them from men who had known Lincoln, and visited the site of New Salem and played about its ruins, for this frontier town was abandoned in the forties and is now "a green cow pasture." In 1880 the Masters family moved to Lewiston, Ill., and here Masters attended a small college and studied logic and Latin. He also began to read law in his father's office and to write for the local newspapers, and to correspond for the Chicago and St. Louis papers. When twenty-one he entered Knox College in Galesburg, Ill., and studied Greek, Latin, and German. Later he studied law and in 1891 was admitted to the bar. During all this time he was writing verses in the formal, classical manner.

This early life must have left a deep impression on Masters for in his later writing career he has made it the keystone of his work. When he came to write "The Spoon River Anthology" he actually portrayed a composite community drawn from his knowledge of the little towns along the Sangamon river. The cemetery at Spoon River might be the Concord cemetery for all one knew —at least the dead who spoke might have lived in New

Salem ages ago and now "all, all, are sleeping on the hill." Among them were those who, like Ann Rutledge and William H. Herndon, bore names nationally known. And the Lincoln theme also introduced itself unawares:

> Where is Old Fiddler Jones
> Who played with life all his ninety years . . .
> Lo! he babbles of the fish-frys of long ago,
> Of the horse races of long ago at Clary's Grove,
> Of what Abe Lincoln said
> One time at Springfield.

As is well known Masters had been writing for a long time when "The Spoon River Anthology" appeared and placed a book of poetry for the first time since mid-Victorian days in the lists of the best sellers. His first, "A Book of Verses," had been published by Way & Williams in Chicago in 1898, and five books and plays had succeeded it, as well as many political and economic essays written for the newspapers. The early verses were very dignified and formal, often stilted and unoriginal. They no more foreshadowed the author of the anthology than the rail splitting of Lincoln forecast the later president. We find in this book, for instance, such lofty titles as "A Dream of Italy"; "Ode to Autumn"—"season of gusty days and cloudy nights"; "Invocation to Spring," and the like. From the start Masters was interested in his own state, for there is a poem to Illinois, with the lines:

> Illinois, an empire is thine of billowy fields of glory,
> Here shall our epic thrive in ages hereafter.

But his knowledge of the classics did not prejudice him against Walt Whitman, of whom he writes: "The soul of him who could find true in false and good in everything." Here too is a hint of his acquaintance with Goethe, for he writes a sonnet "On Reading Eckermann's Conversations with Goethe." Thus in his first book he touches on themes that have always had a marked influence in his life—Illinois, Whitman, Goethe.

Masters had become acquainted with William Marion Reedy and was sending Reedy formal, uninspired verses along the line of those in his earlier books. T. K. Hedrick, who was associated with Reedy in editing the "St. Louis Mirror" at this time, tells me that Reedy said to Masters: "For God's sake, lay off on formal and classical poetry." A short time later Reedy received a group of poems about Spoon River and sent them to Hedrick, asking him what he thought of them, and remarking that he "considered that they had a fine new angle and that they would make a hit." Hedrick was also impressed, and the first of the poems appeared in the "Mirror" on May 29, 1914, over the name of Webster Ford. Reedy immediately tried to obtain a publisher for the verses in book form. They continued in the "Mirror" until January 5, 1915. Alice Corbin Henderson, then an editor of "Poetry," was immediately attracted to them, and Ezra Pound praised them as the work of a great poet, although he did not actually know the name of their author. John Cowper Powys at once introduced them to a wide public through his lectures. When the book was published the outburst of approval was spontaneous, although both in content and in form the poems violated many of America's literary canons. They were in free verse, were realistic and often cynical, deprecated the hypocrisy of the conventional tombstone epitaph, and often dealt with sex in plain terms. They distinctly belonged to the

school of revolt and their author refused to view the
village and the "folks back home" as free from the vices
of the town.

When Masters was writing them he was a member of
a law firm that included Clarence Darrow, whose "Farm-
ington" is also an iconoclastic story of village life. Carl
Sandburg has written of this period of authorship:

"I saw Masters write this book. He wrote it in
snatched moments between fighting injunctions against a
waitresses' union striving for the right to picket and gain
one day's rest a week, battling from court to court for
compensation to a railroad engineer rendered a loath-
some cripple by the defective machinery of a locomotive, having his life round affairs as intense as those he
writes of."

Masters continues to write about Lincoln, about the
small towns, about early days in Illinois. But his is no
delicately embroidered picture of the early days, drawn
by a sentimental artist. The Illinois of Lincoln is to
him a festering sore, and so he has described it in the
letter called "Gobineau to Tree" in "The Great Valley,"
one of the books that succeeded the "Anthology":

> From the photographs
> And the descriptions of your Illinois,
> Where Lincoln spent his youth, I almost sicken;
> Small muddy rivers flanked by bottom lands
> So fat of fertile stuff the grossest weeds
> Thrive thriftier than in Egypt; round their roots,
> Repulsive serpents crawl, the air is full
> Of loathsome insects, and along these banks
> An agued people live who have no life
> Except hard toil, whose pleasures are the dance,
> Where violent liquor takes the gun or knife;

Who have no inspiration save the orgy
Of religious meeting, where the cult
Of savage dreams is almost theirs. The towns
Places of filth, of maddening quietude;
Streets mired with mud, board sidewalks where the men
Like chickens with the cholera stand and squeak
Foul or half-idiot things; nearby the churches
Mere arches to the graveyard. Nothing here
Of conscious plan to lift the spirit up.
All is defeat of liberty in spite
Of certain strong men, of certain splendid breeds,
The pioneers who made your state; no beauty
Save as a soul delves in a master book,
And out of this your Lincoln came, not poor
As Burns was in a land of storied towers,
But, poor as a degenerate breed is poor
Sunk down in squalor.
                              Yet he seems a man
Of master qualities.

Masters' return to the theme of Spoon River so late
as the spring of 1923 is significant of his continued preoccupation with the village in its relation to American
life. "The New Spoon River" is the title given a new
group of poems, serial publication of which began in
the July number of "Vanity Fair." In them Masters en-
deavors to interpret the lives of those who have died
since Spoon River became a "standardized community"
—in other words suffering from all the ailments which
beset the republic itself—foreign influences, materialism,
the madness for money, the lack of high ideals. Spoon
River has been "metropolized," in the phrase of the poet,
and its people have forgotten any spiritual message. One
of them says:

My people came to the U. S. A.
To live in a land of liberty . . .

. . . .

I saw that the thing is money, money,
And the gift of gab for liberty.

And another of the dead complains that "I put walls
between myself and a full life," and "All the while I
could look out of a window upon an America perishing
for life." The author betrays his continued interest in
the themes that engaged him when he wrote the anthology.

Masters may be occupied with the low mentality and
the physical squalor of life in small towns, but he is also
something of a prophet, an exhorter, for he points out,
as in the above poem, that there are great spiritual truths
for those who would seek them, and that the failures
who are strung across his pages somehow have missed
the greatness of the fathers. This is true in his strictures on political affairs. He is a keen observer of the
progress of the republic, and often his verses deal with
a passing political crisis, or lash the stupidities of legis-
lators with a venomous sarcasm. This note also creeps
into his prose—it is present in "Mitch Miller," which
ostensibly is a boy's story of the New Salem country, but
incidentally contains the author's comment on national
affairs.

But most marked is his experimentation, and it is
doubtful whether any author of the Chicago group has
attempted to write so much in so many different styles.
Formal and free verse, rhymed and unrhymed lyrics, prose
in the form of "The Ring and the Book" ("Domesday
Book"), boy's stories, novels realistic and subjective. In
"Children of the Market Place," he attempted a long

prose novel which had for its motive the career of Stephen A. Douglas, but was no doubt also intended to convey a complete picture of the times in which Douglas lived. To accomplish his purpose Masters must have spent long hours over musty files, and must have dug deeply into archives, for the book was freighted with an overwhelming mass of detail of the times, some of it germane to the story, most of it only justified by the size of the canvas. Masters has always been deeply concerned with the influence of environment, and a large part of his books is given over to painting the community in which his characters move and the effect of its restrictions and conventions upon them. This is clear not only in the Douglas story, but also in "Domesday Book," where the death of Elinor Murray exposes a whole group of festering sores. One of his recent books, "Skeeters Kirby," published in the spring of 1923, returns to a more orderly form, and is by far the best prose work that its author has so far done. It aims to be a continuation of the story begun in "Mitch Miller," in that it traces the career as a man of Mitch's pal, Skeeters, and here we have a story of Chicago that comes pretty close down to our day. To write this book Masters must have drawn deeply upon his own knowledge of Chicago of the nineties, for it is with that period that the book principally deals. Through it a youth with a training for law but a passion for the more romantic moods in life views his world; the spark of integrity with which he comes permits him, like Robert Herrick's hero in the "Memoirs," to observe sharp practices in and out of the legal profession with something of a twinge of conscience; still he is the product of his time, influenced by his environment, and he lives the sort of life that one observes compounded out of more realistic materials in Theodore Dreiser's story "A Book About Myself." It was Masters who endorsed the Dreiser book most wholeheartedly, and well he might, for he was able, through his residence here, to appreciate the truth that it contains. "Skeeters Kirby" is, to my mind, evidence of Masters' growth and continued promise. He has never duplicated the "Anthology of Spoon River," but it is not necessary that he should do so. He has gifts in another direction that make him a figure likely to loom large in the literature of the middle west in this decade.

8. Harriet Monroe
Priestess of Poetry

*To have great poets there must be
great editors too.*

WHEN I look over the great number of magazines devoted to modern poetry now flooding the country I wonder how many of them will attain either the age or the record for helpfulness of Miss Harriet Monroe's "Poetry; A Magazine of Verse." It was over ten years ago—almost when the American poetic renaissance was just beginning —that Miss Monroe obtained her first endowment and launched the first number of her magazine, and yet the latest number is as fresh as the first—filled with new names and with poems that make no obeisance to conservatism. This is the more remarkable because Miss Monroe's magazine is not published from a sub-cellar or a garret, but from a comfortable, well-lighted office, and Miss Monroe herself has never had to oil the press, feed the sheets, or work in the bindery in order to live up to her promises to subscribers. . . . There were times when I wondered about this too, and once I sought her out in an effort to arrive at an explanation. The explanation came without my asking, but in an unexpected way. It dawned on me while I sat talking to Miss Monroe and realized that in addition to her mature judgment and undoubted powers of selection she also retained an eagerness for new and beautiful writing, a hatred for restrictions and deadening conventions. Essentially she was a free spirit.

Only recently she was quite willing to break a lance for the new order when she injected herself into the controversy over prosody that Llewellyn Jones and Miss Amy Lowell carry on from season to season, by saying: "The old prosody is a medieval left-over, as completely out of relation with the modern scientific spirit as astrology would be if solemnly enunciated from the summit of Mount Wilson. All the old terms should be scrapped, and a modern science of speech-rhythms should be built up from the too-slight beginnings which have already been made. The lamentable confusion in English prosody is illustrated by the fact that two persons trained in the art, like Miss Lowell and Mr. Jones, should give absolutely different meanings to such simple terms as iam and anapest."

"Poetry" is located "just across the river" in a building once devoted to apartments but more recently transformed for the use of architects, engineers, artists . . . and poets. It lies in the path of commerce and the time is not far distant when great commercial structures will replace even this attractive shrine. I wish that it might be still possible to visit Miss Monroe in her historic office in Cass street, where for a decade indigent poets camped on the broad stone steps and itinerant minstrels rested their packs and exchanged a few lyrics for bread. The picture of Walter von der Vogelweide, clad in colors and caroling his songs down the valley of the Adige may appeal more to the imagination, but to me there is just as much romance and color in the picture of young poets stepping down hurriedly from sooty trains in the heart of an industrial city and hiking before breakfast to the little office in Cass street with portfolios under their arms. To them the need to give their songs to the world was much greater than the hunger of the body for rolls and coffee, and Miss Monroe afforded the only opportunity and hope for both. Vachel Lindsay, David Saul Zolinski, Oscar Williams—one loves to picture them contented to sit on the doorstep in the early dawn, waiting for the coming of their paraclete.

One day when I was comfortably established in a wicker chair in Miss Monroe's office and she was commenting on the rise of poetry, I kept thinking about the part this quiet little woman had played in the renaissance. A great part, surely, and yet I had heard some of the younger poets say that "Poetry" was now a thing established, like the church; that it had gained a certain dignity and reserve with its years and a wariness of youth and novelty. I looked at Miss Monroe and felt that her quiet repose and the low matter-of-fact tone in which she spoke was reflected in the editorials she had written for her magazine these ten years, and concluded that if ever she erred on the side of conservatism one might attribute it to her calm and self-possession. Her chief quality was hospitality; in her magazine at least all schools and voices have been heard; it is to her credit that she was never heard shouting in enthusiastic abandon over one group or another, but that her portals were always open and her doorsteps free. Hers is an unusual service in an unusual age.

The absence of a magazine devoted exclusively to poetry no doubt kept many of the younger poets in America from practising their art; it was their fate to scribble quatrains on desk blotters as they planned advertising campaigns for washing machines, vacuum cleaners and other by-products of a college education. But a revival was already under way when "Poetry" was established in 1912. In that year and those immediately following the trans-Atlantic influence was marked. The Abbey players had helped develop a wide interest in the Irish renaissance a few years before; William Butler Yeats, with twenty years of achievement behind him, was at the height of his powers; men commented on his influence on the writings of Lady Gregory and his espousal of Synge; a young man, Padraic Colum, had just begun to translate from the Gaelic. John Masefield was writing "The Tale of a Round House"; Rupert Brooke had just "come down from Cambridge"; T. Sturge Moore, Lascelles Abercrombie and Richard Aldington were writing often and there was a healthy curiosity about the influence of the *imagistes,* whose aims Ezra Pound published to the world in the famous manifesto.

Before "Poetry" came on the scene Harold Munro's "Poetry and Drama," later "The Poetry Review," was being published in England, but there was no magazine in the United States entirely devoted to poetry and to the encouragement of the new poets. The established magazines had their own formulas that had changed but little from the days of Thomas Bailey Aldrich and Edmund Clarence Stedman, and for the most part used poems to help fill gaps at the end of stories and articles. It was clear that the audience for original work in America was growing but not large enough to support a magazine by subscriptions alone, so that an endowment fund would be needed. Miss Monroe carried her enthusiasm to Hobart C. Chatfield-Taylor, who suggested that if one hundred friends each gave $50 a year for a series of years the magazine could be printed and the poets paid. So Miss Monroe's campaign for the endowment opened in 1911. To say that Miss Monroe's first list of guarantors read like the social register would tell only half the story; the truth was that many of these patrons of the arts were artists themselves and only incidentally members of the first families. For H. C. Chatfield-Taylor, who headed the list, had been writing since the early nineties and had a long list of books to his credit, among which his studies of the lives of Molière and Goldoni were particularly prized; Mrs. Mary Aldis was writing plays and articles for the magazines; Frances Wells Shaw was a poet, and her husband, Howard Van Doren Shaw, an architect of national significance; Mrs. William Vaughn Moody, widow of the poet, had probably done more to encourage authors and poets than any other woman in the middle west; Charles G. Dawes was a keen student of literature and was to prove later his capacity for writing succinct autobiography; Mrs. Emmons Blaine was the donatrix of the school of education at the University of Chicago. It was significant also that Miss Monroe found, among her friends in other cities, Mrs. Charles K. Freer of Detroit, Mich., and Miss Amy Lowell.

There was some anxiety lest the title, "Poetry," which was thought remarkably appropriate, might be used by another magazine about to be founded by the Four Seas company in Boston, but the publication of "Poetry" on September 23, 1912, established the right to the title, and the rival journal appeared in November as the "Poetry Journal." The first number of "Poetry" contained poems by Arthur Davison Ficke and Ezra Pound; an unpublished work by William Vaughn Moody entitled "I Am the Woman"; the "Symphony of a Mexican Garden" by Grace Hazard Conkling, and several other contributions. Miss Monroe announced her aim in the line by Whitman: "To have great poets there must be great audiences too," which the magazine has carried ever since. In the second number Richard Aldington printed his imagist poem, "Choricos," the first he ever published, and Margaret Widdemer and Charles Hanson Towne wrote in rhymed verse. The third number was notable in that it marked the first appearance of Tagore with "Gitanjali"; Yeats had a poem, and a melancholy interest attaches to the publication of "Sangar" by John Reed, dedicated to his devoted friend, Lincoln Steffens. As we turn to the other numbers of the first and second years we become aware of the forcefulness and influence of this magazine. Here was first published "Gen. William Booth Enters Into Heaven," by Vachel Lindsay. The publication of this poem gained an audience for Lindsay in England, and when William Butler Yeats came to Chicago in February, 1914, as the guest of Miss Monroe, he was eager to discuss Lindsay. His remarks to Lindsay as a fellow craftsman, made at the first general meeting of poets in Chicago, deserved especially to be remembered; he spoke of his pleasure in reading "The Congo" and remarked that Lindsay possessed "a strange beauty—but beauty should always be strange," and referred to a remark of Dickens that "there is no excellent beauty without strangeness." . . . By this time "Poetry" had obtained the endowment of two annual prizes, the Helen Haire Levinson prize of $200 for the best poem published during the year, and a prize of $100 instituted by the Friday Woman's Club. And then in 1914 Carl Sandburg's first poems came to Miss Monroe. "They were the 'Chicago Poems,' and I was overjoyed to get them. They had a freshness and force and originality that I liked. It seems that Mrs. Sandburg, who had faith in her husband's work, had submitted them here and there, and finally sent them to me by mail, and they constituted his first acceptance." It was for these poems, beginning with the "Hog Butcher of the World" that Carl Sandburg won the Levinson prize.

Edgar Lee Masters once told the Book and Play club that he would never have written the "Spoon River Anthology" but for "Poetry," and he contributed very early

to its pages. Miss Monroe was also the first editor to
accept a poem by James Branch Cabell, and it was
through her encouragement that Lew Sarett began to
write his Indian lyrics. Miss Amy Lowell, Witter Bynner,
Maxwell Bodenheim, appeared very early in "Poetry";
it was this magazine that published for the first time
"Trees" by Joyce Kilmer, and gave hospitality to the
first writings of Marjorie Allen Seiffert, Hazel Hall, Ivor
Winters, Wallace Stevens, Glenway Wescott, Jessica
Nelson North, Maurice Leseman, Elizabeth Madox
Roberts, and many more. Robert Frost had published
poems in England but "Poetry" gave place to his first
publication in America, as also to the first American
appearance of D. H. Lawrence and John Gould Fletcher
—surely an enviable record for a modest inland publication. As for the inspirational value of Miss Monroe's
example and the benefits of her encouragement, this can
never be accurately measured, but the results are written
in broad characters up and down the land.

9. Lew Sarett
The Prophet of the Thunderdrums

God, let me flower as I will!
For I am weary of the chill
Companionship of waxen vines
And hothouse nurtured colum-
*   bines;*
Oh, weary of the pruning knife
That shapes my prim decorous
*   life—*
Of clambering trellises that hold
*   me,*
Of flawless patterned forms that
*   mold me.*

God, let me flower as I will
A shaggy rambler on the hill!
    Lew Sarett, "The Box of God."

I

ONLY the other day, when I was meditating on the place that Indian legends hold in our literature, and the meager use to which they have been put by our own writers, I tried to reconstruct the picture of Henry Wadsworth Longfellow writing down the story of Hiawatha for the children of America so many years ago. That story became a classic; for generations our teachers drew from it their conception of tribal customs, of native imagery and spiritual values. Longfellow, in his day, might have studied the Indian in his native haunts and in surroundings very similar to those in which Hiawatha lived, yet when he wrote his epic he was a thousand miles away at a desk in a sunshiny room of the Craigie house in Cambridge; out of the diaries of Schoolcraft he extracted this rich ore, and although he had once discussed the theme with Schoolcraft at Mackinac, it was far from the land of the Ojibways and the Dacotahs that he declaimed his stately meters. About him were the amenities of life in an orderly community; Harvard College with its friendly associations, Concord with its group of gentle disputants; the literary shrines of Boston—Park Street, Charles Street, Beacon Hill—with their warm, encompassing hospitality. It is inconceivable that the cloistered scholar who once felt chagrined because a friend did not wear a vest should have tolerated the rough life of a wilderness to gain inspiration for his epic of the red man. . . . Perhaps that is why I think that "The Box of God," by Lew Sarett, means more as an American Indian epic than "Hiawatha." That it will ever achieve the popularity of its predecessor I have no illusions about—the reasons I will discuss later—but that it comes warm and red-blooded from the hidden heart of the American wilderness is to my mind the greatest quality that it possesses. Measure it by such other standards as you will, you must still concede that it owes most of its force to an understanding of the deep spirituality of the Indian. And Lew Sarett came by this understanding honestly and at first hand. He was a wilderness guide before he became a poet; he had tramped across the northwest wilds through all sorts of weather with a pack on his back; had portaged, made camps, cooked frontier meals, and paddled a canoe 9,000 miles in ten summers. And often, even now, when Lew Sarett writes of the Thunderdrums he can see the smoke rising from the wigwams of the Chippewas; when he describes their ancient medicine rites he is within walking distance of the Lake of the Woods or Flute-reed river; when he woos the wind in the pine, the mist of the mesa, or the timberline cedar he is close to the heart of things in Shoshone, or on the upper Yellowstone, or on the Absaroka range. That, perhaps, is why his poetry has in it the essence of native spirituality and philosophy.

Sarett himself draws you to him because there is something healthy and wholesome about him; a big-chested man he is, with large features, bronzed skin, dark hair, dark snappy eyes surrounded by friendly wrinkles, a ready smile, a hearty handclasp. He has won the heart of the Indian as he wins the heart of the white man; he is as much at home in the native attire of the Chippewas, or in the outfit of a forest ranger, as when he presides in conventional attire on the platform of the school of speech of Northwestern University. He is a poet, an orator, a man whose mind is like a sensitized plate, a lover of humanity and of nature—more than that, Lew is an American literary pioneer.

For the rhymes that he has spread before us in his two published books of poems, "Many, Many Moons," and "The Box of God," are the result of his own pioneering. Sometimes they are in rhymed verse and conform roughly to traditional forms; more often they leap out toward you free of all conventional restraint. His most powerful poem, "The Box of God," comes to us uninfluenced by the classic outlines of a "Kalevala." Men in Longfellow's day criticized him for his hexameters, but it was a pedant's quarrel, and the only issue involved was whether or not the classic meter could be naturalized in English. With Sarett the issue is as big and almost identical with that of Sandburg—is poetry something encased within verse forms laid down by another age, or is it simply a cry from the heart, an unburdening of the soul of man in accents and meter that fit the theme and stir the reader with the poet's mood?

Perhaps the answer to that should come from those men and women to whom Lew Sarett has personally carried his message. And that recalls an interesting episode of three or more years ago, when Sarett was just beginning to realize the richness of the treasure he possessed. His first poems, "The Blue Duck," and "Chippewa Flute Song," had been published by Miss Harriet Monroe in "Poetry" and had attracted the attention of Carl Sandburg. Big-hearted Carl wrote Sarett to tell him that he recognized the genuineness of his message. Sandburg had done very little reading in public at that time, and Sarett was practically unknown, so it was arranged that the two men should read their poems from the same platform. Sandburg's part of the program was called "Poems of the City," and Sarett's, "Poems of the Wilderness." Dressed in woodsman costume Sarett sang the love songs of the Chippewas, bellowed the call of the moose and repeated the chants of the medicine men. Some survival of the primitive hates and loves and passions vibrated through the audience as they listened to this eloquent, fiery singer and felt their pulses mount at the incessant beating of his drum. Then came the more deliberate, slow-spoken, deep-toned Sandburg. Poems about men and women toiling in mean streets, of life in the by-ways of the city, displaced poems of the wilderness, of the natives, of the beasts and birds and good and evil spirits of the hills. That was a program to talk about, a rich study in contrasting moods, like the well-remembered lyceum programs of another generation, when Major Pond presented on the same platform James Whitcomb Riley, singer of homely sentiment, and Bill Nye, jokesmith of the frontier settlements, and men laughed and wept in turn. When Lew Sarett came to publish his first book of poems, "Many, Many Moons," Carl Sandburg wrote the introduction. There was one significant sentence: "Many, Many Moons," said Carl, paraphrasing "Zarathustra," "says 'yes' to life."

II

Life—Lew Sarett knows life; he lives it intensely and writes it into all his poems. His is not a surface acquaintance with the greatest of all adventures. His boyhood years were harsh; he had to fight every step of the way. Except for a certain sense of direction he might have come out of his adolescence a finished Halsted

Street tough. His unconquerable spirit ordained otherwise. When he came to write poetry he was not a college
sophomore sitting down to whittle rhymes after the fashion of the parlor poets; poetry simply welled up in him
and commanded him to write. Emotionally he is blood
brother to the Indian of the north. He is brother likewise to all humankind. His is a large heart, open to
large friendships, open to deep, lasting sympathies. Here
is a big, broad-shouldered man, singing loudly of life in
the open, of life with men whose music has become dis-
cordant in alien hands, whose dreams have been made
commonplace through misunderstanding.

Some of his passion for interpretation comes out so
eloquently in the title of his new book, "The Box of
God" (Henry Holt & Co.), that I am going to leave off
talking about the man himself to discuss his poem. True,
it is a revelation of the soul of this man, of his deep
spiritual nature, of his pantheistic approach to the
mystical forces that underlie all nature. But it is more
than that—to me it is one of the great tragic poems of
our generation. It was published originally in "Poetry"
a year ago, and although it evoked a great deal of favor-
able comment, its true significance appears to have been
lost to all save Miss Harriet Monroe, Louis Untermeyer,
Carl Sandburg, and half a dozen other kindred souls. In
brief, the poem recounts the conversion of Joe Shing-ob,
or Joe Spruce, whom the priests call Pagan Joe, to
orthodox religion. Weak of body, wearied of soul,
smitten by wasting disease, Pagan Joe enters the little
Christian chapel which the Indians know as "the Box of
God," and turns his back upon the mystical pantheism
of his fathers which endows the whole face of nature
with spirits of good and evil.

He has already made this decision when the poet be-
gins his story, and the first section of the poem, "Broken
Bird," recounts how the black-robed curés won Pagan
Joe to their cause. The poet's story is a lament; Pagan
Joe to him is the high-flying eagle, who, crippled of
wing, has now been brought into the foursquare "box of
God"—

> To flutter against the bars in futile flying,
> To beat against the gates,
> To droop, to dream a little, and to die.

In the second section, "Whistling Wings," the poet
recalls in retrospect the nobility of the Indian's belief in
the pantheism to which he has become apostate. So intensely moving is this part of the poem that the reader
feels that the poet is giving voice to his own intimate
beliefs and convictions. When we fully grasp the poet's
grief at the apostasy of his friend, the full tragedy is
apparent. The poet has put all his emotional fervor into
depicting the glories of the Indian pantheism, by the side
of which the persuasive arguments of the missionaries
seem hollow, forced, and unreal. Line after line celebrates the wonders of the woods and waters, of the hills
and valleys, the trees, the birds, the wild game, all named
and endowed with miraculous faculties in Indian my-
thology. As if in a last attempt to hold the dying Indian
to his ancient faith the poet recounts their adventures
together, their musings on the forces of nature, and how
Pagan Joe, "companion of my old wild years, in the land
of K'tchee-gah-mee my good right arm," himself was
stirred by the manifestations of a spiritual force in
nature:

Do you recall the cruise to Flute-reed falls?
Our first together. . . . How we talked
Till dawn of the Indian's Keetchie Ma-ni-do,
The Mighty Spirit and of the white man's God.
Don't you remember dusk at Cold-spring Hollow?
The beaver pond at our feet, its ebony pool
Wrinkled with silver, placid, calm as death,
Save for the fitful chug of the frog that flopped
His yellow jowls upon the lily pad
And the quick wet slap of the tails of beaver hurrying
Homeward across the furrowing waters, laden
With cuttings of tender poplar? . . .

And after each reminiscence the poet tells how Pagan
Joe tried to communicate to his companion something
of the Indian reverence for the spirits that dwell in
nature—in the beaver pond, mayhap; in the thrush, in
the bullfrog, on Mont du Père, in the big water of
K'tchee-gah-mee:

Sh-sh-sh. . . . Look Ah-deek—on K'tchee-gah-mee!
Somebody—someting, he's in dere . . . ain't?
He's sleep w'ere black Big-water she's deep . . . Ho!
In morning he's jump up from hees bed and race
Wit' de wind; to-night he's sleeping . . . rolling little—
Dreaming about hees woman . . . rolling . . . sleeping . . .

No wonder that the poet mourns in the accents of a
pitiful threnody:

O eagle, crippled of pinion, clipped of soaring wing,
They brought you to a four-square box of God;
And they left you there to flutter against the bars
In futile flying, to beat against the gates,
To droop, to dream a little, and to die . . .

Ah, Joe the pagan, son of a bastard people,
Child of a race of vanquished, outlawed children,
Small wonder that you drooped your weary head
Blinding your eyes to the suns of elder days,
For hungry bellies look for new fat gods,
And heavy heads seek newer, softer pillows.

Here in the place of death—God's fenced-in ground!—
Beneath these put-in pines and waxen lilies,
They placed you in a crimson gash in the hillside . . .

I have said that it is the poet's heart speaking. Let us go back and see where it all began.

Before you open a book of Sarett's poems you must know that the wilderness is his passion. It stirs him as nothing else does. It got into his blood when he was a kid, and it still survives. He was born in Chicago but the biggest part of his boyhood was spent in Marquette, Mich., on Lake Superior. That's where he first came to know the woods. As a youngster of ten years he would hike out into the woods far from human habitation and observe the habits of the birds and the beasts. In the summer he would hit for a trout stream; in the winter he set traps, followed trails, observed the habits of the wild creatures. He got to know the meaning of a bit of turned-up moss, of a bunch of woodpecker feathers, of moose tracks in the muck; he collected bugs, butterflies, agates, quartz and strange rocks, bird's eggs, bear tusks, moose teeth, old antlers, arrow heads, and war clubs of a forgotten age. He slept out in the open or in improvised shelters. This was the foundation for his love of the wilderness which was to color all his life and all his writings.

Later on, at nineteen, when years of privations and

drudgery had intervened, he took up camping, studied woodcraft carefully, and began guiding expeditions into the north. He went into the timber country of Ontario, Can., tramped in lands near Hudson's Bay, became acquainted again with the wild life of forests hardly touched by the hand of man. That is where nature got into his bones—as he once said: "I don't merely 'admire' nature; I don't 'enjoy' the 'beauty of nature'—it's more than these merely esthetic emotions, more vital, more elemental; it's a passion that I feel and that I try to put into my poems."

Lew Sarett confesses to belief in a pantheism that differs from that of the Indian only in that the Indian believed in both good and evil spirits, whereas Sarett believes only in good spirits. "It seems to me that God shows himself in the wild, naked country as he shows himself nowhere else," Sarett once told me. "And by God I mean the great creative power, a wild, pagan god —my god—I use the word in that sense in 'The Book of God,' and in all my poems. He is not a personal god, but a pantheistic god; I am assured that he can be reconciled with our Christian God, but I make no effort to reconcile him. In the woods you feel his presence as you can never feel it in the city. He shows himself as nowhere else in the sleeping mountains, in the quiet valleys at dusk, in the night-skies. There is one great spiritual fact upon which I have a tight grasp; that fact is the fact of God; the consciousness, the belief, the intuition that some great power is loose in this world, is working constantly through the universe, sees and moves and talks in a hundred mysterious ways. It does not matter what we call it—some call it "the great spirit"; some call it "all-harmony"; the Indians call it "Keetchie

Manido," the big spirit. Whatever you call him, it is in the woods that you feel his presence most keenly; it's in the woods that you hear him talk and see his hand moving. And there you come to know him, and learn to talk with him. That is how I came to write these poems. I hardly ever write a poem without feeling that this spirit is clamoring for expression."

And so we came to talk about "The Box of God," and the feeling he had put into it, and what it all meant.

He had been meditating for a long time on the deep spiritual reserve of the Indian and on the latter's inability to utter it. He had been out hunting and fishing and berrying with Indians for the fun of the thing, and found that as twilight came on and cloistered silences of the woods invoked confidences between men, the Indian would invariably fail in an attempt to formulate his consciousness of God in words. His religion was mystical, intangible—there was the feel of the thing, but it was too evanescent to capture. The Indian recognized and communed with the minor spirits in the bodies of animals—especially in the bear, the beaver, the eagle, the snowy owl, and the frog, all good spirits; then the more powerful spirits in the four winds, and finally with the Keetchie Manido, the big spirit. And the Indian feared the bad spirits in the wolverine, the snake, and in the little red toad that lives in the stumps of trees—the latter most of all. And then the bigger evil spirits—the big sea snake, the thunderbird, who comes with the electric storms, and the spirit that lives in the center of the earth, the Muchie Manido. Yet the Indian is powerless to express himself concretely and vividly.

"I remember one night when I was out in the big timber with an old Indian named Fine-Day," said

Sarett. "We got talking about it. Fine-Day pointed to dusky Mt. Josephine and said: 'Somebody, he's in Josephine.' He pointed to Lake Superior and said: 'Somebody, he's in K'tchee-gum.' He pointed to the moon and said: 'Somebody, he's in Tee-bee-ke-gee-siss.' That was all he said."

The setting for the poem seemed to spring up overnight. When Sarett was a wilderness guide he lived at Grand Marais, Minn., nearly one hundred and fifty miles northwest of Duluth, thirty miles from Grand Portage and not reached by any railroad. It is a wild country— two miles back from the shores of Lake Superior lies a wilderness unspoiled by man. Grand Marais itself has a population of only four hundred, of which two hundred are full-blooded Indians and the rest French-Canadians, many of them half-caste. Grand Portage has a handful of Indians and is an old Hudson's Bay post. Fishing, hunting, and trapping is about all the neighborhood affords, and with this the Indians keep themselves occupied.

One day in the forest behind the village on the Pigeon River Reservation, Sarett discovered the log cabin of a little mission. He had heard in Grand Marais that a missionary priest came once a month to this place to conduct services and make converts. He looked through the windows of the house and then went inside the little chapel. It was primitive and must have been built much like the crude chapels erected in the western wilds hundreds of years ago by the earliest missionaries. There were a dozen wooden benches for the congregation; in front, a small, wooden altar; on the walls a few cheap, tawdry chromos of saints; a few plaster casts. All over the interior hung long streamers of gaudy colored tissue paper, green, red, yellow, and blue, with rosettes and glittering tinsel.

To Sarett, with his poet mind wide awake to the spiritual implications of nature displayed so lavishly outside the log house, all this colored paper and tinsel was a weak attempt to interest the child mind of the Indian with toys. White men, contemptuous of the religious feeling with which the Indian endowed all nature, asked him to desert the god he found in the open and come within this house and acknowledge God when the priest invoked his presence in an alien ritual. The missionaries spoke of the Indian as a pagan, and yet the Indian probably came as closely into communion with the god of us all in his own humble way as the white man—still disputing with his fellows over the true revelation—did in his. True, the Indian had peopled the hills and the woods with sprites even as did the ancient pagans, in a fashion said to be abhorrent to the true god, and yet his Keetchie Manido, the great spirit, hovered over all and enfolded the red children within his love even as did the god of the white men, and the Muchie Manido was there working evil even as the white man acknowledged the existence of a devil who ruled in hell. Sarett contemplated all this and came to the conclusion that there was great cause for recognizing the simplicity and beauty of the Indian pantheism.

"I can't describe how I felt," he told me, "except to convey to you a feeling of weariness that I had when I considered the cajolery and brow-beating that passes for religious evangelism among us. And I knew and felt the beauty and sweep and immanence of the religious world of pagan Indian thought, and I felt that the god of the Indian and the church of the Indian were big and real with the colors and power and mystery of all the earth, coming out of a passionate love for the beauty of God as he shows himself in the rippling muscles of the deer and caribou, the marten and the mink, in the gleam of stars and the falling snow, in the sweep of big waters, in the language of the rapids and the winds. What might be revealed in a house of logs, thirty by forty feet in size, seemed to me inconsequential in comparison.

"I threw all this feeling into my poem. I have never written anything with such fever and passion and joy. I worked at it about a year and the first draft was fully several thousand words long. I was voicing my own feeling and what I really knew about the heart of the Indian. I reveled in Part Two—"Whistling Wings," which is a series of lyrical pictures strung together on a thread of narrative, and in which I endeavored to picture the Indian's pantheistic conception of the universe, and you will find in it the note of fear, of dreadful power, of impersonality; the harsher, more fatalistic side of the pagan god. God is not always kind and beneficent; he is as much concerned in protecting the enemies of the human race as protecting man against them, for otherwise the Indian cannot explain rattlesnakes, wolves, famine and pestilence, forest fires and drought. I felt the existence of that god as the Indian did; I was ready to bow my knee before him, before his beauty, his power, and his will. And so in Part Two I wrote with a passion because I was writing about the most powerful force, the biggest inspiration in my life, from which I get what strength I have and what happiness I have found and what zest for living and working and fighting that is within me. That is the story of the origin of the poem, and for that matter of all of my poems."

I reminded Sarett that a critic had once commented that no priest would use the line he attributes to the black robed curé in his poem: "Pagans, ye men of bastard birth! Bend, bow ye, proud heads, before this hallowed shrine!"

Sarett pulled at his pipe a bit before he replied. "And yet I heard the very epithet used by a priest," he said. "In fact I once heard a missionary say to the Indians: 'If I say to Mt. Josephine, Move!—she will move!'"

III

Sometimes Sarett comes down to Schlogl's, and we sit at the big table and talk. He gets out his pipe, and fills it from an ample pouch of Indian workmanship, and puffs complacently. Bit by bit he told me about his career. It is in itself an eloquent life story.

His father was French and his mother of Polish and Lithuanian stock, and their American residence began in 1880 when they came here as steerage passengers. Lew Sarett was born in Chicago amid airless, treeless tenements. But in his childhood his parents moved to Marquette, Mich., and here, until he was twelve years old, he grew up with a love for the open. The pastures, the hills, the timberlands—all nature became his very own.

When he was twelve years old he came to Chicago once more, and through a series of family misfortunes he was left stranded here with his mother; without friends or relatives and no one to turn to for help. The boy immediately took upon himself the burden of supporting his mother. They found two barren rooms in a ramshackle house in Solon Place, just off 14th Street and Blue Island Avenue, which was then the breeding

place of pickpockets, prostitutes, and "snow-birds." His
mother tried to get money by doing odds and ends of
household work, but her earnings were meager; she suffered severely from want and cried a great deal. It fell
upon the lad to do most of the fighting in this uneven
battle for existence.

He picked up all sorts of odd jobs. He could play the
piano fairly well and once he got a job in Hull House
playing at a dance for a party of Italians. He earned one
dollar there, and although he and his mother needed food
he bought a valentine for two bits and brought it to her,
thinking she would be happier and not cry so much.
Eventually he landed a job selling papers for the
Chicago "Daily News." He had a route and got the
papers for peddling in the loop late in the afternoon;
often he would sleep in the alley behind the publication
office of the newspaper, lying in front of a grating
through which the foul warm air of a restaurant was
blown into the alley. "And twelve years later," said
Sarett, in telling this incident, "I went into the office of
the 'Daily News' by its front door as an accredited lec-
turer on its free lecture staff, with my photograph in the
paper. I can't explain the joy I felt, and the feeling of
security that it gave me."

From newspaper peddling Sarett turned to the stores;
he became a cash boy in a large clothing house at $2.50
a week and to save car fare he walked to and from his
home; his lunch was just plain bread and butter. The
two rooms that he and his mother lived in cost $4.50 a
month. There were no friends, his mother cried a great
deal, and the lad himself was heartsick for the woods.
He had no intimates; the boys and girls he met around
Solon place were tough and given to committing petty

offenses; the girls were foul-mouthed and the boys took up thieving and sometimes, at twelve and fourteen, became cocaine fiends. "Every once in a while I find the name of one of those lads in the criminal records," said Sarett. "Four especially, that I knew, went the route. All of them were sent up—one for holding up a saloon-keeper, one for petty thieving in the Y. M. C. A., one for rape, another for peddling cocaine on Halsted Street. Poor kids, it wasn't so much their fault—they lived in neighborhoods filled with saloons, gambling hells, houses of prostitution; Chicago of that day did very little for its adults, much less for the young and impressionable children who were condemned to live near these hell-holes.

"On the hot summer nights the folks in these ramshackle tenements would be driven out of doors by the heat. They would go into the street, or on the roof, and you can guess how it affected a kid who had loved the woods like I did. Lots of nights I would walk down to the lake front and out on a pier in Lake Michigan and I'd fling myself down and lie there all night long, never sleeping, just lying in the cool lake breeze. I used to listen to the chugging of the lake steamers as they slid down the river and out into the open sea, and often I wondered whether they hit Marquette. And then I'd study the stars and locate my old friends the bear and the north star, and figure out the direction of our old home on Lake Superior. I may have been starving physically in those days but I was a whole lot more hungry for the woods and the wild things."

Sarett's next job took him to a department store; he got a raise to $2.75 a week and for this consideration became chief factotum in an employees' lavatory in

Schlesinger & Mayer's store. The lavatory was under the sidewalk; here the lad suffered even more, for he had no chance to get out into the light of day during working hours. There was a chance that if he hung on he might eventually get a job on a truck, but before that happened he found a want advertisement calling for a boy to do errands. He ran all the way to the place and captured the job. This paid $3.00 a week and for this sum he carried bundles, delivered packages, oiled machinery and swept out in a sweat shop, a skirt factory in Chicago's wholesale clothing district. It was while in this occupation that he made friends with Pat Mulcahey, whom Sarett remembers affectionately as a bartender in "Hinky Dink" McKenna's saloon at Clark and Van Buren streets. Pat had a good heart—he permitted Sarett to sneak into the place and make an ample meal off crackers and nippy cheese without exacting the tribute of a drink at the bar.

About this time the skies cleared up a bit; Sarett's father recovered from his incapacity and again became the breadwinner for the family. Sarett in the meantime had been trying to study nights at Hull House, and had begun to read books. The father obtained a job in Benton Harbor, Mich., and there the lad and his mother joined him and Sarett got a chance to go to high school. He worked on fruit farms, caught fish and sold them, picked berries, and got a chance to swim and play. He learned to debate in the high school debating teams and for the first time began to feel the urge of a better education. He went in for long distance swimming and at various times saved persons from drowning in the St. Joe River. For this he received several medals and this was indirectly the reason for his getting a place as life guard in the Chicago south park system when he was graduated from high school.

During his high school experience Sarett began to put in his summers camping. He first worked in a summer camp at Mercer, Wis., coaching athletics, swimming, life saving, and woodcraft. His scope increased and several years later he was doing woodcraft work and guiding campers into the north woods. From this time on his development became more rapid. He determined to work his way through the University of Michigan and began his studies there. In his second year Beloit College offered him the position of assistant athletic director in track, wrestling, and gymnasium work. He accepted this and entered into all the college activities with a will—oratory as well as athletics claimed him and he went in for football, track, and intercollegiate debate. He won his baccalaureate degree in 1911 and then entered Harvard College to study law. This proved a severe physical strain for he had to work to earn money for his studies. Three nights a week he taught English in a Boston settlement house, coached the athletic teams of several Boston clubs and organized a small class of retail merchants and taught them business law. His work and his studies occupied him until two A.M. every night and for one whole year he stuck to this routine. Then at twenty-three years of age came an offer from the University of Illinois to join its public speaking staff as an assistant at $800 a year and he accepted. There Sarett taught public speaking and studied law and in 1916 took his law degree. He remained at the University of Illinois until 1920 when he joined the school of speech of Northwestern University, where he is now professor of argumentation and persuasion.

IV

It is perhaps necessary to know this much about Sarett to realize how his strong and powerful personality developed; but by far the most interesting phase of his career is that which deals with his tramps through the woods. These began in his Benton Harbor days and from that time on he let no summer go by without his spending two or three months in the wilds. As his knowledge of woodcraft developed he became acquainted with strange out-of-the-way places where white men rarely penetrated. It was then that he learned to know the Indian in his native haunts and to understand his philosophy and spirituality. In the Ontario country, where all travel is by water and where there are no roads, Sarett became an expert canoe man; in the Rocky Mountains, which he first visited in 1920 as a forest ranger in the United States forestry service, he learned how to handle a horse on mountain patrols. In 1919, when he was working among the Indians of the Brule river and Pigeon river country, he was given a Chippewa name, Pay-shig-ah-deek, or Lone Caribou, in tribal ceremony. It was during these pilgrimages to the wilderness that the urge to write came upon him, and his first work, produced purely on impulse and as the result of a desire to sing about the wild life, was not actually intended for publication.

An interesting sidelight on the character of Lew Sarett is his love for Carl Sandburg. As in the case of so many poets he expressed it in a poem, which he called "The Granite Mountain." It reads:

> I know a mountain, lone it lies
> Under wide blue Arctic skies,

Gray against the crimson rags
Of sunset loom its granite crags,

Gray granite are the peaks that sunder
The clouds and gray the shadows under.

Sarett said of the poem: "I wrote it—well, because I loved Carl, and because Carl is a granite mountain. Odd —when I had completed the poem, I thought I had failed. It was too cold, didn't say all I felt. Later William Marion Reedy took it for his 'Mirror,' and the critics who reviewed 'Many, Many Moons' praised it."

Once I asked Lew Sarett how he came to choose his medium. "I owe it all to Harriet Monroe," he said. "I was teaching at the University of Illinois when Miss Monroe came there to lecture on the new poetry. Her advice: 'Build your own vehicle' made a tremendous impression on me. I then wrote as I felt and in the form that best expressed my thought. When I had finished 'The Blue Duck' I sent it to Miss Monroe and she printed it in 'Poetry' for November, 1920. I wouldn't change a word of it to-day. I also owe a great deal to the inspiration of Stuart P. Sherman. He is a fine friend and a wholesome influence at the University of Illinois."

Lew Sarett's poems are not translations or transcriptions, but rather original poems built up from the suggestion received in Indian dances, songs, and chants. The underlying philosophy, that the great spirit is everywhere and in everything, Sarett has made his own; it permeates all his work. "I know of no race that has a more real and more spiritual contact with nature than the Indian," said Sarett. "Every act of his life, the most ordinary and the most highly organized ritualistic ceremony, has some spiritual significance; his dances, his legends, his manner of smoking, his trapping, his incantations—all are bound up with some phase of nature. And as I am so thoroughly in sympathy with much of his philosophy I find it easy to use Indian themes as vehicles for my own feeling." How successful he has been in this may be inferred from the comment once made on his work by Mrs. Alice Corbin Henderson, who declared that Sarett uses both the Indian method in his poetry, getting thoroughly inside the Indian's heart and soul, and the objective method from the standpoint of the white man. And part of this immersion into the Indian's mind is due to Sarett's close participation in the practices of the grand medicine society of the Indians, to which only pagan Indians belong. No white man actually belongs to this organization, but Sarett has been able to take part in its ceremonies, its medicine-making, and its conferring of degrees. He has recorded in notes the whole theory of creation of the Chippewas, the development of their medicine society, its beliefs on death, life, and religion. "If ever I work up these notes from an anthropological and scientific standpoint I promise you it will be interesting," said Sarett. "I have drunk so deep at the fountain-head of Indian paganism that I am constantly tempted to give expression to its beauty and mysticism in poetry."

Often friends express their preference, among all his poems, for a bit called "The Great Divide" [in "Many, Many Moons," Henry Holt & Co.], which is sometimes compared to Tennyson but which, according to Lew Sarett, is a pantheistic poem, filled with Indian imagery:

> When I drift out on the silver sea
> O may it be

A blue night
With a white moon
And a sprinkling of stars in the cedar tree;
And the silence of God
And the low call
Of a lone bird—
When I drift out on the silver sea.

10. Wallace Smith and the Symbolical and Diabolical Straight Black Line

> *Art . . . is being chained to a galley oar and exulting in the clean sweep of the graceful blade; it is pulling at tendrils hauling at a stone that will be part of the pyramids and rejoicing that one may thus serve divinity; it is a mother dog eyeing her latest litter and proudly assuring herself of its technique and originality.*
>
> Wallace Smith.

THE oddest fact about Wallace Smith is that he is a man of warm friendships—an emotional man, of great depressions and glad rejoicings, and yet a careful student of his fellows; a man who loves colors and color contrasts, who responds quickly and intensively to beauty in mountain and valley, in seashore and plain;—this man, who draws with his black pen strange, distorted creatures that seem to be writhing in the torments of hell, that seem to express in their tortured aching limbs all the woes of humankind.

One year ago Wallace Smith was still drawing newspaper caricatures, and perhaps few persons who watched the evolution of his race track tout from day to day dreamed that the pen that gave that portrait birth could portray irony, satire, pain, and intense. emotional suffering in powerful sketches in black and white. Since that time, in one year, Wallace Smith's drawings have become a distinctive phenomenon in American illustration. They have appeared chronologically, in these books: "Fantazius Mallare," by Ben Hecht (Covici-McGee, 1922); "The Shadow-Eater," by Benjamin de Casseres (American Library Service, 1923); "Blackguard," by Maxwell Bodenheim; "Actor-views," by Ashton Stevens and "The Shining Pyramid," by Arthur Machen (all Covici-McGee, 1923), and "The Florentine Dagger," by Ben Hecht (Boni & Liveright, 1923). They signalize the strange, unheralded artistic emergence of a man who combines with his knowledge of what a black line can do a gift for luminous, colorful prose. And in addition to these drawings Wallace Smith now comes forward both as author and artist in a collection of melodramatic tales "out of the dust of Mexico" called "The Little Tigress" (Putnam), in which he has dropped his symbolical style and presented forceful drawings along more conventional lines—although still strongly individual—and descriptive and imaginative prose that places him in a category with W. Somerset Maugham and easily surpasses the writings of John Russell and Llewellyn Powys among recent arrivals.

"All strength and beauty lies in the straight line," is a favorite remark of his. Over and over again he has used the straight line as against the curve, applied to it his tremendous creative fecundity, developed it, pursued it with brilliant technical skill. Over and over again the straight line becomes the backbone of his art. He stands tall and erect like a young sapling. He is at his best in drawing men. Those versed in symbolism may find this a logical deduction.

Externally there are half a dozen Wallace Smiths. There is Wallace Smith in khaki, riding over the Mexican foothills, strong, robust, radiating health and energy. There is Wallace Smith of the editorial room, quick, nervous, chafing at confinement within four walls. There is Wallace Smith as you meet him on the Avenue—a jaunty air, a springy step, clear-eyed, well-groomed, a marigold in the button hole of a double-breasted serge coat; swinging a cane. And then the Wallace Smith of the room in which he works, bending over an improvised desk, drawing with an old pen and a withered ruler, applying himself to the task, hour after hour, through daylight, dusk, dark, into the dawn—six hours, eight hours, twelve hours, fourteen hours at a stretch, working like an engraver with tremendous industry and concentration upon one drawing—the Wallace Smith who comes to us with a new note in interpretative illustration.

Like Carl Sandburg, like Sherwood Anderson, like Ben Hecht, like Edgar Lee Masters, Wallace Smith owes his skill to no man. No art institute can claim him as an alumnus; no commercial art house can boast of giving him "his start"; no social teas in dimly lighted studios ruined him, no "movements" marked him for their own. His drawings are the product of the desire to express himself artistically; as in the case of Sherwood Anderson this desire might have been diverted into music or literature. This desire—plus a power of concentration.

Only a man with these two qualities well developed could have produced these disfigurements of the human form, these emaciated, clongated creatures that live in the diseased imagination of Fantazius Mallare. Look at the eight tableaux (if the law permits) and observe how firm the hand, how powerful the grip upon the pen that drew even these bony caricatures of men in torment. Follow the lines and see where the artist's keen sight has placed them—the black lines and the white lines—and then reflect that these white lines are simply an absence of black, for Wallace Smith never uses white paint; he never corrects a lost line; he never stultifies his idea by scratching or painting in; that is the cardinal sin—rather would he tear up his drawing and begin anew. On his table stands only one inkbottle—of black—and there is only one pen. And until a few weeks ago, when a friend insisted on the acceptance of a gift, Wallace Smith had never owned a drawing table or even a T-square.

In the days when I first came to know him Wallace Smith was sitting at a reporter's desk in our old local room. He had just turned twenty then, I believe, but he was already the star reporter of the staff and there were few assignments that did not, some time or other, fall to his lot. Even in his earliest newspaper days Wallace stood apart from the whole reporter tribe by his careful attire; often he was a study in black, perhaps with a black stock in the days when stocks were first worn, and maybe carrying a black cane with a silver head. He worked quickly, and between editions he had time for leisure, and I recall that he often sat at his desk drawing heads and hands while gossiping with his colleagues; always heads and hands, hands with strange, swollen knuckles, chins with warts and stubbles, noses with unnatural protuberances. His "line" was human interest, but there was no incident, however minute, that he could not develop to first page dimensions; he possessed the gift of expansion, and as Keith Preston once said of another, "given a bone he could reconstruct a whole dinosaur." And the "desk" had use for him; it used him for comedy and tragedy, for politics and crime, and Wallace got close to the hearts of simple folk by that attitude of sympathy and comradely understanding which makes friends for him to-day. At times he enjoyed a hoax—it was Wallace Smith who discovered that high on the apex of the figure on the Montgomery Ward tower perched an eagle, and for days Chicago thronged the streets and alleys to watch this motionless creature, only to be convinced after long straining of necks that the bird was part of Mercury's wand. His salary was always big, his stories were always expansive, his expense account always leaned to the side of generosity to all men; he came and went in princely fashion; in olden times he might have been preceded by a roll of drums. And when we lost him to Hearst we mourned.

During all those years that Wallace Smith was drawing bones and knuckles and reporting golden weddings
and hangings he used to sit up nights with his old pen
and a sheet of white paper. "You must have had the
urge," began a friend. "I never had an urge," inter-
rupted Wallace Smith. "I never knew what an urge was.
I had a bread board for an easel and a yardstick for a
ruler and I kept as far away as I could from artists with
great big terrible goatees and long hair. Once I enrolled
in an art school; but the instructor had on make-up and
thought everybody ought to draw like he did, so I walked
out and never went back. Then I thought I would study
lettering. I took my place in an evening class and began
to draw, and finally the instructor came to me and said.
'That is wrong, Mr. Smith. The letter H is drawn like
this: a shaded line here, a thin line there.' 'But mine is
a new letter,' I replied. 'My dear Mr. Smith, there are
no new styles in lettering; Larsson in Sweden was the
last man to invent a series, and you must follow the accepted form.' 'You mean that I can't draw the lettering
I want to draw?' I said. 'I am afraid not.' 'Good-by,'
said I and never went back. So you see I have never
had any art training. And I know nothing about artists.
In spite of that fact I have impressed Ben Hecht with
my knowledge of art. Ben and I used to wander over
to the Art institute once in a while, and I would absorb
valuable pointers on what not to do. I used to hear Ben
talk about Botticelli. Once he stopped abruptly before
a large painting and said: 'Who painted that?' 'Botticelli,' I said because that was the only word I knew.
And it was true. After that nothing could shake Ben's
faith in my knowledge of painting."

But when Wallace Smith speaks like that—when he

deliberately tells you how poor his preparation, how weak his knowledge of the classical painters, you suspect that he is "playing down"—that he is presenting himself at an unfair valuation. Years ago it was manifestation of a lack of confidence in himself; of a discouraged feeling that the world with its standardized painting would never accept him. Artists who belonged to the elect and were hung in fashionable galleries confused him, but unlike another youngster who would have become a rebel and declared war against all schools he merely buried his dissatisfaction within himself and kept aloof from the groups. Keenly sensitive, sometimes nervous, often haunted by moods of depression, he became a victim of the delusion that the heights were not for him. He avoided art and artists; he sought out men decidedly his inferiors, perhaps from an inverted and mistaken notion that among his equals he was not accepted at full value. He came to know and cultivated prize fighters, gamblers, ward politicians. Their picturesqueness appealed to his eye, but their openness and lack of snobbery won his heart. Criminals interested him and there is cherished in our local room the fact that once a murderer, whom Smith had come to know in his reporting at the county jail, refused to mount the gallows until assured that Wallace Smith was present. For his daily task he drew a series of newspaper pictures of a race track tout with comment in that worthy's vernacular. Neither his work nor his choice of friends represented his real self.

The studio in the Chicago apartment where Wallace Smith makes his drawings is, in matter of fact, merely a bedroom, but there is a strange fascination in the drawings that are tacked up about the walls—drawings that compel the eye to turn now this way, now that. A single

electric lamp with an improvised shade hangs down over
the drawing board, throwing all its light on the solitary
figure that bends over the paper. If Wallace talks, like
as not his preoccupation is with Mexico, with the open
roads of California, with the deep skies and wide plateau
of the southern ranges. He enjoys the saddle; likes to
go on long tramps through virgin woods; makes companions of mountaineers and forest rangers. To hear
him tell about it is a delight; his narrative is lived intensely in the re-telling; he is emphatic and colorful and
his gestures are original and widely known. Best of all
he likes to talk about wild rides after Villa in Chihuahua,
for there the freedom from conventional restraint and
the intensity with which each moment of life was lived
won his heart. While with the Pershing punitive expedi-
tion and the Carranzistas as a correspondent he witnessed
skirmishes, bull fights and executions; in the hands of
the Villistas in lonely Chihuahua he narrowly missed
execution as a spy and international fame. What im-
presses him is that death always stalks along by the side
of the living in Mexico, leering in their faces; but it is
the careless attitude toward death, the flourish with which
men meet their end, the dramatic staging of events we
consider tragic, that live in his imagination. It is this
milieu that appears in his "The Little Tigress."

"Wonderful people! Marvelous people!" exclaimed
Wallace one night in his studio, and I slumped down in
a comfortable wicker chair and let him ramble on: "How
they die! Think of it—always the same ritual, always
the same courage. The prisoner is marched up to a
wall, the firing squad takes position. The sentence is
read to him. Has he anything to say? Yes, he will
make a speech. An oration—a glowing oration in which

he justifies himself, his party, his country. The firing squad stands silent. The captain stands politely attentive. The captain offers to roll him a cigarette. No, he will roll his own cigarette, to prove that his hands don't tremble. He will permit the captain to light it for him? Yes,—that too, a part of the ritual. And his last words in a ringing voice: 'Viva Mexica!' Always that, no matter what party he belongs to, Villistas, Carranzistas, —always 'Viva Mexica!'

"And talk about a sense of the dramatic, of the fitness of things—one day I saw three brothers shot, one after the other. They took a stand before a wall and when the first brother fell his head struck the wall. When the second brother fell his head also struck the wall. The third brother saw the undignified attitude in which this left the corpse. He took his place in turn, faced the firing squad and then marched three steps forward so that he might not fall against the wall. Always dramatic—in Mexico!"

We fell silent for a space, and then:

"I tried to draw an execution once," said Smith. "In tempera. But I didn't finish."

"Life would seem to be rather trivial and useless after a turn at Mexican executions," was my comment.

"Let me tell you where I had that impressed upon me," was Wallace's quick reply. "Out in the Malibu district of California, out of Los Angeles by the Santa Monica road. When I go there in the fall, to forget the city, and to roam the hills and to look a mountain lion in the face now and then, I hear the great roar of the sea again and again, night and day. One day I had been tramping about a lot and I hit a high hill and climbed it, and lo—this like Balboa, understand—there lay the

sea. I looked at those great waves rolling out over the
sand and I said to myself: 'There she is pounding like a
great fist against the land, and she's been doing that for
hundreds of thousands of years, for all eternity perhaps.
And life, compared with that, is what? And here I stand,
and nothing accomplished. 'If you're going to do any
thing you've got to do it fast,' I said to myself.

"I think I found myself out there.

"In Mexico there was a campanero of mine who was
a growling, sullen beast in camp and a light-hearted,
cheerful fellow in a skirmish. I asked him why once,
after he had sung a merry little song through a gallop-
ing exchange of shots, and he couldn't explain except
that when there was action life seemed to straighten
itself out and become beautifully simple. 'Either you
do or you don't in a fight,' he said, and no petty squabbling about it; no bickering with the bullet of the bandit
whose curse sent the shot away from the Mauser muzzle
no less vehemently than the charge of powder. He was
an honest enemy.

"Maybe that's what I've felt in this last year—though
I never sensed it on other journeys west—the ancient
battle line where the sea and land carry on their heroic
and ancient warfare. A splendid place to live and a
glorious place to die. I ask my gods for both blessings—
and a little while to make black lines on white paper.

"Black rocks dripping in the sun and lifting their
proud breasts from the eager embrace of the sea. The
delicate white veins of the sea threaded through the
sullen gray of its crushing waves. The sea sounding its
eternal tragic note, like the battle chant of a barbaric
army.

"It is something to flatten out against a sudden rise

of rock and cling to a two-foot trail, three hundred feet over a mad maelstrom where the sea beats in tireless patient fury.

"On the headland are the pioneer trees, scourged by the wind that has screamed at them for centuries. Scourged and beaten, tortured and deformed and grotesque in their agony, but holding their ground with their arms and legs thrown about each other in a deathless, desperate effort.

"In back of them the great army of giant trees. To have heard one of these magnificent beings brought down in its full strength and whimpering and groaning as a strong man brought down in battle—not whimpering because he is dying but because he can no longer fight— is to have heard something of the tragedy of the universe.

"These things I have seen and done and heard. And they have been translated for me. They have become the symbols of the world's miseries and struggles, told in a nobler way than in the conflict and clash of human bodies. With them comes a clean perspective and a clear vision—as clear perhaps as we can approach the vision of the first artist who scratched lines on the bone of the reindeer.

"They have told me that it is all very well to listen to the song of the sea, to worship in the infinite hush of the hills and the forests. But that it was impossible to work in their overwhelming presence. It may be so, for those who seek with puny tools to decorate the majestic simplicity of the sea and the hills and the trees. Perhaps it is better for them to work their tools far away from these things.

"What I have to tell is of men and women. And perhaps it is better for me, after years of being close to men and women, to be there, and away from them to tell their story. There, whatever they theorize—and the *Bien Dios* knows I know nothing of their theories—I work best. And there, if I may make that humble boast, I became an artist."

The pen moved slowly over the paper. I reflected in the interim on the masculinity that stood out in all of the drawings by Wallace Smith. When he has drawn women they seem to have something robust about them. I remembered a tableau where a woman stands before a couch, facing her mirror. The lines of her torso are those of a youth, with no suggestion of gentle voluptuousness, no seductive curves. I spoke of this to Smith.

"I prefer to draw men," he replied. "And I use only men as models. The reason is very simple. I get my anatomy direct from the human body and all my studies are made on living men. You can't conveniently take hold of a woman's limb and trace a muscle or a ligament. They would yell for help.

"I'm pretty hard on my models, so my brother is my principal victim. Sometimes I throw him into a position and expect him to keep it. I nearly put his shoulder out of joint once when I drew a crucifixion—"

I have not spoken of Wallace Smith's sense for social satire—of the fact that many of his drawings often strike home with a biting bit of irony. There is "Snobs" for instance, in which half a dozen males are straining every muscle to push a great block of stone up an incline for the pyramids, under the eye of a superior task master. There is "The Worshiper"—a drawing of unusual force in which three-quarters of the space is taken up with a conglomerate oriental idol that combines perhaps all forms of idolatrous effigies throughout the ages, and one-quarter is given to a puny human who grovels in the dust before the shrine. There is "Matrimony"—two nude figures, male and female, bound tightly together breast to breast by thick cords, struggling vainly to loosen their bonds before a great closed door. And from satire Smith swings to fantasy and to poetic concepts. There is in his room a little drawing that appears to be a series of black hands reaching out towards the observer from quiet waters.

"I happened to see that picture one day when I was out in a boat," said Wallace. "The wild grass that grew in the water seemed to reach up to me like hands and pull me down.

"One day Carl Sandburg saw this little drawing. 'That's poetry,' he commented, as he mused over the picture and quietly murmured to himself 'the hands seemed to reach up and pull me down.' That's poetry."

"What interests and to some extent amazes me," said I, "is the flexibility you have achieved when you have limited yourself so decidedly by your own technique."

"Look at the Egyptians," replied Smith. "Elie Faure tells how the priests restricted the artists to the severe forms in decoration. Everything was prescribed and within those limits the artists achieved permanent beauty, wonderful technical results and purity. They were the born artists—the Egyptians."

"Then you do know Elie Faure!" I said, pleased beyond words.

"I have just got acquainted with him. A friend comes in and reads to me when I work and the other night he brought Faure. Sometimes he reads to me in French."

"I didn't know that you understood French."

"I don't. But I like the sound of it."

And then Smith told me that he had something to show me—a drawing that he had just completed and that he had called "Mother." It proved easily superior, it seemed to me, to all his published work. No sentimentalism this—but the bitter truth that tugged at the heart of one and filled it to overflowing. An aged woman sits in a chair nude to the waist. Her face is the face of old age that has seen years of suffering, her muscles are flabby, shrunken; there stand out the outlines of the bones of the great wide thighs. A mother tired, drawn, weary from long years of child-bearing, the matrix of all the race.

"I had the idea some time ago," continued Smith, "but I had not completed the picture when I went to the hospital recently for a minor operation. Just as I was being prepared for my turn and was in the hall and about to be wheeled into the operating room an old woman in a chair was drawn past me—a woman with the face that I had been looking for all these weeks. Hastily I took my pad and pencil and sketched in the outlines while the attendants watched with a strange sort of curiosity about me, and when I got out, I went to work, and there it is."

I stood before it for a long time in silent admiration. Smith seemed to divine my mood and met it in airy fashion.

"Tell you what a girl once said about me," he commented, as he tied up his portfolio, "said I was a bitter little boy making black lines on white paper. . . ."

11. Ben Hecht
Pagliacci of the Fire Escape

*Perhaps the greatest miracle is
that which enables man to tolerate life.   It is the miracle of san-
ity . . . a stupidity which has already outlived the gods.*
From the journal of Mallare.

I

"BEN HECHT is an iconoclast," says one, "a smasher of idols"; "Ben Hecht is an intellectual mountebank, an insincere fiddler," says another. "Ben Hecht tramples on that which men have built up through the centuries and hallowed with their tears," says one; "and destroys shams and that which is foul and diseased," says another. "Ben Hecht is a combination of street urchin and skeptical intellectual," says a poet; "he is the incomprehensible lover," says his friend, "the man who hovers always between ecstasy and disillusionment; who welcomes the dawn with a sneer and folds away the twilight with a caress." "Ben Hecht is—"

But let me add a line of mine own. It is as Ben told me. At the age of eighteen or thereabouts, Ben Hecht was an acrobat in Costello's road show in a Wisconsin country town. . . . Make of that what ye will!

Incomprehensible acrobat! Incomparable mountebank of the emotions! Unexplained dreamer and poet, scorner and critic, philosopher and friend.

And so he comes into our view, a lad just passing the twilight zone of youth, with the face of a man who dreams at times, and at other times plans; a round face, which will be chubby, or florid, at fifty; the face of a Balzac, or an Alexandre Dumas. A man with a certain careless air about wearing clothes that hang loosely upon him, and a certain recklessness in knotting his tie, and yet making occasional overtures to fashion in the manipulation of a heavy cane; a man with soft, dark hair often disheveled, falling loosely over his forehead;

brown eyes soft, kindly; the mouth, most expressive of all, sensitive with a touch of the sensuous, and on either side two deep furrows that come out sharp and clear when the lips part in disdain, or mockery, or sarcasm, or mild, quiet invective.

When first I saw him he was reading Burton's "Arabian Nights"—their spell has been upon him ever since. The next day it was Gautier, and then Dostoievsky's "The Idiot," which he urged upon me as the greatest novel of modern times. And finally "Penguin Island," and "Spiritual Adventures." And so my earliest memories of him are associated with books, and when I take down these treasured volumes from my shelves I think also of the man who first enlisted my interest in them, and the occasions that called it forth. Not so long ago it was, either, by human reckoning, for he has just turned thirty at the most and I, who indite these memories, am still hovering on the sunny side of a certain meridian despite my palsied hand and furrowed brow. Those were days that seem ages gone now—days when we waged war upon the city hall, or held monotonous vigil in some undertaker's drab rooms, or sat in noisy hotel lobbies waiting for the passing celebrity to come down and give us the platitude for the hour. He could talk then as he talks now—volubly, incessantly, fascinatingly—holding all who came within hearing by his subtle innuendoes, his philosophical observations, his penetrating irony, his vehement indignation, his gentle persuasiveness, his dubious facts. And so to-day.

When I ask newcomers now: "Well, what do you think of Ben?" the answer is ever the same: "An amazing man. Such words! Such conceptions! Such enthusiasm! Such facts! *Such facts!*"

Ben Hecht has published in the last two years: "1,001 Afternoons in Chicago," a series of sixty-two journalistic sketches chosen from over four hundred written originally as a daily task for the Chicago "Daily News"; "Erik Dorn," a romance of a disillusioned man's vain search for an ecstatic outlet, written in the manner of an expressionist; "Gargoyles," a drab, colorless, fairly objective dissection of hypocrisy and the sex life of dried up, illy-nurtured Americans; "Under False Pretences," also known as "The Egoist," a comedy of stage life prepared for and acted by Leo Ditrichstein; "The Florentine Dagger," a detective story; "Fantazius Mallare," a strange, wayward, biting analysis of society under the pretext of a study of insanity, published in a limited edition and withdrawn at the request of the federal government. He has in preparation and not yet published ———, but lack of space forbids a detailed chronicle.

Keith Preston and I had wandered rather aimlessly to Ben's room in an ancient building that ran back to the days of the great fire. A strange, Dickensian sort of pile, like those that appear in the funereal prints of the sixties and seventies, a place in which the appearance of Abraham Lincoln and Stephen Douglas even to-day would not seem out of harmony. Quaint, old-fashioned mahogany elevator cages, still propelled by a tug at a cable; a great wide court roofed over with a skylight and surrounded by heavy mahogany balustrades. Offices that permit a glimpse of old, high-backed secretaries with pigeon holes stuffed with musty, yellowing papers; of men, bearded and unkempt, bent over wide blue blotters frayed and covered with inkstains. Insurance; real estate; steamship agencies; the law. Two doors at the right—the second door is his—through the first one discerns a tailor in shirt sleeves industriously applying a steam press to pantaloons. His workshop—a strange anachronism. Across the street the false Corinthian pillars of a modern city hall, and just beyond that the thousand glowing candles of an office building encased in terra cotta. But here, within his walls, great hangings of green burlap depending from the ceiling, and soft mats of thick, green wool just underfoot, and deep enveloping chairs and soft lights and hours for idling. And Ben Hecht, sunk down within the generous arms of a deep leather chair, saying in a melodious monotone: "I've got something to read to you boys. My first act. Yes, I'm doing another play for Leo. We stayed up until daybreak to try it out, and here it is. Quattrocento this time. Florence, Venice, Rome, Milan; swords, loves, swashbuckling, romance. Leo likes that sort. Gives him a chance to make love gracefully and swashbuckle all over the place."

And then he reads. A play on the life of Benvenuto Cellini, as revealed by himself in his incomparable memoirs. A swashbuckler with a soul. A mountebank with a heart. An acrobat with love and laughter and hope and tears. And an artist. Thus Ben Hecht has captured him and portrayed him. He reads on, and we listen.

And how he reads! You are attracted by his fecundity, his versatility, his humanness, his shifting aims. You wonder, as you listen: What next? Where? And how? Already at thirty he is the most talked about, the most praised, the most reviled of the Chicago group. Already at thirty he defies analysis. Stay away from him and you will judge him harshly. Come close to him and his gentleness, his knowledge of human motives and acts, his kindliness, robs you of an objective judgment. His acerbic criticism, on paper, stings; spoken, it amuses. To-day, condemned by some, vilified by others, praised by those who know him best, he stands as a strangely aloof, irreconcilable figure in American writing, an example of the new, uncompromising spirit born with Dreiser, of the new unassimilated spirit that has bade defiance to the New England tradition within the last twenty years. And yet he is one of us, born on our soil, nurtured in our middle west, educated in our public schools; the product of living in a crowded, rude, tempestuous city, a representative of the shifting, restless, uncatalogued writers of the new age.

II

Ben Hecht was born in New York City, acquired a high school education at Racine, Wis., and then came to Chicago to work as a newspaper reporter. College never beckoned him, and to-day all that it stands for is hateful to him. No doubt this attitude is partly protective; on the other hand he is so thoroughly out of sympathy with classicism, puritanism, the didacticism of college English courses and the lack of modernity in college reading, that much of his feeling is sincere. Many of the books exalted in high school gave him a distaste for further reading in the conventional English and American novel. He had always read much on the outside and on coming to Chicago found himself drifting toward the authors who dominated the latter part of the nineteenth century. Sometimes he would merely skim through a book, catch an idea here and there, and hold on to it; at other times he would become profoundly impressed with style and method and read a book again and again.

Of the three men who are so closely related in the young Chicago group—Carl Sandburg, Sherwood Anderson, and Ben Hecht, Hecht was more influenced by his reading than the other two. Sandburg's reading was desultory, and largely to acquire information; Anderson's reading, or the lack of it, reveals his naïveté. But Hecht read omnivorously, and soon found unusual merit in those authors whose books agreed with his views, his habit of thought, his own innate iconoclasm. "We cannot be sincere in our own work and admire the very opposite to ourselves," writes George Moore somewhere. Ben Hecht's reading tastes reflect his mind, just as everything he writes reflects his mind. Moreover we find that the two things coincide, that Ben Hecht has written, or tried to write, exactly the sort of work that he most admires in others. The predominant traits are a fondness for realism, naturalism, and iconoclasm; a leaning toward sex psychology and neuropathic and psychopathic studies; a love for glittering phrases and word combinations that arrest eye and ear; a dominant preoccupation with the mind and especially psychiatrics. He is the exact opposite in his thinking from Sherwood Anderson, for where Anderson sees in the liberation of our unconscious a relief from the repressions, conventions, and inhibiting laws that bind our conscious life, Ben Hecht thinks entirely in terms of our conscious life, and while despising the shackles man has laid on himself looks for liberation solely in breaking them and beating them down without taking the subconscious into consideration.

Thus very early Hecht found himself drawn toward the color, the romanticism, the paganism, and anti-

puritanism of Théophile Gautier and the verbal gorgeous-
ness of Huysmans. He bought Gautier in a set and
consumed him. "The Red Lily" came across his path
and he knew that Anatole France must be his; out of his
meager earnings as a reporter he captured the whole set
of red-bound volumes and was in debt to the bookseller
for months. Arthur Symons' "Spiritual Adventures"
made a deep impression on him, and George Moore likewise interested him in the French modernists; he thereupon read Mallarmé, Verlaine, and Baudelaire, and
talked Baudelaire weeks on end to attentive friends. His
dislikes are also characteristic. "I could not stomach
Victor Hugo and Balzac," said Ben. "I was bored to
tears by Balzac. Rousseau I considered a great, big
thumping fool, especially in his "Confessions." But for
action and romance give me Dumas; I have just bought
a fine leather set of his books. At that I think I got
more out of Huysmans than anybody else."

When Ben Hecht mentions Huysmans it is as if he
had found a choice morsel for the tongue. Huysmans
impressed him particularly with his intensity, his fire,
his beauty in expression. He read "En Route" and "The
Cathedral" in translation and then went around searching for a translation of "Là Bas," to no avail. Finally
an obliging friend made a free translation and night after
night Hecht sat by and listened to the rippling prose.
His views on Huysmans reveal his intense preoccupation
with decadence in the French, and his fondness for
verbal acrobatics. In contrast the writers of America
seemed tame and colorless. "The culture which loves
the cadence of line, the sparkle of words, the piquant
acrobatics of phrase, is still unborn in America," said
Ben. And in "Erik Dorn" no doubt he sought to cap-

ture some of this beauty and color. He has put his admiration for Huysmans into an enthusiastic panegyric that is characteristic of him:

Huysmans is the rajah of writing, his brain the splendid macaw of all literatures. He illumines the *fin de siècle* of his Europe like some effulgent and exotic Napoleon of words. His work, from beginning to end a fulgurating panorama of phrases, forms the rarest and most precious pages in the thought of France. To him may all stylists be compared—Verlaine, Mallarmé, De Gourmont, Barres, Nietzsche, Louys, Pater. For beside the flame of his strange genius the Salome of Wilde, jewel-phrased courtesan that she is, pales to a shadowy bawd. . . . Huysmans' decadence is the most virile and furious manifestation of beauty in any language. It is the apocalypse of imagery, the tortuous hallelujah of style. His vision is of a demonical intensity. His eye, turned critically upon life, upon canvas or upon any other of the arts, kindles with unholy lights. He can present in his matchless cataracts of words the beauty of Chopin, the sataniques of Rops, the splendors of Moreau. All color and movement he can evoke by the mellifluous devices of phrase and clause which impale upon their rapturous points the soul of beauty. His "Certains" and "A Rebours" remain the apotheosis of verbal splendors, of volcanic nuances. His trilogy, "Là Bas," "La Cathédrale," and "En Route," inspired by the exotic loveliness of medieval Catholicism, contain the vivisections of Dostoievsky, augmented by a lyricism which rises, page after page, to unearthly harmonies.

Ben Hecht is still devoted to Huysmans and only recently, when the subject came up, he remarked that he would like to obtain a good translation of "Là Bas" so that he might submit it for publication—if the boobs and brahmins would permit. His love for the decadents

as well as his fondness for beautiful writing early made
him admire "The Hill of Dreams" and "The House of
Souls." When he reached London in 1918 he had in
mind two pilgrimages that meant much more to him
than the Abbey or the Tower—the first to the humble
home of Arthur Machen, the second to the rooms of
Ezra Pound. For Machen he had conceived a strange
personal fondness, wholly out of keeping with his usual
disgust at hero worship. It must have been an odd
experience for Machen, at that time still unpublished in
America, to find himself venerated and his books inti-
mately known and understood by this cool, sophisticated
youth from Chicago, and no doubt Machen can, if he will,
tell an arresting story of how Hecht sat at his feet wide-
eyed and plied him with questions and examined the yellowing manuscripts that Machen pulled from out an
ancient cabinet, among them the book that has since been
published in America as "The Secret Glory."

Of the early American writers Hecht approved Poe and
Hawthorne, for he liked the excitement and movement in
Poe and the activity that Hawthorne projected into the
essay, together with the latter's freedom from prudery.
Holmes, Lowell, Whittier, and the other New England
authors bored him; he saw in them only an echo of
English literary currents, nothing that was American, and
felt that most of them wrote down to the level of high
school boys. When he reached Stephen Crane, however,
he recognized a new note in American literature. Crane
was at once a realist and an artist; all the reporter's
admiration for clean, straightforward story-telling and for
the genuine human element went out to his tales. But he
found in Walt Whitman little to hold his interest. Moreover Whitman had become a sort of god to persons who

had no other literary traits to recommend them; this immediately offended Hecht, and he deprecated the sentimentalism which had become a pose among certain American intellectuals. There is still recounted the story of a dinner of the Walt Whitman fellowship of Chicago which Hecht chanced to attend with a friend. Clarence Darrow, Dr. Preston Bradley, and Llewellyn Jones delivered addresses; Ben Hecht, nauseated by the adulation, went from the dinner to his typewriter and wrote an indignant screed which was printed later in the "Little Review" under the title "Slobberdom, Sneerdom and Boredom." He inveighed against "saccharine drool at the expense of a great man," and asked: "Leave justice to the graybeards? Why should a soul which has the capacity for inspiration quibble in prejudices?" Some of those who had attended the dinner were angered; others professed to be amused; Ben was happy at having relieved himself of an outburst at the expense of the "mob"; the Whitman dinners continued year after year, even until now.

In his views on American culture Hecht is one with H. L. Mencken. He has always read Mencken and agreed with most of his opinions, but it is doubtful whether he derived from Mencken at all. Hecht esteems him highly. He said once: "Mencken is what you might call a healthy force. His attacks on our brahmins are delightful. Of course he is no judge of literature. His approval means less than that of any critic in America— it means simply that you have good literary manners. Mencken is unable to fix the type of the artist he examines. He is America's soapbox orator, street corner shouter and table thumper. He has no feeling for moods, rhythm, or style. He could not see Sherwood Anderson at first, in fact called him one of the imitators of Dreiser, and got nothing at all out of Bodenheim's best early work. But he has always been helpful to me. When I first began to examine novels critically I saw that most novelists appeared to suffer from obsessions, like programs and propaganda that they wanted to put over. I wrote Mencken that I had no program in me, nothing to tout. I just had a skepticism that was born of nothing; it simply existed and wanted to get out. Mencken replied: 'Go ahead anyhow. That will be a new start for a novel.' "

Hecht has not imitated Mencken, and yet some of his strictures on American writing read strangely like Mencken. Take this excerpt from an essay of several years ago:

Beautiful writing in America is regarded with the usual American sneer for all manifestations beyond our aboriginal appetite, stupidity, and morals. This sneer, which is the highest critical expression of our highest critical classes is in its own way a low and baleful thing. It is a blight which has stunted American literature with the exception of such decadents as Poe, Hawthorne, and Whitman, to the weedy level of mediocrity. More than this, it has asphyxiated the taste of an English reading people, and without taste, without pudding. There are some pathetic exceptions. For instance, the heavy jocundities of Chesterton, the sizzling platitudes of Shaw, the profound banalities of Masters, the garrulous flapdoodle of Mackaye, the petty journalism of O. Henry, the walla walla of Henry James are a few of the white cows of conventional fame. But even concerning them there is still a stubborn yokelry abroad in the land which objects to them because they sometimes write in epigram, because they sometimes essay to relieve the monotony of thought with the word adroit, the phrase polite, the clause colored. For it is the unwritten law of American almanac culture that any wight who scribbles cleverly is by the Zodiac and all the sacred rumble bumble of our professors a superficial fellow, a mere juggler of words, a low backstairs Andrew. Likewise and by the same fascinating tokens is it the unwritten law of this almanac culture that any Rollo who writes stupidly, whose style is that of the mail order catalogues, whose phrases are full of "good old Anglo-Saxon English and simplicity"—that such a yawn brewer is automatically an Honoré Balzac, Marcus Aurelius, a creature and philosopher whose fingers rest shrewdly upon the pulse of life.

In the matter of technique, then, he also drank deep at the fount of Wyndham Lewis of "Tarr," and James Joyce. Both the "Portrait" and "Dubliners" impressed him, and he sympathized immediately with Joyce's amazing irreverence and his disregard of the sacred cows of conventional life and thought. When "Ulysses" began to appear in the "Little Review" he became deeply interested. Other books that left a more or less lasting impression were "Homo Sapiens," "Taras Bulba," and "The French Revolution" of Carlyle. He saw in the latter an admirable way of handling large masses and playing with big canvases—and practically all his many references to the revolution are inspired by this one book. He read most of the Irish writers—the coming of the Irish players and the popularity of William Butler Yeats led him to read Synge, Yeats and Stephens, but only the latter aroused his enthusiasm with "The Crock of Gold."

But a most profound influence in Ben Hecht's work was Dostoievsky. He had read a sprinkling of the Russians—Tchekov, Gogol, Andreyev and Turgenev, although for some reason or other he always thought of the latter as a Frenchman. He had never liked Tolstoi. When he came to Dostoievsky he recognized a fellowship that went below the surface. "There is only one plot in the world after all and that is the human mind," Hecht had said, and Dostoievsky had believed that. Dostoievsky hated life, hated the humiliating groveling that human beings performed in their interpretation of certain ideals, inspirations, dogmas, and systems of faith; he was intensely interested in abnormal and subnormal mentalities; he dealt with people who suffered intensely, mentally and physically, because of the indignities that they inflicted on themselves or that were inflicted on them by others; he saw humankind nailed to a cross of its vices and its virtues, sinning despicably more often through infirmities than through volition; again and again he came back to the mental struggle and dissolution of an individual caused largely by his attempt to overcome an abstraction, to surmount a new intellectual obstacle. Hecht found himself drawn to this strange, powerfully equipped writer as to no other. Certain passages in "The House of the Dead" captivated him. He preferred particularly the passage relating to human crucifixions in Siberia. But "The Idiot" held him spellbound. He regarded it as a masterpiece and spoke of it as the greatest novel ever written.

There is much more similarity between Ben Hecht and Dostoievsky than meets the eye. Hecht's makeup is such that he and the Russian are kin. Hecht, like Dostoievsky, is an intellectual rebel, fighting against life. Hecht sees life through the same lenses—he views human beings as distorted and perverted by their adherence to false ideals, shams, taboos, complexes, laws in which they do not believe and which fail to liberate their mortal souls. He understands sensuality and its relation to the simple acts of life as Dostoievsky understood it and pictured it in "The Brothers Karamazov." Hecht's definition of the artist might have been that of Dostoievsky, put into American prose: "The mob taboos, censorships, fatuous idealizations, and doltist tyrannies eternally designed for the comfort of the feeble-minded and for the propagation of the illusions which contribute to their feeble-mindedness, are phenomena under which the egoist of every age finds himself struggling to exist. It is his inability to annihilate the obscene realities that turns him toward the minor anarchy of evading them or denouncing them or weeping over them or sometimes merely hopelessly cataloguing them; in short, which causes him to transform himself from a natural into an unnatural animal—the artist." Where Hecht differs from Dostoievsky the difference is a matter of physical makeup; in many other things they are alike. Dostoievsky was an epileptic, a border-line case mentally, a man who had suffered intensely, physically and mentally, and who had been persecuted; whose ill health was continuous, even while he wrote, and who had a tendency toward inflicting suffering on himself in minor ways for the sake of the sensation it produced. He was a mystic and deeply concerned in abstract arguments on God, religion, immortality. He wrote intuitively of insanity and morbidity, without any research whatever in medical history. . . . Ben Hecht is a man of tremendous physical energy, who was known at one time as an excellent boxer and ball player, whose health has always been good and whose mental reactions are normal. He is able to judge men intuitively, but much of his knowledge is acquired not from an analysis of himself, as in the case of Dostoievsky, but from close observation and reading. He therefore lacks Dostoievsky's sureness of touch, and often offends with his journalistic mannerism of overstatement. His characters are more sharply defined in their vices and in their aberrations than those of Dostoievsky, and there are fewer persons of mixed and jumbled emotions and action in his books. He has had to reinforce his "hunches" on psychology and neurotics by much reading of medical lore. He is strongly egoistic and intensely subjective, but he lacks Dostoievsky's mysticism and religious faith, although he has a deep curiosity about exotic religions and tribal forms and ceremonies. The tendency to inflict suffering, Hecht, however, shares, but it is not on himself that he practises. Making no compromise with conventional taste or feelings, his principal characteristic is to say and write what will be most effective and to send an arrow unerringly to the sore spot where it will give the most intense pain to his victims. To make an audience writhe, to bring to a reader sharply the consciousness of physical and mental lacks and defects, to plunge a dart home with the most intense mental pain is so thoroughly characteristic of Hecht that it is always mentioned as part of his make-up. That he can do it so much more forcefully and effectively than Dostoievsky did in his milder and smoother manner is proof that Hecht enjoys health and vigor far superior to that of the Russian he so earnestly admires.

III

Ben Hecht is in revolt against the forms in which life has become crystallized, but he is thoroughly a part of it and in love with life itself. He plays the game wholeheartedly, and apparently gets a great deal of fun out of it. In spite of his strictures on the world, he has no program for remodeling the world. He would like to destroy a great many conventions, but he has made no effort to formulate an ideal program of living to take their place. He says of himself that he is simply possessed of a skepticism, and that he was born perversely. Not long ago, when Samuel Rudens asked him for a paragraph about himself, Ben typed the following and sent a copy to me. It was written almost immediately after the federal government had sequestered his book, "Fantazius Mallare," which was the signal for a number of sycophantic friends to desert him:

Born perversely. Out of this perversity, a sentimental hatred of weakness in others, an energetic amusement for the gods, taboos, vindictiveness and cowardice of my friends, neighbors and relatives; a contempt for the ideas of man, an infatuation with the energies of man, a love for the abstraction of form, a loathing for the protective slave philosophies of the people, government, etc., a determination not to become a part of the mind which the swine worship in their sty. A delirious relief in finding words that express any or all of my perversities. Out of this natal perversity I have written "Erik Dorn," "Gargoyles," "Mallare," some of my "1001 Afternoons," three dozen stories. I have only one ambition; to get away from the future caresses of my friends, from the intimidated malice of their praise, from the grunts of my enemies, and live in a country whose language is foreign to me, whose people are indifferent, and where skies are deeper.

Much of this, of course, is a reaction against the proscription of his book. There is small reason to believe that Ben Hecht would be contented in a foreign land, among indifferent persons who spoke another language.

His whole career so far contradicts that. Indifference is the last thing he would hope for; even in foreign lands he would need an audience. He might find a much more sympathetic and intelligent one than in America, and a larger one at that, but he would also discover that the seas do not wipe out the foibles and weaknesses of human-kind. It is likely also that he might find himself even more misunderstood than in America, for after all he has developed an American method. "I consider myself thoroughly American," he told me once. "All my work is American; my ideas are the result of my living in Chicago alone. Except for my search for better writing in foreign authors I have not been influenced by them."

And one might write voluminously of his infatuation with the primal energies of the American people, and with the material results and symbols of that energy; buildings, streets, houses, fire escapes, chimneys, bridges, railroad trains. He has interpreted streets as no writer before or since. Windows, umbrellas, hats, street cars—all these have become symbols in his mind. He often speaks of his affection for city themes. "Why do artists always disregard streets?" he asked once. "No one paints streets and yet these streets are very close to the people. The earliest art was entirely a part of the life around it. I like Madison street and I always look for a building to come down and a new one to go up. I watch people walking up and down these streets. What's in their minds? Success? Money? Power? Yes, if they are up and coming. Amusement, for some of them."

He has always used city themes. His earliest writings grew out of his experience as a reporter. He was a part of the group that included Sherwood Anderson, Maxwell

Bodenheim, Margaret Anderson, Stanislaus Szukalski, Alexander Kaun, and others. When Margaret Anderson started the "Little Review" Ben was one of its first contributors. He wrote some of his best sketches for this magazine, expressing a certain tendency toward subconscious elements and abstractions that he has since buried under an avalanche of objective writing. He first met Maxwell Bodenheim in the office of the "Little Review" and was attracted by the poet's attempts to capture nuances in colorful phrases. Soon the Hecht-Bodenheim debate, formal and informal, became a legend.

"Nobody really knew what the 'Little Review' was aiming at," said Ben, "in fact I doubt whether Margaret knew. Everybody had an idea of his own and we all wrote what we pleased. I recall talking with Margaret about imagist poetry when she was living on the beach at Glencoe. The 'Little Review' had been running articles on the imagists for about three quarters of a year and Margaret exclaimed: 'Ben, you tell me what these imagists are all about.' I wrote some of my best sketches for the 'Little Review.' Among them were 'Broken Necks,' 'The Yellow Goat,' 'Lust,' 'Decay,' 'Nocturne,' 'Fragments,' and 'Black Umbrellas.' I also wrote 'Laughter' for them but recalled it. It was published in the 'Milwaukee Arts Monthly' in September, 1922."

Of the sketches that are well remembered was one called "The American Family," which appeared in August, 1915, and in which Ben tried to satirize the typical American home. It was one of his first investigations into sex aberrations. He pictured the mother as having suppressed joy and life within her to attain social goals, the daughter as trying for self-realization. Of the man he said that "honor toward his woman expired when the mysteries of

her sex paled." The family thinks of virtue in terms of
legs and always "plays safe." Hecht also wrote twelve
sketches of Chicago life called "Dregs." Of these, three
were used in the "Little Review." They included "Life,"
the story of a beggar with vermin in his beard, and "Sorrow," the story of an outcast in a café weeping because
her pal had died. The first was selected by Edward J.
O'Brien for inclusion in his anthology of the American
short story for 1915. It was the first outside recognition
that came to Hecht. He was then twenty-two.

Some of his views are included in sketches that he
ironically signed "The Scavenger." Among them is this
estimate of Theodore Dreiser:

Hark you who have stultified your artists and buried them
under the gingerbread morality of your own monotonous lives.
Dreiser is the one novelist being published in America to-day
who does not listen to you, who describes you at your various
bests, who wrings the pathos and joys out of your little worlds;
who paints in with the brush of a universal art what you and
I are doing in Alexandria, and Chicago, and New York, and all
the little milk station stops between. . . . I am not a disciple
of the Dreiserian gospel. I would like to argue with him the
certain superiorities of monogamy for the artist. But he has
limned a hero who is not a sugar-coated moralizer. He has
ignored superbly the mob-begotten mandates of literary excel-
lence. Whatever his faults of composition or construction, and
there are not so many as his friends endeavor to make out, he
has magnificently booted the reading public, the morally sub-
sidized critics and the very publishers in the coarsest regions
of their bodies—their souls. . . . And for these things I hail
him as the greatest novelist in the country and I acclaim him
as the only real uncontaminated genius of these States—and
pray to God that my friend Sherwood Anderson will hurry up
and get published, so that there will be two of them.

Sometimes, but not often, he threw his thoughts into an easy verse form, as in "Humoresque":

Faces, faces.
Swimming like white fever specks away;
Faces coming close.
See the meaningless odd bumps on them called features.
Yellow bits of paper blanks blown along the street.

The rain is like laughter,
The black devils of my brain,
Have leaped outside the window
And are laughing at me.

"Most of those earlier sketches in the "Little Review" furnished me with backgrounds which I put into 'Erik Dorn,' said Hecht. "My first book was called 'Moisse.' It was a weird, fantastic thing, and I sent it to Edward J. O'Brien, who had been prodding me to write. O'Brien said it was the first great novel of the twentieth century and accepted it on behalf of Small, Maynard & Co., and then nearly lost his job trying to get them to print it. I rewrote it eventually, worked long hours over it, and then put it aside. Then I wrote another novel called 'Grimaces.' I sent it to Mencken and he said it was not good. The ideas were unoriginal, the whole thing was incoherent. I threw it away. When I came to write 'Gargoyles' I followed some of the themes I had put into these two books. I wrote 'Gargoyles' twice, so I have really been over some of the ground five times. And it can be rewritten again. In fact when it came out I realized at once where I might have improved it."

In spite of the fact that Ben Hecht has been before the public as a novelist for only two years he has been writing like mad for nearly ten. And all the work that he has already piled up, be it juvenile, or amateurish, or actually full of merit, bears the marks of vehemence, of enthusiasm, of boisterousness, of depth of feeling that one finds in his later work. He has always been an iconoclast; he has always been able to pump up a hearty indignation. He has always had a gift for facile expression. He has never been afraid to work hard and despite all sorts of distractions around him will sit hours at a typewriter, pounding away on his favorite theme, discarding and rewriting, with but little show of effort and without any pretense to the hocus-pocus of authorship.

"I used to write plays incessantly and must have turned out twenty or thirty of them," he told me. "They were sad specimens compared with what I wanted to do. Three or four I wrote with Bodenheim out of our conversations. Bodenheim used to sit around, say a sentence full of color and charm, and I would reply. Then we would write this down. I never expected any of them to turn up but last fall without any warning I found that they had put 'The Master Poisoner' into 'Frenzied Fricassee' at the Greenwich Village Theater. I swear I knew nothing of it. It was terrible . . . well, ask some one who heard it. Eventually I became acquainted with Kenneth Sawyer Goodman. He had studied plays for technique and knew a lot more about stage directions and limitations than I did. We wrote several comedies. One of them, 'The Wonder Hat,' still turns up in amateur theaters now and then. It is one of those sweet little plays about Pierrot and Pierrette—that's about all you can say for it. 'Dregs' I also wrote as a play by myself, and 'The Hero of Santa Maria,' composed with Goodman, had a small run in New York."

At about the same time Hecht was writing short stories for the "Smart Set." He took characters from round about him and made them serve his purpose. The stories were sometimes grim, more often caricature. He speaks of these tales as "second rate stuff." "Once I wrote two stories on the same theme," said Ben. "I worked three weeks on 'The Yellow Goat' and six hours on 'The Eternal Fugitive.' I sent both to Mencken and he took the latter. Then I sent 'The Yellow Goat' to the 'Little Review.'

"The 'Little Review' was the only fearless literary magazine that the country has ever had. We had a lot of fun with it. We used to go to Margaret's office in the Fine Arts building and sit around and debate. Poets and authors would drop in, most of them unpublished then. Once Margaret turned an issue over to Alexander S. Kaun and myself and gave us the key to the office. We opened all the mail and whenever we spotted a manuscript that seemed to be just ordinary conventional writing we sent it back with a caustic note. There was a whole box of poems from Vachel Lindsay and we fired it back with the memo, 'Rotten.' Then Dreiser sent a play which he explained had been knocking about in his desk. We wrote back that if that was the best he could do he might let it knock around another ten years. Finally a story from Galsworthy. We wrote something about 'cheap stuff' across the face of it and mailed it back and I don't know whether Margaret Anderson was ever able to fix things up with him after that escapade."

One recalls in this connection a remark credited to Galsworthy by an eastern publisher, who informed him that he had in his desk the manuscript of a story by Ben Hecht.

"But isn't he rather an erotic writer?" asked Galsworthy.

IV

It is as a reporter that one loves best to remember Ben Hecht, for there was a nonchalance, a recklessness, a boisterousness, an enthusiasm about his reporting that sat much better upon him than his later and more serious mood. He was always intensely interested in human foibles and life's trivialities, and seen through his eyes they became magnified and important. His ability to tell a story, to write quickly, to grasp the contents of a situation intuitively, to conjure up images in great profusion without apparent effort, made a newspaper career inevitable for him. He could make any situation alive, interesting and human, because he invariably drew on his imagination. A few words uttered by some one, a fragment of thought begun, but not completed, were enough to start trains of thought in his mind and to let loose the resources of his creative power. He therefore became a romantic reporter, one to whom the meticulous accuracy of a stenographic report was abominable and uninspired, and who loved to let the imagination play over the dull, prosaic routine of a commonplace event. He had the faculty for making a drab world seem gorgeous and full of color; he had the dissector's skill for laying bare the sores of humankind in all their vileness.

There are innumerable anecdotes extant of his proficiency, of his ability to "deliver." His "angle" on a story was always different from that of the conventional reporter. I recall half a dozen instances. On one occasion three of us waited for Winston Churchill in the lobby of the Blackstone hotel. Churchill had just written 'The Inside of the Cup" and had been indulging in philosophical research work at the University of California. A young woman, Miss Marie Armstrong—who, by the way, is now Mrs. Ben Hecht—was there to get a "feature story" on how Churchill planned his woman characters for his novels. My own task was to get an expression on political primaries, in which the author had been interested in Vermont. But Ben's preoccupation was with the philosophers and scientists that Churchill had just been reading in Berkeley. Churchill talked volubly about Renan, Darwin, Compte, Schopenhauer, Spencer—Ben Hecht's tendency toward modernism and iconoclasm immediately made itself visible; he listened long, and the next day the Chicago "Journal" bore on its front page, under scarehead lines, a long interview with Churchill on God, life, matter, divinity, immortality, and what not, all of it in strange juxtaposition with the murders, jury reports, thefts, and political scandals that make up a reader's daily fare in Chicago, and no doubt much more interesting. There is an anecdote that once when Ben was working at an out-of-town hanging and was sending his own frank story of the proceeding his editor wired him to tone down the gruesome details. Hecht's reply came at once: "Will try to make hanging as pleasant as possible."

Life to him was not always a matter of reporting catastrophes; he loved to linger in second-hand bookstores, to converse with old men on a bridge while his eyes were fascinated by the play of lights upon the water, to sit in strange eating houses and consort with men of various talents and occupations. Sometimes he would write stories about a scene or a mood. One day he wandered out to a tiny city park, where old men sat about in the sun, and the unemployed loungers fingered through dirty newspapers. Squirrels were running over the grass, hunting for nuts, and the comment of one of the old men was nothing more than a simple statement of what his eye beheld. Ben returned to his office and wrote half a column of conversation and description which, in the opinion of the reader who looks for a fillip at the end, "got nowhere." Yet it expressed a simple, homely setting, conveyed exactly the feeling one got in the park and in its implication gave the reader a thought on the futility and aimlessness of life. In many a newspaper office it would have gone into the waste basket; in this instance the story found first page position because of an editor who could see beyond his desk. In similar vein was written one of the best tales Hecht wrote for "The Daily News" in his series of "1001 Afternoons in Chicago," which is to be found in his book of those tales, entitled "Grass Figures." He describes men who are lying on the grass in Grant Park just off Michigan avenue. "Funny thing about them," he remarks, "they lie there on their backs all in the same position, all looking at the same clouds. So they must all be thinking thoughts about the same thing. Let's see; what was I thinking about? Nothing." And then he reaches the conclusion: "I was just waiting and so are they." And he reads the following out of their attitude:

"Everybody was waiting. On the back porches at night, on the front steps, in the parks, in the theaters, churches, streets and stores—men and women waited. Just as the men on the grass in Grant Park were waiting. The only difference between the men lying on their backs and people elsewhere was that the men in the grass had grown tired for the moment of pretending they were doing anything else. So they had stretched themselves out in an attitude of waiting, in a deliberate posture of waiting. And with their eyes on the sky, they waited."

Of similar meditative origin are several other sketches written for this series—among them: "Fog Patterns," Waterfront Fancies" and "The Lake."

The apogee of his reporting experiences is reached in his book, "1001 Afternoons in Chicago" (Covici-McGee, 1922), which pictures, better than anything that has been written so far, the conglomerate mob life of a big industrial center. It is a selection of tales made from his contribution of one a day for over a year to the Chicago "Daily News." The contents of the book range over the gamut of the emotions, they touch philosophy, comedy, cheap burlesque, tragedy and tenderness, and represent the mental processes of Hecht and his ability to spin a yarn out of simple themes. Ben refers to the stories as hack work done for a meal ticket, as a reporter's relief from the more disturbing and engrossing details of life. No doubt many of them are that—"ground out on the typewriter," as the phrase goes—but some touch heights which their author has not reached in his more strained and ambitious writing. Some represent his philosophical reflections, his views of people, his attempts to spin colorful combinations of words, which became so marked a characteristic of "Erik Dorn." When one has read these tales, people and incidents remain in the memory, isolated sentences keep recurring, pictures detach themselves from the themes and demand recognition:

The fog tiptoes into the streets. It walks like a great cat through the air and slowly devours the city.

The office buildings vanish, leaving behind thin smoke pencil lines and smoke blurs. The pavements become isolated, low-roofed corridors. Overhead the electric signs whisper enigmatically and the window lights dissolve.

The fog thickens till the city disappears. High up, where the mists thin into a dark sulphurous glow, roof bubbles float. The great cat's work is done. It stands balancing itself on the heads of people and arches its back against the vanished buildings.

He has always been interested in the fog, in the smoke, in the street. "Michigan Avenue" is the story of a street —a street of refinements and material satisfactions. He sketches it thus:

This is a deplorable street, a luxurious couch of a street, in which the afternoon lolls like a gaudy sybarite. Overhead the sky stretches itself like a holiday awning. The sun lays harlequin stripes across the building faces. The smoke plumes from the I. C. engines scribble gray, white, and lavender fantasies against the shining air.

A deplorable street—a cement and plate glass Circe. We walk—a long procession of us. It is curious to note how we adjust ourselves to backgrounds. In other streets we are hurried, flurried, worried. We summon portentous frowns. . . . But here—the sun bursts a shower of little golden balloons from the high windows.

The high buildings waver like gray and golden ferns in the sun. The sky stretches itself in a holiday awning over our heads. A breeze coming from the lake brings an odorous spice into our noses. Adventure and romance! Yes—and observe how unnecessary are plots. All the great triumphs, assassinations, amorous conquests of history unravel themselves within a distance of five blocks. The great moments of the world live themselves over again in a silent make-believe. . . .

And his theme is that Michigan avenue is the street of day-dreams, that given five minutes it becomes a street of heroes and heroines; we are actors all, living over in our minds the great events of the ages under the inspiration of this "Circe of the streets."

It is of the tales in "1001 Afternoons," and of those now entombed in the newspaper files and not placed in book form that Henry Justin Smith, Hecht's editor, wrote in his introduction to the book:

Of the thousand and one Hechts visible in the sketches there were several that appear rarely, if at all, in his novels: the whimsical Hecht, sailing jocosely on the surface of life; the witty Hecht, flinging out novel word-combinations, slang and snappy endings; Hecht the child-lover and animal-lover, with a special tenderness for dogs; Hecht the sympathetic, betraying his pity for the aged, the forgotten, the forlorn. In his novels he is one of his selves, in the sketches he is many of them. Perhaps that is why he officially spoke slightingly of them at times, why he walked in some days, flung down a manuscript and said: "Here's a rotten story." Yet it must be that he found pleasure in playing the whole scale, in hopping from the G string to the E, in surprising his public each day with a new whim or a recently discovered broken image. I suspect, anyhow that he delighted in making his editor stare and fumble in the dictionary of taboos.

V

When we omit "1001 Afternoons" from our consideration and examine the three books and one play that Ben Hecht has published in the last two years, we find a curious thread of similarity running through all of them. This is all the more striking because outwardly the books do not appear similar, and Hecht does not, on the surface, appear to be a writer who uses a uniform style and form. "Erik Dorn," his most colorful book, is the story of a man who rebels against his drab surroundings, strives to rise to ecstatic heights, and fails; "Gargoyles" is an analysis, so far as its chief character is concerned, of an American who strives for high political office, gains that at the expense of his self-respect, becomes an accomplished hypocrite and a disillusioned man; "Fantazius Mallare" is the story of a man who revolts against his surroundings, tries to overcome the tyranny of his senses, and fails miserably; the play, "The Egoist," is a comedy in which an actor tries to find ecstatic release in a perfect love adventure and fails. In each case the principal character is at war with the limitations, the thralldom of life—and loses.

"Erik Dorn" (Putnam, 1922), was the first of the books and remains the most satisfying and the most revealing. It disclosed evidence that Hecht had labored long and faithfully over his characters. In plot and style it gives a better glimpse of the real Hecht than any of the other books. It is a clear-cut story, and much of it Hecht himself lived, notably the experiences in Europe, which are based upon Hecht's trip to Germany, immediately after the armistice in 1918, for the Chicago "Daily News." Part of the story embodies events observed by Hecht as a reporter; part of it is imagined. The book reveals his infatuation for the physical side of the city, his close acquaintance with city life, his leaning toward philosophical reflection, his preoccupation with sex as a motive power in life, his passion for colorful metaphor, his love for words and phrases, his ability to write swiftly-moving prose. Like many another first novel it is packed full of things observed and lived over a long series of years; this accounts for the fact that no book of Hecht's written since has surpassed it.

Erik Dorn is an editor who takes an active part in the routine of newspaper making. This brings him into intimate touch with city life and gives Hecht an opportunity to describe the atmosphere he knows best. As he passes through the city Dorn observes "a zigzag of windows, a scribble of rooftops against the sky." He sees "the city alive with signs, smoke, posters, windows; rising, flinging its chimneys and its streets against the sun." The men and women that he meets remind him of "faces like a flight of paper scraps scattered about him." . . . "Bodies poured suddenly across his eyes as if emptied out of funnels. The ornamental entrances of buildings pumped figures in and out." We learn of Dorn that "no drawn picture stirred him to the extent that did the tapestry of a city street. The nature of Erik Dorn was a shallows. Life did not live in him. He saw it as something eternally outside." At thirty Erik Dorn had explained to himself: "I am complete. This business of being empty is all there is to life. Intelligence is a faculty which enables man to peer through the muddle of ideas and arrive at a nowhere."

The description runs on. We find it revealing, as if in Erik Dorn Ben Hecht had in mind a concise prototype. We wonder. . . . "He often contemplated with astonishment his own verbal brilliancies which his friends appeared to accept as irrefutable truths of the moment. His phrases assembled on his tongue and pirouetted of their own energy about his listeners. Smiling, garrulous and impenetrable—garrulous even in his silences, he daily entered his office and proceeded skilfully about his work. He was, as always, delighted with himself."

In his picture of the editorial room, Ben Hecht has

tried to give the counterpart of the local room of the Chicago "Daily News," using here and there an author's license in dealing with characters we all know. The picture of a newspaper in the process of making is done with short strokes of the brush and infinite power of suggestion. The bedlam is conveyed in fantastic sentences: "A curious ritual—the scene—spreading through the four floors of the grimy building with a thousand men and women shrieking, hammering, cursing, writing, squeezing, and juggling the monotonous convulsions of life into a scribble of words." Erik Dorn has stated it in an epigram: "The press is a blind old cat yowling on a treadmill."

Two women enter the life of Erik Dorn—Anna, the complacent, unemotional wife, exhausted after seven years of married life with Dorn, and Rachel, "a morose little girl with a dream inside her." Anna to him is duty, a recognition of the material side of life; Rachel is a sensitive and beautiful being who stirs in Erik spiritual and ecstatic desires. Rarely have two influences been sketched with such precision, such happy verisimilitude. Hecht is most successful in his passages describing Dorn's relations to Anna and to Rachel, and in his descriptions of the old father, Isaac Dorn, who seems to move as a symbol of futility through the book. It is Rachel who prompts Erik Dorn to begin his ecstatic pilgrimages, and who realizes that he looks for something beyond her, beyond himself, whereas she is falling in love with his bodily self. "Of what do I complain?" she writes him. "Of your ecstasies and torments of which I am not a part, but a cause? Forgive me. I adore you. I am so lonely and such a nobody without you. And I want you to write to me that you long for me, to be with me, to caress me and talk to me. And instead you send phrases analyzing your joyousness. . . . I have found happiness—all the happiness that I desire—and hold it tremblingly. And you have not found happiness but are still in flight toward your faraway one, your dream figure."

But our interest is not so much in the story as in the author's treatment of his theme. The episodes of Ben Hecht's life as a reporter crowd into the picture. Everything that has been a part of his experience is grist to his mill. Erik Dorn proceeds to Germany and here lives the most fantastic adventures of the book. Rachel has gone out of his life, Anna has become alienated. Into the postwar confusion he throws himself, observing the red uprising, playing about the edges of the holocaust. Life becomes tolerable when he meets von Stinnes, a quaint ironical figure who illuminates this part of the book. The love episode with Mathilde is commonplace, and saddens Dorn. In the end he returns to America to find that his wife has obtained a divorce. Thus with Rachel gone, Anna gone, there is nothing left for Dorn but his task at his office, which remains as it was. The book ends as it began, with a picture of the old father, Isaac Dorn, mumbling futilely and falling asleep. Dorn's search for the beyond has come to naught.

Several episodes in the book, not in harmony with the rest of the story, forecast the method Hecht used later in "Gargoyles." One is the dissection of the character of Hazlitt, the lawyer, who conducts the defense for a woman who had murdered her betrayer, and then finds himself drawn to the same woman. Another is the surrender of Rachel to her lover, Frank, after he beats her in plain, cave-man fashion. Both episodes are elementary and not of consequence to the story.

"I had another long section in the book devoted to German politics," said Hecht. "It was a 15,000 word monograph that I wrote on shipboard upon my return in 1919. I read it to Sherwood Anderson and he was greatly impressed, in fact aghast at what I said. I tried to put it into 'Erik Dorn' in the section devoted to Dorn's adventures in Germany, but Mencken and George P. Putnam both voted against it as off the subject, and so I let the publisher drop it out." . . . John Macy, in a review of the book, pointed out the technical merit in Hecht's method of beginning and ending "Erik Dorn" on the same note—that of the old man, thus completing a cycle of futility. "It is interesting to find other men discovering merit in one's accidentals," was Hecht's comment.

Between the publication of "Erik Dorn" and "Gargoyles" something happened to Ben Hecht. For one thing he determined to use the surgeon's knife on society as he saw it, and to cut deep into the living flesh. There were flashes of that spirit in the ruminations of Erik when he reached a low level of depression between his various pursuits of ecstatic adventures. But on the whole "Erik Dorn" was an amiable book; it contained concessions to beauty, both physical and spiritual, and an undertone of pity and sympathy warmed certain episodes. That is perhaps why, by contrast, "Gargoyles" seemed the work of a cold and hardened cynic. The style and approach of the author had undergone a change; attempts to capture beauty by feats of verbal acrobatics were absent; the characters were commonplace persons, with no aspirations worthy of record, no dreams fit to inspire poetic raptures. The method of Rémy de Gourmont had got into his blood; he deprecated an allegiance to the form of the well-rounded novel, which had come down to us from the 19th century, and in which a character was visualized wholly and complete; like his French *maître* he preferred to make characters merely the vehicles for ideas. Ben Hecht had recast his theme and his mood, and for his people he had come down to a gray and fetid earth with a vengeance.

Ben Hecht said of "Gargoyles": "I wanted to take a section of society, say people in the professional class, like a judge, a lawyer, a writer, and strip them of their veneer and show them as they really are. I wanted to expose their lying, hypocritical, toadying souls." And so he did. And the result was a cold analysis of a group; a dissection on a stone table which left them nothing to call their own. The author had striven for objectivity, although the book was still strongly subjective. He had tried for a formidable result. He had avoided the colorful words and phrases that he himself so dearly admired and tried to write in a vein of unrelieved realism. As a result he puzzled many of his admirers. "Erik Dorn" had been welcomed east and west, had been commented on favorably by certain conservative critics, had even achieved a printing in England. "Gargoyles" seemed to invite criticism, although in the end it will probably have been read more widely than "Erik Dorn."

The plot of "Gargoyles" is strung rather loosely on the rise of George Basine to the position of judge, but actually the book is a series of cross sections, in which Hecht takes up his characters by twos and threes and exposes them in various situations. None of them seems to be so much a living person as a trait personified. All of these are unlovely; there is not a character in the book who is really what he purports to be; nearly every one is dominated by some form of sex hunger, or sex aversion; and the conduct of each is determined by some hypocritical or insincere motive, or is brought about as the result of unsatisfied physical desires. Gargoyles all—strange, twisted humans, leering at the reader; shapes that bear little resemblance to reality because all warmth, pity, sympathy, kindly intention, hope and joy has been excluded from their make-up.

To write "Gargoyles" Hecht again drew on contemporary history as he had seen it made in Chicago. Out of his stock of police reporter's memories came the incidents of the vice commission at work, the crusade against private banks, the liberty loan rallies. The spectacle of the vice commission is still well remembered in Chicago. A lieutenant governor of the state instituted an inquiry to determine why girls went wrong, beginning with the thesis that low wages were responsible. Every form of publicity was seized upon and exploited. Men and women meeting at midnight in a public restaurant of spotless repute were dragged out to testify before the commission on what they knew about gay dining out. Heads of great corporations were interrogated in public about the wages of their stenographers and clerks. Politicians presented ill-digested summaries of vice conditions; in one instance the commission demanded that one large corporation state its profits, and when this was refused, arbitrarily fixed the profits at a sum that ran into many millions because the chairman suspected this to be true. Fallen women elbowed club leaders; shopgirls told of supporting their families on meager wages. The whole situation proved a glorious opportunity for exploitation by the newspapers, who assumed no responsibility in reprinting the comical antics of the state investigating body. The effect of this hilarious travesty was felt for many months;

motion picture houses were deluged with films insincerely depicting the war on social evils, boys and girls read lurid stories of the enslavement of girls in opium dens, the work of serious investigators and scientific bodies was retarded and disrupted and no practical result was achieved outside of keeping the names of certain self-seeking politicians in the headlines. It was one of those typical "exposures" to which Americans give their time and energy under questionable leadership, and which produces in every instance the same result—nothing. Ben Hecht was assigned to the investigation and so became acquainted with its methods, which he detested. In "Gargoyles" he has pictured not only the situation but also its effect on certain of his characters.

"Gargoyles" provided more than a ripple in the New York publishing pond. Originally Hecht sent it to George P. Putnam, who viewed it favorably but hoped that certain changes and excisions could be made. Ben Hecht had written the book with a fine indignation and a feeling for those strong Anglo-Saxon words that have fallen into disuse in the best social circles because their strength has gone largely into their smell. There were also situations that demanded deodorizing, but this Hecht refused to admit. He said that he saw no reason why an artist should quibble over words; he had written a straightforward account of things as he saw them, and so expected it to be printed. He wired east that he would accept no changes in his copy. After considerable discussion Hecht went to New York, withdrew his manuscript from the Putnams and decided to submit it to Horace B. Liveright. Liveright was at that moment at his home in New Rochelle with a cold, but this did not deter Hecht. "I need an immediate decision," said Hecht to Liveright, so the

story goes; "I leave in six hours and you can have the
book if you print it as it stands." Liveright, confronted
by "Gargoyles" on the one hand and the prospect of
another mustard plaster on the other, chose the lesser
of the two evils and replied: "I'll take the book." The
humorous aspect of the situation is that when the book
was finally published Hecht said that it appeared practically in the form suggested by Putnam, with certain
offending lines neatly dropped somewhere between New
York and New Rochelle.

This was the first concrete encounter Ben Hecht had
with the censorship of the printed word. He had tried to
pick quarrels before; he had vented his indignation on all
sorts of abuses and real and fancied grievances, and had
been rewarded by the applause of friends who followed
him with doglike eyes and patted him on the back without
getting much wrought up over the issues themselves. The
idea that a censorship in New York could influence the
writing and printing of books gave Hecht more than a
windmill to tilt at and he made the most of it. His best
essay on the subject appears in the book called "Non-
sensorship," published by Putnam's in 1922, to which
Heywood Broun, Charles Hanson Towne, John V. A.
Weaver, and others also contributed. This contains a
caricature of Hecht in the rôle of Don Quixote. Hecht's
antagonism to the censorship was also used by Gene
Markey for a caricature, in which he depicts Hecht cere-
moniously shaking hands with John Sumner.

And so we come to the unexplained and abortive appearance of "Fantazius Mallare," with its weird story, its
fantastic drawings, and above all, its amazing preface.
Every one knew of Ben Hecht's contempt for the commonplace, of his indignant thrusts at hypocrisy, cheating,

lying, and the gaining of worldly honors under false pretenses, but no one suspected that Ben meant to take on all
the hypocrites, cheats and liars as his personal enemies.
Yet in the dedication to this book, which runs eight pages
long, Hecht has enumerated all those he considers his
personal enemies, and none of the prophets of old made
a more sweeping denunciation when he thundered against
the sins and vices of the cities of the plain. Then comes
the story itself, written largely in the form of a journal,
in which Mallare recounts how he tries to rise above the
thralldom of the senses and detach himself from his
material and physical surroundings, ending in complete
disaster and the dissolution of his mind. "Mallare," said
Hecht once, "is my favorite character." It may well be
believed. He appears in various guises. His first bow
was in the respectable circle of "Harper's Bazar," where
Hecht introduced him in a story called "The Adventure
of the Broken Mirror." He also promenaded innocently
enough in the Chicago "Daily News" in one of the "1001
Afternoons." And he may well be heard from again.
For he is the clearest character that Hecht has visualized
so far. The book contains some of the author's best writing, and some of his worst. It suffers from an unfortunate unevenness, from a preface that has no relation to
the story, from coarseness in situations that call for
subtlety. Mallare is mad, but it is the madness of irony,
and in his categorical denunciation of the world his madness becomes a satirical episode. For Mallare "considered himself mad because he was unable to behold in
the meaningless gesturings of time, space and evolution
a dramatic little pantomime adroitly centered about the
routine of his existence . . . his eyes were lifeless because
they paid no homage to the world outside him. . . . We

keep alive only by maintaining despite our intelligence
an enthusiasm for things which are of no consequence or
interest to us. . . . Perhaps the greatest miracle is that
which enables man to tolerate life, which enables him to
embrace its illusions and translate its monstrous inco-
herence into delightful, eddying patterns. . . . Man, alas,
is the only animal who hasn't known enough to die. . . .
Unable, despite his shiftiness, to lie the fact of his mor-
tality and decomposition out of existence, he has satisfied
his mania for survival by the invention of souls. And so
behold him—spectacle of spectacles—a chatty little
tradesman in an immemorial hat drifting goodnaturedly
through a nightmare. . . . It is for this ability to exist
that he has invented the adjective sane."

The author's satirical purpose was apparent, but he
was not sufficiently master of his technique to overcome
the objections sure to be raised by the custodians of the
public morals. Even in past times writers have been
subjected to the rigorous prohibitions of church and state,
but the great masters have been known by their ability
to circumvent all restrictions by adroit phrasing and
subtle devices of writing. Ben Hecht, himself an admirer of subtlety and cleverness, failed to discern any
difference between frankness and vulgarity. His own
maladroitness made it possible for the postoffice department to step in and charge author, artist and publishers
with misuse of the mails. About 700 copies still in
sheets were confiscated, and 300 bound copies also were
seized, so that out of the 2,000 copies to which the
edition was to be limited less than 1,000 actually reached
the public. The book has now become much sought
after, not solely because its publication has stopped, but
also because it contains the first drawings by Wallace

Smith. After this episode, which was the one topic of discussion for months in literary circles in Chicago, Ben Hecht printed a personal card with this quotation: "There are no obscene words. There are only obscene readers."

In portraying the mental dissolution of Mallare and his repressions, his complexes, his dissociation and his phantasy, Hecht had recourse to a little book by Bernard Hart of University College, London, entitled "The Psychology of Insanity," which gives, in compact form, a survey of the simpler forms taken by mental disease.

"And now I have in mind two serious books," said Ben Hecht the other day. "In fact I have done some work on them. For one there is the character of Cesare Borgia. Cesare Borgia lived a completely individualized life. He was absolutely without restrictions and inhibitions, assumed no responsibilities toward others, or toward the state. He did whatever pleased him. Into that book I am going to put what I left out of 'Gargoyles.' Then I am writing a book about the so-called average American. A long time ago I wrote a sketch called "Mr. Winkelburg.' He was the little man for whom the flag waves, the bands play, the trains run, for whom movies are made, advertisements are written, factories work. In other words he is the real American. I have his name and address and telephone number.

"In these books I want to write truth. I want to write them absolutely true. They will be more outspoken than 'Gargoyles.' As a writer I want to be able to tell exactly what I see in the words it pleases me to use. I cannot conceive of a writer adjusting himself to the sensitiveness and vanities of men who have nothing in common with him or his art and who want to put restraints on him.

When I write I don't want to think of the business of putting my words into books, of printing them and selling them. I want to ignore censorship and repression."

The influence of Rémy de Gourmont's disregard of social responsibility is patent here.

VI

Strange, how a simple title may call to mind a whole series of forgotten episodes. "The Contemporary One-Act Plays of 1921," edited by Frank Shay, came to my desk a few months ago, and upon turning the pages my eye fell upon "The Hero of Santa Maria," a comedy by Ben Hecht and Kenneth Sawyers Goodman. An insignificant trifle in itself, but holding a vivid fascination for me, for I had arrived in Chicago from a foreign trip just in time to witness the grotesque incidents that gave birth to this social satire. Ben Hecht was then in the heyday of his newspaper reporting and it fell to his lot to witness how the funeral of a simple soldier lad was turned into a gigantic political rally by the forces then seated in the city hall. The idea of publicly honoring a soldier who had fallen with his boots on was at bottom worthy of respect; it was observed in various American cities, but probably no community but polyglot Chicago could deflect it for selfish political purpose into a huge rally. The lad when living might have begged his bread on the streets and been ignored; his family might have stood in line for hours before the desks of political pygmies without gaining either recognition or word of sympathy; dead he became the excuse for an overwhelming agitation. Politicians in office and out elbowed one another in a rush to lay wreaths upon his bier; the slightest reason for association with the funeral was seized upon by half illiterate ward heelers as an opportunity for oratory and flag-waving; decent respect for the dead was forgotten in the desire to get in front of the camera. I have often wondered whether the politicians who were so ready with their flowers and tears and fulsome resolutions ever recalled the family of the dead after the ceremony long enough to pay their respects, for, with perhaps one exception, the politicians belonged to one party—"hogged the show" in fact—and all of them suffered defeat soon after. Ben Hecht stood by while this typical American farce was being enacted; it must have afforded him a delicious study in mass psychology, in hypocrisy, in the buncombe attached to hero worship, for soon thereafter the episode of "The Hero of Santa Maria" suggested itself to him and he drafted the plot and some of the lines. . . . The scene is the living room of the Fisher home. Nate Fisher has tried for many years to get a civil war pension, but has always been refused, and the latest rebuff has just come to him. His son Toady is a good-for-nothing who has arrived home unexpectedly, but because the father considers him a thief, a liar and a drunkard, his uncle Marty hides him temporarily in an adjoining room, the better to prepare for his reappearance. Word is suddenly brought to the group by a local dignitary, Squire Hines, that Toady had enlisted in the United States cavalry, had entered a town of "Santa Maria del something-or-other on the Mexican border," and had been killed. "At the very foot of the enemy's position," intones the florid Hines, "Edward gloriously gave up his life for our beloved flag, the first American killed. When you have been duly informed of your bereavement by the war department the remains will be shipped here for interment, via El Paso, Tex." The astonishment of the sister who contends that "Toady never rode a horse in his life" and that "he wasn't the kind to expose himself" is equaled by that of the father, who says somewhat grimly: "This here corpse is one I'll take a heap of interest looking at." At this point Hines announces that the party plans to hold a large public demonstration with a military funeral and that the expenses will be borne by the local newspaper, Congressman-elect Foss and the Hon. Theodore I. Wilkinson, Democratic candidate for sheriff. Nate comprehends in a trice that his family is to be turned into a Democratic rally while he remains cheated of his civil war pension. If his son's funeral is to be made capital of by the community he will forbid it unless he can get his "rights." Ably seconded by his daughter Elmira, and by his brother Marty—the only one who knows that Toady is alive and well in the adjoining room—Nate holds out for a promise that the party leaders will see that he gets his pension. This agreed upon, Hines leaves. Then Marty stages a family upheaval by calling the defunct Toady into the living room. And Toady, selfish, irresponsible ingrate, drives his own sordid bargain with his father. He explains that he once met a man in Madison Square, New York, with whom he swapped names. The other man enlisted in the U. S. cavalry and was no doubt shot at Santa Maria. He is the "Fisher" whose body is now being sent to the town for public burial. Toady is willing to stay dead, if his father will split the pension with him. The discussion that follows tears the veil from any pretense of patriotic conduct:

TOADY. I want four hundred dollars or I'll walk down the street to Hopper's hotel and get drunk where the hull town'll see me.

NAT. That's a fine way for a son to talk to his father. Here's Hines and Foss, come around to do the right thing, after ten years' crookedness, and just when it's all fixed up for me to get my just deserts.

ELMIRA. Yes, and mebbe your pa'd have got his pension long ago except for your carryings on, putting everybody against us.

TOADY. Don't make me laugh. Everybody's heard how Pa tried to buy a substitute when he was drafted only he couldn't raise the coin.

NATE. That's a lie, you blackmailing young skunk.

TOADY. I got my feelings the same as other people and just for that word skunk it'll cost you an extra hundred before I leave this house.

And Toady, without a spark of pride or patriotism, indifferent to virtues great and small, agrees to stay dead for eight hundred dollars of his father's pension money. The band comes blaring down the street, the governor, the senator, the tadpoles and the polliwogs crowd into the little living room, the resolutions are unfolded and read, telling pompously of the courage of the son and indorsing the claims for pension of the father.

The play is crude and the author's shafts are often only too obvious, but the beginnings of a social satirist are there. It required a certain degree of courage to write so unconcernedly when the episode was still fresh in the minds of the public and when any imputation of selfishness in a patriotic demonstration was likely to be regarded as high treason. Hecht drafted the play and took it to Goodman, who polished it with his knowledge of stage technique. Sometime in 1916, I believe, it became a part of the repertoire of the Players' Workshop in a store on East Fifty-seventh street. The performances at the Workshop failed to attract much attention and there is little to record about them except that Laurence Langner, Edward Goodman and John V. A. Weaver took part. John acted the rôle of the irascible father! Then the Washington Square Players caught it up and produced it in New York City, and it became one of the most popular satires in the one act theater.

But "Dregs" provoked a tempest from the start. Even the members of the cast at the Players' Workshop, who were Afraid of Nothing, must have trembled when the curtain rose and the principal character galvanized the audience into a quivering alertness with his famous first line. The line was simply an ejaculation of profanity and marked the extreme opposite of the innocuous opening sentences pronounced by the maid and the butler in the conventional British comedy of manners. For terseness It has never been surpassed. The story of the play was simple. A half-drunken bum, at midnight, stands on a street corner, and looking at the window of a drug store opposite, mistakes his own reflection for that of the Christ. He talks to him in his own vernacular, hoping that he has found a pal. In the meantime the low, degraded life of the street—brawls, drunkenness, police, a fallen woman—is enacted in the background. The vag discovers his mistake: "It was me in that looking glass all de time." Beyond the monologue there is no action to the tale.

J. Blanding Sloan mounted the play and Laurence Erstine took the leading rôle, and the Players scheduled "Dregs" for two weeks. The rehearsals, applauded by a small group of cognoscenti, went encouragingly. The first audience quaked and walked out in whispers. The second audience trembled. Percy Hammond, then dramatic critic for the Chicago "Tribune," attended the third performance and commented on "the unbelievable squalor of the words." A few days later Ben Hecht walked into the Workshop and found the actors rehearsing a new play. He has told how it feels to be a discarded author. "Nobody said anything to me," he said, "so I sat down in one of the back seats and listened. The actors stumbled about in their lines, and now and then I thought some one was going to come up to me and explain why my play had been withdrawn. But no one did. Their courage had ebbed away. They were going on with something easy and sure fire. After a while I felt chilled. I went out."

But "Dregs" went on again, eventually, at the little audacious circle known as the Dill Pickle, in Tooker alley, where it was one in a repertoire that included "Cocaine" and "Suppressed Desires." The Washington Square Players also negotiated for it, but they wanted to change its most effective lines. And that was more than its author could stand, for its lines had made it live.

VII

He is the most enigmatic figure in Chicago, if not in the nation, and curiosity about him refuses to die. Readers who have been captivated by "Erik Dorn," repelled by "Gargoyles," puzzled by "Fantazius Mallare," and amused by "1001 Afternoons," conjure up the strangest sort of phenomenon to fit their surface deductions. Students at universities, coming stifled out of the fine New England calm that pervades the libraries of English literature, call him an iconoclast, link him with Shaw and Wilde, and extol his vehemence. "Fantazius

Mallare" has been circulating sub rosa at various colleges at twenty-five cents an hour or more for the reading alone, and has helped pay many a student's bill for taxi-cabs. Illustrations from that book have appeared both in the "Wisconsin Literary Magazine," published by students of the University of Wisconsin, and in the "Circle," published by students at the University of Chicago. An experience Carl Sandburg had at the University of Texas is typical. Sandburg had gone there to make an address and during the day was asked repeatedly to tell something about Ben Hecht. At about eleven P. M. a member of the faculty took him aside and suggested a smoke in a quiet nook. "Now that we are uninterrupted," he began, when they had seated themselves, "I want you to tell me about Ben Hecht." "Have you read his books?" asked Sandburg. "No, but—" "Then I would suggest first that you read his books," said Sandburg. "I have delivered a lecture on Hecht four times to-day and I am not going to give another to-night."

All sorts of men call him "Ben"—laborers who talk broken English, and heads of corporations who covertly admire his contempt for conventional thinking. He has traveled in all sorts of company and can draw something out of any one he talks to. After he had published "Erik Dorn" he received "mash" notes from women moving in different social strata—little Jewish garment workers on the west side wanted him to look at their poems; actresses playing the leads in loop theaters sought to enlist his interest. He laughed and tossed the letters to his wife. He finds that every man is a "story" and when he talks about people he does not recount their inane gossip and repeat their platitudes; he analyzes their motives, charac-terizes them in terms of their inhibitions, restraints, and repressions. Once after visiting for several nights the colored theaters on the south side of Chicago, Ben came back with a fund of observations on the social and thinking habits of the negroes—on what jokes they laugh at and why, and wherein their response to the drama differs from that of the white man. One day at a fashionable restaurant, at which he had been asked to meet George Marion, the actor, and half a dozen others, Ben entered with a guest whom he introduced as "Mr. Johnson." Remarks of courtesy to the effect: "What are you interested in, Mr. Johnson?" were parried by Hecht with the reply: "He writes, but he hasn't published anything yet." During the luncheon Mr. Johnson remained politely attentive but silent and then slipped away. "That man Johnson," explained Ben, "is a nifty little check raiser and con man. He just got out of the bridewell and needed a meal, so I brought him along."

A whole series of legends has been woven about the friendship of Ben Hecht and Maxwell Bodenheim, the poet, which began years ago before Bodenheim had written "Minna and Myself." The two men used each other as foils for their wit in public and for a time they collaborated on plays in private. Their estrangement came about when Bodenheim wrote Hecht asking for the loan of $200. "I am very glad to be of service to you," wrote Hecht in reply, "enclosed please find check." No check was enclosed, however, and when Bodenheim made inquiries, thinking that it had been lost, Hecht enjoyed the joke hugely. For a number of years thereafter Bodenheim referred to Hecht as "an enemy of mine." Hecht reciprocated in kind, but when the report got abroad that Bodenheim was seriously ill in New York Hecht wrote a long story about him for the "Daily News" in which he praised him as one of the foremost American poets, who was likely to die in obscurity because an obtuse and illiterate world had not discovered his poems. In 1922 Bodenheim came to Chicago and Hecht sent him this note: "After seven years you and I are still the best hated men in American literature. Why not pool our persecution mania? My hate is getting monotonous. I confess that even yours lacks variety. I will be here Monday at 4 with a bottle of gin. I shall expect you. I salute the possibility of your fatheadedness." Bodenheim did not act on this overture, but a few weeks later both men met and renewed their relationship, and safely ensconced in the Hecht home Bodenheim finished his novel, "Blackguard," which was published by Covici-McGee through Hecht's advocacy in the spring of 1923.

Ben Hecht presents the strange case of a writer with certain continental habits of thought set down in the midst of an American environment. Had he been born and educated in Europe he would easily have acquired the background of culture that is innate in every European novelist, at hand to be used as a jumping-off place when he begins his own independent thinking. Ben Hecht had to get its equivalent by reading and observation, but the American habit of doing things quickly and superficially captured him and he missed a big, solid, scientific foundation for his thinking. His social knowledge, in so far as it rests on observation and experience, is accurate; in so far as it rests on his reading it is often faulty and full of holes. Contemptuous of many authorities, Ben Hecht accepts those that please him, and often considers an original thinker a man who is only the echo of some one else. His judgments on men and books prove him to be an emotional reader, an enthusiast who leaps quickly at a decision without further inquiry. This is shown by his ready acceptance of the diluted sociology of Gustave Le Bon, a vendor of other men's ideas, and of his exaltation of the genius of De Gourmont in "The Natural Philosophy of Love," a medley of scientific, pseudoscientific and questionable statements about the processes of procreation, thrown together in brilliant disarray by the Paris journalist, but scarcely permissible as first-hand evidence. College, which Hecht has often derided as useless and enervating, might have saved him from this naïve disclosure; at least certain courses in anthropology, sociology, and the medical sciences might have taught him that some of the discoveries on which he has placed the most value were made years before by other men and had reposed in musty libraries for decades.

He is a man of dreams and fantasies, of plans and reorganizations, of ideas that hold him enthralled one day and are gone the next. He has the faculty of tying up his most extravagant schemes with what appears to be a practical method for realizing them, so that his friends are always enthusiastic followers. His brain leaps ahead and visualizes the possibilities of a situation quicker than most men. And his aim always is to produce an effect, to gain a hearing, by a big, forceful, emphatic attack. Once the publication of a literary journal in Chicago was being discussed. "We will start the first issue with a street parade," said Ben. "We will have wagons carrying authors, critics, and poets, and each will have banners telling who and what they are. We will make the whole town know there is a new magazine." Similarly the Chicago group was thrilled and stirred when Ben proposed to transplant the London sandwich men to Chicago for literary purposes. The plan was to have one member of the clan write every week a ballad on some contemporary event which was to be printed in folio leaflets. Half a dozen sandwich men, dressed to suit the occasion, were to parade the streets selling the ballad for a small sum. The first ballad was the story of a murderer who was about to be hung, and the sandwich men were to march in dolorous costumes, each with a noose about his neck. When the murderer was granted one stay of execution after another, the ardor of the marchers cooled and Ben turned to other themes. When the Chicago "Literary Times" was finally inaugurated as a literary newspaper under Ben's editorship, it needed no blare of trumpets to announce that it differed from other journals. Ben had rolled up his sleeves and plunged in, and in his most powerful vein he had attacked everything, high and low, that to him had a semblance of weakness, ineffectiveness, dignity and prudery. He was particularly antagonistic to any show of dignity and declared that dignity meant an empty mind. There was nothing dignified about the "Times." It laughed heartily in loud, boisterous laughter; it made fun of everything not approved by the spirit of modernism, naturalism, and expressionism; it eliminated staid, respected authors in a line and exalted rebels in a paragraph. It carried a chip on its shoulder. It was also characteristic of Ben that when it appeared he no longer thought of it as an eight page newspaper issued once every two weeks. He considered it the beginning of a great Chicago daily, one that would eventually offer spirited competition to the "Daily News" and the "Tribune," and for the consummation of his dreams he was ready to go out and borrow a million.

He is full of contradictions and anomalies. Embittered against the Babbittry, contemptuous of the herd, he is

personally warm and friendly and always ready to go out
of his way to help some one he likes. Hateful of mass
hypocrisies and shams, he cheerfully allows himself to be
plucked like a pigeon and sponged upon by men who are
neither sincere nor clever. He believes audiences have a
low level of intelligence, and reviles them to their faces,
yet everything he writes is planned with an audience in
mind, and he is one of the most earnest students of
effects in the novel and in the theater. Ostensibly a
cynic, a disillusioned man, he is devoted to his home, loyal
to his household. An ardent worshiper before the
French decadents, he is actually a strong, virile character
to whom decadence is an acquired taste and whose books
prove him to have great resources of primal life and
power that he sometimes tries to deny for the sake of an
enfeebled pose.

VIII

We who have worked side by side with him, who have
listened to him between editions while he sat with his feet
on his desk, his felt hat pulled down over his forehead,
and talked and talked and talked; we who have rejoiced
at his first nights and despaired of his prefaces, look upon
Ben Hecht as the most baffling, and for that reason the
most promising writer of the whole Chicago group.
Robert Herrick is a known quantity; Edgar Lee Masters'
career holds no more surprises; Sandburg can be plotted
in straight lines and curves; Anderson can only repeat his
apologia pro sua vita with more and more intensity and
verboseness. But with Ben Hecht anything is possible.
He is the only young writer whose vehemence, whose
spirited indignation, has not been diluted by association

with people. He has so much fight and vigor in him that, once having harnessed his powers, he may present the most amazing results at fifty just as he now arrests attention at thirty. All that he has written thus far may be regarded as the faint forecast of a talent the depths of which none of us can gage. He cannot get sour on the world now and dissipate his gifts in grumbling, for he began sour and that is mainly responsible for his tremendous hammering, his undoubted fecundity. His greatest failing is his superficiality, his greatest enemy is the editor or the publisher who will print everything to which he signs his name. Once he gets away from his journalistic ballyhoo, from his superficial estimates of people, from his desire to walk the tight rope and do acrobatic tricks in mid-air to the delight of a gaping mob, he will be able to dig deep and search for the really lasting treasures of literature. He is to-day a man whose promise is better than his performance, whose gifts are better than he knows, whose mental processes cry aloud for discipline and direction. His fine sarcasm, his biting irony, his social irresponsibility, may yet make him a first rate force for striking at the worthless idolatries of an industrial civilization. To-morrow may find him a prophet and a seer; to-day he stands there, a Pagliacci on the fire escape, singing his heart out over the streets and alleys of a city whose very stones he loves but whose people fill him with sad and mournful soliloquies.

K